The Moral Case

D0865042

considerations and contradictions. From the philosophical to the practical, Furedi gives us a handy toolbox of arguments and cutting-edge reflections. This book will embolden advocates—and confound opponents—of bodily autonomy and freedom of conscience."

—Jon O' Brien, *President, Catholics for Choice, USA*

Ann Furedi

The Moral Case for Abortion

A Defence of Reproductive Choice

Second Edition

Ann Furedi
Faversham, UK

ISBN 978-3-030-90188-2   ISBN 978-3-030-90189-9 (eBook)
https://doi.org/10.1007/978-3-030-90189-9

This Palgrave Macmillan imprint is published by the registered company Springer Nature Switzerland AG
The registered company address is: Gewerbestrasse 11, 6330 Cham, Switzerland

In memory of Dr. Wilbur Larch,
a moral standard bearer
for doctors everywhere who believe a pregnant woman
should be able to make her own choice.

Larch was the finest abortionist and obstetrician who never lived
except in the pages of John Irving's The Cider House Rules

Foreword

I first met Ann Furedi in Washington, DC when we were both honored to share an award for promoting values in science. In the previous year, we had both published books explaining how we saw our work with women seeking abortion as a moral mission, but our paths had never crossed. On the surface, we could not have been more different—except for being about the same age! I'm a black man from Alabama, in the Southern United States and she is a white woman from England. Yet on a stage talking together before several hundred colleagues we spoke exactly the same language and shared the same values.

I am honored to write a Foreword for the second edition of *The Moral Case for Abortion*. I could not pass up the opportunity to herald an update to the depth and precision of thinking in this seminal work. As a long-time abortion provider who has also written about this subject, I am pleased that the life of this critical book will extend the important work of the moral agency of women. The update includes the author's retrospective, upon retiring, of a long career heading the premier abortion service in the United Kingdom. She explores the original thesis of abortion's significance as a universal human right and the affirmative morality of such a decision to the lives of women making it. This new edition also intersects, perhaps controversially, with issues that have become more prominent since the publication of the first edition. Insights on issues such as transgender identity and the role of conscience in both the refusal and decision to provide abortion by practitioners are explored for the first time. As the dynamism of change related to reproduction must pervade any issue relevant to it, the author has honored that truth by revisiting, revising, and adding to the profound thinking captured in the first edition. Two new chapters have been added to this edition: a chapter on conscience and the another on her perspectives about the Reproductive Justice movement. Fully cognisant of the fallout and potential blowback to be had by readers feeling antagonised by her positions in these additions, the author has included them in a spirit of encouraging discussion. Some speak what they claim as truth *in order* to offend others, and I believe this author is one of these, who speak bravely what they believe as truth *even though* it may offend.

The first edition of *The Moral Case for Abortion* made clear that there is nothing sentimental about abortion for the author, and yet she is not cold, distant, or aloof about it either. She is rigid where we all need to be: on the non-negotiability of the right of women and pregnant people to have the final say, resources, and respect necessary to decide on whether or not to give birth. Not solely on whether or not to become a mother, because the fetishisation of motherhood by those opposed to abortion prompts false volunteerism about adoption, care provision, and maternal assistance that is never supported by data, but rather on what is uncomfortable to many: the prospect and reality that a woman or trans-man can decide to end the process of reproduction that occurs only in their bodies with the affirmation that it does not violate the moral code of humanity, however that is defined. This edition furthers the conclusion that the intellectual capacity and moral authority of women to end pregnancies should not be subject to the interpretation or regulation of legal or religious authorities, but rather should be a function of their human rights.

The second edition is more timely than ever in the current climate of reproductive oppression worldwide. The growth of organised efforts to undermine abortion access has been facilitated increasingly through patriarchal claims of the moral authority to control the lives and bodies of women through misogynistic representations of faith to create hazard in reproductive decision-making. This has made necessary advocacy to secure abortion rights via rigorous counter-narratives to moral under-standings about abortion that lead to the coercion and oppression of women. This second edition represents a refinement of that work accomplished by the first edition.

On a final note, whatever identity one holds, religious or not, the field of engagement for moving public discourse and the politics of reproduc-tion forward resides in our willingness to make a case for the morality of abortion. It's the only stone left unturned. *The Moral Case for Abor-tion* helped to flip that stone, and the profundity of that effort has been enhanced in this edition. Given that the case has been made that abor-tion is safe, that foetuses cannot feel pain at the gestational age where the majority of abortions occur, and the various other facets on which abortion has been challenged have been rebutted, what has remained is our need to put forth the case that women are inherently deserving of the freedom to care for themselves and should have the sovereignty to control all processes occurring in their bodies, including reproductive ones. This second edition will continue the effort to make that a reality.

Alabama   Dr. Willie J. Parker, MD, MPH
August 2021   Author, *Life's Work: A Moral Argument for Choice*

Preface and Acknowledgments to the Second Edition

Since the 2016 birth of *The Moral Case for Abortion* I have been asked repeatedly why it is dedicated to a fictional male doctor. Typically, women in my position—that is those who have worked in abortion services for decades—dedicate subsequent literary endeavours to the women in whose interests they have worked or the colleagues with whom they have toiled.

So, yes, I see why it may seem strange that as a woman, writing on an issue that affects women particularly intimately, my thoughts and gratitude were drawn to the masculine character, Dr. Wilbur Larch, who was imagined by a masculine writer, John Irving, in a novel published in 1985.

My answer to the question is always simply, "read the novel."

To me, Wilbur Larch, flawed as he is, is a picture of the best of us: we who have worked in ways that help women exercise their self-determination. That he is a man, imagined by a man, is insignificant. His empathy and understanding is not a product of his masculine body or male identity but his reasoning, his understanding mind, his deeply held values and his kind and empathetic spirit. I have enjoyed the privilege of working with just such men. Dr. Willie Parker MD who has generously provided a Foreword to this edition is one of them. David Paintin FRCOG, my long-time mentor, now sadly deceased, and John Parsons FRCOG who more than anyone I know has worked in the UK to bring assisted conception and termination of pregnancy into the same field of vision are also latter-day Larch's.

Irving says of his creation: "He was an obstetrician, he delivered babies into the world. His colleagues called this 'the Lord"s work.' And he was an abortionist: he delivered mothers, too. His colleagues called this, 'the Devil's work,' but it was *all* the Lord's work to Wilbur Larch … the true physician's soul cannot be too broad and gentle."[1]

Larch understood the complex muddle of people's lives. What has stayed with me always is Irving's description of how Larch saw "the great ambiguity in the feelings people [have] for children."

> "There was the human body, which was so clearly designed to have children—and then there was the human mind, which was so confused about the matter. Sometimes the mind didn't want the babies, but was so perverse that it made other people have babies they knew they didn't want … No one, he believed … should ever make a woman have a baby she didn't want to have. NO ONE!" (pp. 24–5)

I share that view.

In a life of advocating for, and running, abortion services, I have never made a secret of my own, personal, presumption in favour of "life." Each human embryo has the potential to be the most wonderful creation on our planet: a human person that adds to our collective humanity. Each one of us is a unique outcome of all the evolutionary processes that have spanned the aeons. Every embryo is quite literally "awesome."

To support abortion is not to deny the value of life in the uterus. It is simply to value the lives of those who carry them even more.

This book is an argument for the humanness of human life, which I consider is more than flesh and bones, a beating heart and species-specific

---

[1] John Irving (1985). *The Cider House Rules*. Jonathan Cape: London, pp. 93–4.

DNA. This is an argument for respect for our capacity to shape our own lives.

There are two substantial new chapters that address issues on which I have been challenged and have considered at length since the publication of the first edition.

The first new chapter (Chapter 7) considers the place of the value of conscience which I consider to be vitally important in moral decision-making. I have a particular debt of gratitude to my close friend Jon O'Brien for many inspiring conversations and help with sources for this chapter. Jon ran Catholics for Choice during the years when later abortions were under particular challenge. He was, and still is, an enduring and fierce advocacy partner of those doctors who were compelled by conscience to provide abortion.

The second new chapter (Chapter 9) is a strengthened case for choice and autonomy in the face of arguments that this is no longer an appropriate framework in which to consider reproductive decisions. I know that some readers will consider this inclusion to be provocative and inappropriate since it challenges the direction taken by organisations led by young women of colour and I am an older white woman of privilege. But I say what I believe needs to be said.

Between the last edition of *The Moral Case for Abortion* and this one, I spent time back on campus, reading philosophy and engaging with a student community. I have emerged even more convinced that our ideas matter more than our identities, and nothing should be regarded as unsayable or beyond debate.

In that spirit I would thank all those who have invited me to speak on platforms opposite those who hold different views; those who have challenged me in debate, and especially to those who have written to say where they think I error. This new edition takes many of these comments into account and I hope is more nuanced and convincing because of it.

I have let my original Preface stand. My obligations to those I acknowledged remain, with an additional acknowledgement of my recently deceased dear friend and BPAS Board Member, Amanda Callaghan, who provided me with endless encouragement.

Professor Ellie Lee has offered challenges and incisive comments that have inspired me more than she can imagine.

My son Jacob was referenced (much to his embarrassment) as a young child in the Introduction, and now has grown up into a formidable editor and, without his exacting criticism on style and content, this book would not be what it is. He is now teacher; I am student.

My husband Frank is an intellectual giant on whose shoulders I both stand on and, periodically, lean on. He puts up with a lot.

Finally, I want to say thank you to a young student, Perdie Hibbins for encouragement she will not even have known she has given. This summer, Perdie brightened my day by saying she is considering studying philosophy after reading *The Moral Case for Abortion* which she had used as the basis for a debate with one of her teachers. She said she liked that, while arguing strongly for what I believe, I seem to try to understand, respect and answer the challenges of those who disagree. That is indeed my intention. We should never stop listening to those with whom we disagree, and we should always seek out ways to engage. It's how we learn and how our ideas grow. That is as true for my generation as it is for Perdie's.

Faversham, UK   Ann Furedi
2021

Preface and Acknowledgements to the First Edition

This short book has had a long gestation and I have been privileged to receive the support and encouragement of some very special people.

Professor Frank Furedi, author of many books on which I have drawn, has been an intellectual inspiration and rock and provided much advice, constructive criticism and encouragement. His work and conversation over many years has guided my own thinking. Being my husband, he has been subjected to my incoherent musings, obsessive preoccupations and random lines of thinking that went nowhere. As has my son, Jacob Furedi, who has played more of a role in this project than he appreciates. My concern that women should be able to choose abortion was, initially, triggered by compassion. When I was in my early twenties, I met a woman of a similar age who, pregnant in her early teens, was sent from her home in the Republic of Ireland to England for the duration of her confinement. Her father died when her pregnancy was well advanced, and she returned to his funeral unable to express her own grief. Being so concerned to show no sign of her pregnant belly, she was unable to accept the embraces of her relatives for fear they felt the swelling. After thirty years, I still think often of the barbaric emotional isolation of this girl who, following birth, would have her child adopted.

But compassion is not enough to justify abortion, and it is a feeble rebuttal to the challenges of those who claim abortion is murder and counter compassion for a woman with compassion for an unborn baby.

This was brought home to me when my above-mentioned son was about 10 years old. One evening, he turned his attention from the TV news on which we had watched an item on late abortion and, asked me: "Is that what you do ... kill babies? Because that's horrible." At home, we had always discussed my job running the British Pregnancy Advisory Service (BPAS), but the images of late-gestation foetuses used in the programme had clearly hit home. I explained how I thought abortion was necessary even though it might seem a bit horrible. But although it was a convenient and simple explanation—drawing on some of what I explain in Chapter 2, even while I was talking—my mind went back to a question the same boy had asked many years earlier.

We were passing a field of sheep on the way to the nursery when a question floated from the backseat of the car, "Mum, do sheep *know*?" We then had as rich a conversation as one can have with a four-year-old about what amounts to the difference between human beings and animals. The boy was concerned that sheep might dread becoming lamb chops if they knew they were intended to be someone's lunch.

The question of what a living entity knows has preoccupied me a lot over the years. How can sheep dread their future if they have no under-standing of "lunch" or "meat" or "life" or "death" or "future"? Not all lives are the same and not all minds are the same. Whatever thought processes a sheep has, it cannot know and fear in the way we do. And it is human *knowing*, about situations and ourselves, that shapes our thoughts and feelings and fears—and makes us the persons we are. The connection of this to the morality of abortion may seem eccentric, but bear with me. When you reach Chapter 5, you will see where I have gone with this.

Deepest thanks are also especially due to Jon O'Brien, past president of Catholics for Choice, a long-time friend and partner in many projects, who has taught me much about faith and the individual conscience and tolerated much impolite interrogation about Catholicism. In 2012, O'Brien and I convened an international meeting (supported by Catholics for Choice and the BPAS) of abortion providers, advocates and interested academics to discuss what it means to be "pro-choice." The meeting helped to frame many of the ideas discussed here, and a Declaration of Prochoice Principles (Chapter 8).

Dr. Jennie Bristow and Professor Ellie Lee, both influential writers, university teachers and founders of the Centre for Parenting Culture based at the University of Kent, have challenged and shaped my thinking greatly, especially as regards ways that contemporary motherhood is seen and how that impacts on the abortion debate.

Dilys Cossey, Diane Munday, and also Madeleine Simms and David Paintin FRCOG (both now deceased) campaigned for legal abortion in the 1960s and their support for me has encouraged me more than they can know. David was the first abortion doctor I ever met, and he is still the most morally principled man I have ever known.

I owe a huge debt of gratitude to colleagues at the BPAS, who have provided intellectual and practical support. No one on earth has more insight into what women need from abortion than the leadership of the BPAS. Special thanks are due to Professor Sally Sheldon for her advice to "never, ever open emails before you start writing." Without this instruction, I would never have completed the project.

This book has been far harder to write than I expected. It brings together empirical, sociological and philosophical reflections as inter-preted by someone who has spent more years in abortion clinics than at university. It will be too academic for some and insufficiently academic for others. Intellectuals may find it too shallow; activists may find it too exploratory. But it is what it is. It is my explanation of why women's choice must be set at the heart of abortion politics and abortion provision, and why those of us who strive to offer women choice do "good."

Faversham, UK   Ann Furedi
2016

Contents

A Note on Terminology

Throughout this book I use the term "women" in referring to those who are of reproductive age and have the reproductive capacity to become pregnant. I acknowledge that some individuals who do not identify as women (such as trans-men) also may have the reproductive capacity to become pregnant and I appreciate they may experience additional stigma, prejudice and misunderstanding when they access reproductive health services.

In these pages, "women" is used for brevity, clarity and consistency and because it is in the tradition of the movement that has fought for the freedom of the female body from the burden of fecundity.

1

Introduction: Why Abortion Needs a Moral Defence

In 1945, the year of France's liberation from German occupation, Jean-Paul Sartre published the first novel of a three-volume sequence, *The Roads to Freedom*. The central narrative theme of *The Age of Reason*,[1] set in Paris in the summer of 1938, concerns Mathieu Delarue's urgent search for money to pay for a clandestine abortion for his lover. It is a story of ambiguous relationships, struggles with principles, values and commitments, and above all the meaning of freedom.

It is not surprising that Sartre, a philosopher who rejected all forms of determinism, should choose the effects of a woman's unintended pregnancy on those in her world as a way to explore the relationships between freedom and responsibility, and individual rights and the claims of others. Induced abortion[2] is now a safer and more straightforward clinical procedure than it was in 1930s France, but it is still heavy with significance for individuals and also for society.

---

[1] Jean-Paul Sartre (1945). *The Age of Reason*, 1986 edn. London: Penguin Books.

[2] Every country's legal statutes will contain its own definition of "abortion." The one I use here is: "the intentional destruction of the fetus in the womb, or any untimely delivery brought about with intent to cause the death of the fetus." G. L. Williams (1983). *Textbook of Criminal Law*, 2nd edn. London: Stevens.

A. Furedi, *The Moral Case for Abortion*, https://doi.org/10.1007/978-3-030-90189-9_1

Abortion sweeps up and collects together attitudes to sex; to death and life; to women's roles. responsibilities and their freedoms; to children and family life; to our understanding of humanity and personhood; and to our attitude towards self-determination, individual agency, personal autonomy and tolerance. We read abortion as a metaphor, a *leitmotif*, for all of these things—although, for a pregnant woman, it may simply be the answer to an urgent personal problem.

Abortion, although practiced throughout human history, remains contested, stigmatised and demonised. Typically, in modern societies, it is seen as a moral "wrong," which is sometimes the "right" thing to do. Even societies that value planned parenthood and accept that abortion should be "safe and legal" wish it to be "rare." Many liberal doctors, who support women's reproductive choice, speak of abortion rates being "too high" and view the need for their services as a matter of regret and a marker of failure—failure by these women to prevent an unwanted pregnancy, and failure by society to enable them to do so.

Decisions about abortion drip with moral reasoning, regardless of whether it is a decision made by a woman about her own pregnancy, or a politician about a country's law. There is always room for subjectivity. Facts alone are never enough to settle matters relating to abortion. As much as abortion is a fact of modern life, so it is a matter of morals—a matter of what is right and what is wrong—that speaks to, and draws on, our fundamental values.

Abortion is almost never "just abortion."

In modern Western societies there is little talk of morality and little space for conscience. There is no longer a sense that core values should shape our lives. Nor is it accepted that, because an issue rests on moral premises, it should be left to individuals to decide privately, according to their own judgement, how they should respond.

Liberal thinking no longer tries to define what is "right" by appealing to deontological principles. Instead it looks to find what is "acceptable," what is "reasonable" or what "works." In polite liberal circles, expressions of belief in values, and opinions about rightness and wrongness, come across as rather old-fashioned and judgemental.

This does not mean, however, that policy-makers are prepared to let people make personal moral decisions for themselves. While they avoid arguments about right and wrong, they still seek to bring about social change but by "nudge"[3] and not by challenge. Conflict and argument to change opinion seems rude; conviction seems suspect—one-sided and unbalanced.

Appeals to individual conscience are seen as unreliable and fanciful. Indeed, the concept of individual conscience, once taken to mean our "inward knowledge" "our inmost thoughts," and the "internal recognition of the moral quality of one's motives and actions," is mistakenly seen as confined to religious matters.[4] In today's world it seems eccentric to claim that conscience, this faculty by which, we, as individuals, pronounce on the moral quality of actions, is "the simplest and clearest expression of the exalted character and dignity of human life."[5]

Over the recent decades this well-documented shift in thinking[6] has caused the abortion discourse to be redrawn to fit the frames of value-free non-judgemental thinking. One of the intriguing developments in policy deliberations around abortion is the narrow pragmatic and technical narrative that surrounds it. Moral concerns about whether abortion is right or wrong are replaced with concerns about whether it is safe or appropriate. It would be fine if these pragmatic debates rested on the foundation of resolved normative values, which held the provision of abortion as an expression of beneficence, and, above all, a private matter of conscience for a woman. But that battle of values has not been resolved—and abortion is still seen as something rather awful. Consequently, there has been no resolution to the abortion debate that separates the "rightness" or "wrongness" of the personal *choice* of abortion (situating it as a private matter for a woman's conscience) from the technical and logistical issues of how abortion should be provided (which are, indeed, a matter of public interest). The result is a hopelessly tangled muddle of the personal and the political, which satisfies no one.

One example has been the discussion in Britain about when and where medications used in early abortion might be provided. Although the law

---

[3] See Richard H. Thaler and Cass R. Sunstein (2009). *Nudge: Improving Decisions About Health, Wealth and Happiness.* London: Penguin Books.

[4] *Oxford English Dictionary* definition.

[5] Ole Hallesby (1933). *Conscience,* 1950 edn. London: Intervarsity Fellowship, p. 9.

[6] See *British Social Attitudes Survey* (2015). London: NatCen Social Research.

contains a clear provision for abortion medication to be provided in facilities outside the abortion clinics that require formal approval, until the COVID pandemic in 2020, successive Health Ministers refused permission. The medication was demonstrated to be safe to use in a "home" environment, but no politician wanted to be responsible for action that might be seen to make abortion easier. In other areas of medicine, improving access and ease of application would be seen as "the right thing to do." But the morality of enabling easier use of abortion drugs, even when the abortion is legal, remains suspect.

A further example of British moral–medical compromise is the legal system, which requires two doctors to certify not just the details of how an abortion is provided, but the "legal grounds" under which a woman's personal request for abortion was approved. Put bluntly, the law insists that the moral rationale for her request must be coded and recorded as a quasi-medical reason. A woman's choice to end her pregnancy because she feels it would be wrong to have a child is translated into a rationale that pregnancy would damage her mental health. In truth, this might be the case, but that is beside the point. Government and policy-makers should limit their concerns to matters of state, not matters of the morality of a personal choice about which they have no knowledge or understanding.

The withdrawal of the state from moral matters should be welcomed. Moral decisions are best left to individuals. But for this to happen, policy-makers and politicians need to accept that there *is* a moral component to abortion and not everything about it can, or should, be resolved by law or regulation. If the state were to recognise that the rights and wrongs of abortion were a matter of private conscience, it could leave those issues that arise from beliefs and values to one side and focus its attention on the proper regulation of clinical practice. This is the basis for proposals that abortion be "decriminalised"—removed from criminal statute.

Until now, the marginalisation of the moral discourse has benefitted liberal reformers. There is a robust and convincing evidence base to support the arguments that abortion has a personal and public health benefit. The harm reduction impact of legal abortion is compelling. International non-governmental organisations report regularly on the high death rates resulting from *illegal* abortions provided in unsafe, unsanitary situations without basic medications to treat the inevitable infections. The high maternal mortality rate during childbirth, especially in the most unstable and poorest regions of Africa, adds to the toll of tragedy.

When modern healthcare is available, it is evident that abortion has relatively few medical risks.[7] Thus in a pragmatic and practical world, where "good" is defined as maximising life chances, the case for legal, safe abortion should take precedence.

But is that really enough? For some people perhaps it is. But for many of us, this logic falls short. An argument for abortion based solely on personal and private health is not only shallow, but laden with problems, because it side-steps important questions concerning the nature of our basic values when it comes to maternal health and life.

Abortion has never been simply an issue about individual health. It has been directly enmeshed with the choices and calculations women make throughout their lives. The issue of abortion also raises questions about the meaning that society attaches to human life.

A risk–benefit calculation of the number of lives saved and lost is never sufficient to justify policy. Perhaps more lives might be saved if health services transferred expenditures from palliative care for the elderly and applied it to the research and treatment of childhood cancers. We would expect such a proposal to be challenged, because it is wrong to neglect the elderly and defies our respect for human life. Our moral values matter and it seems bizarre to strip them from the debate on abortion when society as a whole is yet to be convinced that abortion can *be right* and should be seen as *a right*.

We regard people's individual lives as inviolable, and we believe certain freedoms are bound up with these lives. We believe that human life is more than just one's physical existence. For example, we salute the nineteenth-century campaigns to end slavery because they were based on people's right to live "human" lives and for their bodies not to be owned or used by others.

---

[7] E. G. Raymond and D. A. Grimes (2012). The Comparative Safety of Legal, Induced Abortion and Childbirth in the United States. *Obstetrics & Gynecology,* 119(2 Pt 1), 215–219.

Stripped of concern for the fundamental values of human life, which include autonomy and self-determination, the discussion about abortion is partial and impoverished. Denuded of a focus on values based on individual freedom, campaigns aimed at legalising abortion are subject to misdirection towards social engineering, where abortion is legalised to meet what politicians and policy-makers think is necessary, rather than what individuals decide for themselves.

Finally, one of the most significant problems with the liberal estrangement from moral principles is that it has left the moral high ground free for occupation by a small, but loud, minority of those who are fundamentally against reproductive choice for reasons based on faith and doctrine. A moral case as it relates to abortion is assumed to be a case *against* it, not an argument, as made in these pages, that morally *defends* its choice.

Paradoxically, even many advocates of the case against abortion are now loath to engage in moral justification and reasoning. An original supposition of this book was that opponents of abortion had retained their commitment to a moral mission. However, it quickly became apparent that their case against abortion is as disaggregated from any defence of moral principle. As is discussed in Chapter 4, disputes about abortion are less likely to be based on moral claims about the value of life, and more likely to be on whether it benefits or damages women's health, and the circumstances that are seen, by both sides, to drive women to abortion.

That abortion can be a woman's moral preference and the outcome of a personal and private choice, which she should be free to make for herself, is rarely considered and even more rarely stated.

This book is a modest attempt to argue that, regardless of claims based on personal health or social benefit, there is a moral case for abortion. More importantly, there is a moral case to empower a woman to decide whether to have an abortion on the basis of her own moral reasoning. Indeed, not to allow this is an infringement of her autonomy and self-determination, her right to call her body her own and to shape her own future.

I make no claim to be disinterested; I have advocated for women's reproductive rights and freedoms my entire adult life. I certainly make no claim to be a professional academic. For seventeen years I directed the work of not-for-profit abortion service that was proud to meet the needs of almost 100,000 women every year. This book, however, is no justification for my work, which I believe needs neither justification nor apology. Rather it is an attempt to explain why I believe that the struggle for a woman's right to choose is so important.

The chapters that follow fall into two sections—one that describes the debate as it is, and one that explores the arguments essential to a moral defence of abortion that is situated within a frame of individual choice and autonomy.

Chapter 2 reviews why abortion is a necessary part of women's lives. It makes the argument that modern democratic societies with their commitment to equality are based on an assumption that people can, and should, control their fertility. Sex is no longer associated only with reproduction. Even those with conservative beliefs and values mostly regard sex as an expression of love and intimacy, closeness and enjoyment. Because we do not always want sex to be followed by childbirth, it would follow that abortion is necessarily a part of birth control. Contraception sometimes fails and sometimes we fail to use it. If we want our families to be planned, and parents to be responsible, then abortion must remain part of healthcare. We recognise, however, that this pragmatic view of abortion as a foundation of modern society is not unchallenged. Chapter 3 reviews the main arguments for restricting abortion and Chapter 4 looks at how these arguments are countered by those who support legal abortion, and in particular why we fail when we try to distinguish between "good" and "bad" abortions. Chapters 5 and 6 scrutinise arguments concerning the moral equivalence between the life of the woman and the life of the embryo, looking at what it means to be alive, a human and a person. We consider what gives human life its special value and meaning, and what it means to take away a woman's moral agency to make her choices about her future, and to know that her body is her own province.

Chapter 7 is new to this second edition and explains why I believe it is wrong from many perspectives to try to force clinical staff to provide abortion care when they believe it is morally wrong—in any other than the most exceptional cases.

Chapter 8 examines why the principle of autonomy is so important to this discussion; why it is right to elevate the principle of choice and why it is so wrong to see reproductive choice as secondary to other claims. It argues that a strong case does exist for recognising individual moral autonomy in decision-making about personal reproductive intent. True respect for humanity, and for life that is truly human, demands regard for individual agency, for the application of intellect, knowledge, integrity and conscience. When we prevent a woman from making her own moral choices about her pregnancy, we undermine her humanity by taking away that ability to exercise her agency.

The new Chapter 9 that follows this discusses how differently the word "choice" has been used by the movement for reproductive rights and access, and examines the critique that has more recently been constructed by the Reproductive Justice movement. I suggest that this critique is a representation and popularisation of certain critical gender perspectives that do not fully understand principles of moral autonomy and self-governance. The final chapter explores just how even the most oppressed among us have areas where we decide and shape our stories.

There is a strong Enlightenment philosophical tradition that privileges the principles of moral autonomy, human agency and tolerance. It lays the foundation for a strong moral defence of reproductive choice. This book is my attempt to marshal these arguments to support the moral integrity of those who provide abortion care, those who advocate for it and those who use it. The public health evidence for abortion is strong, but it is time to put the pragmatism to one side and to mount an assault on the moral high ground.

Freedom is not, as suggested in the song made famous by Janis Joplin, "just another word for nothing left to lose." Choice is not just the privilege of the privileged. When a woman is pregnant, her freedom to choose her future for herself—and to act on that choice, is the most powerful expression of human agency there can be.

Since the first edition of this book, there has been a disturbing trend for those who support a woman's right to abortion to argue that the issue is "above debate" and it is inappropriate to indulge in discussions with those who consider it wrong. I disagree. I consider that all the issues that call for decisions at the margins of human life require constant scrutiny and challenge.

2

Why Abortion Is a Fact of Life

Two things about abortion are beyond doubt. One is that women have relied on it throughout history to take control of their lives. The other is that, even where it is legal and safe, abortion remains a moral and social battleground.

Abortion is a paradox. With modern medical knowledge, instruments and medication, it is neither difficult nor dangerous to end a pregnancy. The World Health Organisation (WHO) accepts that abortion carries fewer risks than having a baby, a fact reflected in estimates that globally there are around 56 million abortions each year.[1] Abortion is significantly safer when it is legal but even when prohibited it is still thought to be almost as common a female experience as the childbirth it prevents. Women will take extraordinary risks to end pregnancies.

Yet despite this, abortion remains contested and controlled. Almost all countries have laws that define when and by whom abortions can be performed, and under what circumstances a clinician can meet a woman's request to end her own pregnancy. Nowhere is abortion seen

---

[1] B. Ganatra, C. Gerdts, C. Rossiter et al. (2017). Global Regional and Subregional Classification of Abortion by Subregion. *Lancet* 390: 2372–2381.

© The Author(s), under exclusive license to Springer Nature Switzerland AG 2021
A. Furedi, *The Moral Case for Abortion*,
https://doi.org/10.1007/978-3-030-90189-9_2

as just a normal part of healthcare. Even where it is not criminalised, it is stigmatised, "awfulised"[2] and politicised.

In the USA, although abortion (at least in early pregnancy) was conceded as a "privacy" right in 1974, almost fifty years later it remains a focal battle in the culture wars. it seems strange that many of those who passionately assert the importance of freedom from the state and support the Second Amendment "right of the people to keep and bear Arms", oppose the right of the people to voluntarily end pregnancy.

Britain[3] vividly reflects the modern abortion paradox. Abortion is not available to any woman simply at her request; it remains a criminal act, punishable by imprisonment, unless two doctors certify that a woman fulfils the requirements of the Abortion Act 1967 (as amended in 1990). The law provides for doctors to approve abortions when they are determined to be a health benefit, and most doctors acknowledge that forcing a woman to deliver an unwanted child is likely to be harmful. Thus hundreds of thousands of women each year have state-funded abortions. Yet abortion remains as politicised as it ever was. Members of the national parliament who object to abortion try to restrict the law further and activists protest at clinics making wild allegations against abortion providers. Meanwhile, providers and women's rights groups advocate for changes that will decriminalise abortion and allow it to be subjected to only those restrictions faced by comparable treatments. Those against abortion aim for it to be restricted and exceptionalised further, while those who support its legality want it normalised and decriminalised.

For most women in need of one, abortion sits above, below and beyond politics. It is a practical solution to a problem pregnancy. Usually, they just want to be treated safely, professionally and confidentially just as they would when receiving any other medical care.

And so it is that many different, disaggregated factors of political and personal spheres of existence are crunched together in a tangle of facts and opinions. It often seems that there is much about abortion's place in

---

[2] Janet Hadley (1996). *Abortion: Between Freedom and Necessity.* London: Virago.
[3] The law in Northern Ireland is different to England, Scotland and Wales as it was excluded from the provisions of the Abortion Act 1967.

society that we have yet to understand. However, there is also much that is straightforward.

Women Need Abortion as Birth Control

In any society where fertile women have sex with fertile men without wanting a child, abortion is needed as a means of "family planning." Ultimately, there is no other way to control fertility. Given a choice, women almost invariably prefer preventing conception to ending pregnancy, but when contraceptives fail, we need abortion as a back-up.

It has always been this way. Ethnographers and anthropologists have documented how in every society, woman have found substances to ingest, or devices to insert, to abort unwanted pregnancies. Even societies with the most minimal medical knowledge and technologies have found ways to put a stop to unwanted pregnancies. In the 1950s, having spent years compiling the most comprehensive review on record of abortion in what were then referred to as "primitive societies,"[4] the French-Hungarian ethnographer George Devereux concluded: "that there is every indication that abortion is an absolutely universal phenomenon, and that it is *impossible even to construct an imaginary social system in which no woman would ever feel at least impelled to abort*" (my emphasis).

Pregnancy is, quite literally, life changing. Even when women are able to share the responsibilities of motherhood with a willing father, and the state provides support through social benefits, the impact of pregnancy qua pregnancy is on her alone. The claim that adoption is a "better option," with the double benefit of freeing the birth-mother from her responsibilities and providing a baby to be loved and raised by someone else, is strikingly naive. Women seeking abortion do not just want not to be mothers, they want not to be *pregnant*.

At best, pregnancy is demanding, sometimes debilitating and always disruptive. Trades unions and human rights organisations, struggling

---

[4] George Devereux (1955). *A Study of Abortion in Primitive Societies: A Typological, Distributional, and Dynamic Analysis of the Prevention of Birth in 400 Pre-industrial Societies.* New York: Julian Press, p. 1.

for women's equality at work and in public life, draw attention to the "pregnancy penalty" of reduced earnings and promotion prospects that mothers pay even in liberal, democratic societies committed to the advancement of women. Of course, some women in robust health, usually in stable relationships, with an income to pay for support, with empathetic employers and colleagues, and a determination to keep on working, manage to bounce back to the desk in weeks. New technologies and more flexible working contracts have helped, but any employer who does not feel a tinge of despair when an employee announces her pregnancy has the tolerance and fortitude of a saint. Pregnancy is an unpredictable state that cannot always be overridden by determination and commitment to the job.

This is not to say the pregnancy is per se an "illness," it is not; the female body is formed for it. But, for some women pregnancy it can feel like an illness, and certainly pregnancy can *cause* illness.

The topic of how the foetus develops in pregnancy is discussed at great length; how woman develops is rarely considered. Yet the impact of pregnancy is transformative.

The physiological changes of even early pregnancy can leave a woman feeling exhausted and experiencing nausea and sickness. Morning sickness is often likened to a slight hangover; yet for some women sickness can be so debilitating as to cause hospitalisation. It can in itself be the reason for the termination of a planned and wanted pregnancy. In the final months of pregnancy few women are fortunate to escape raised blood pressure, breathlessness and extreme tiredness, and no one escapes the extreme physical discomfort and limitations that accompany a swollen belly that comes to feel like a medicine ball.

There is a good reason why a pregnant woman's delivery is described as "labour"; at best, it is agonisingly hard work. Even an uncomplicated vaginal delivery can result in perineal tears that make even sitting painful. If a woman decides against breastfeeding, she still has to manage lactation. And then there are the permanent scars—stretch marks, perineal repairs and so on. When a woman wants a child, she may see this as a small price to pay, but it should not be beyond anyone's imagination to understand why women insist that enduring pregnancy against their will is intolerable—even torturous.

Of course, compared with the lifetime of mothering, the actual pregnancy makes relatively little impact on women's lives, and is relatively short-lived. When a woman *wants* to have a child, this is something she resigns herself to. Pregnancy is the price she pays for the joys to come. But it seems nothing short of bizarre to expect a woman to have to face all of this when she doesn't want to be pregnant at all. This is why most women do not think of adoption as an alternative to abortion. In Britain, while there are more than 200,000 abortions a year, fewer than 200 newborn babies are offered for adoption.[5] Normally, women only see adoption as realistic when abortion is not an option; typically when she is "too far along" for a legal procedure. Adoption is an alternative to motherhood, not an alternative to abortion.

For women to study, work, be involved in politics or local community life they must be able to manage motherhood. Part of that is about managing the raising of a child, but it is also about managing the timing of pregnancy. A man can sire children and carry on regardless. A woman with ambitions and aspirations needs to consider the impact of pregnancy, birth and her responsibilities for the children she bears.

The responsibilities of family life, and the need for women to be able to shape these responsibilities, have been seen as key to the struggle for women's equality since its inception. The demands for "free contraception and abortion on demand" and "free 24-hour childcare" were adopted as two of the four original demands of the Women's Liberation Movement in the early 1970s.[6] The other two demands are related to equal rights and opportunities in education and at work. The childcare demand recognised that women's involvement in public life was not reducible to "the right to work," and that childcare during working hours is not enough to give women freedom, because not everything we want to do happens at work. Simply getting dad to do more was never seen as an answer for women who wanted to organise and socialise and generally have a life that was more than "being a mum." Women's liberation

---

[5] Abortion Statistics, England and Wales (2020). Summary information from the abortion notification forms returned to the Chief Medical Officers of England and Wales. Published to gov.uk in PDF form only.

[6] Anna Coote and Beatrix Campbell (1987). *Sweet Freedom: The Struggle for Women's Liberation.* London: Virago.

in the 1970s was about liberating women from the things that held them back from developing as people. It was about freeing our choices from unnecessary constraints, including our choices about sex.

When sex risks a pregnancy that can *only* be terminated by the birth of a baby, then it carries with it either a serious commitment, or total disregard of commitment. The second option is only realistically available to the man since only he can "walk away" from a pregnancy—even if a woman plans to give up her baby, she must wait until it is born. Without fool-proof birth control, the only way for women to avoid the unwanted consequences of sex was to abstain from sex altogether.

Women marched chanting for "free abortion on demand" and banners that claimed, "our bodies, our lives, our right to decide" were not "anti-child" or "anti-life." They simply wanted to take control of their own personal futures. They too wanted to be able to enjoy sex as an expression of love, intimacy or fun. They wanted to free sex from reproductive intent, and why not?

Many wanted to have children and looked forward to the experience of pregnancy and birth and nurturing and raising a new generation. But they wanted to do it deliberately at a time of their personal choosing and not by biological chance. Many marched with the children they already had (often in pushchairs or slings), and loved and wanted to enjoy, adding more siblings to the family (or not) as part of their plan.

The people who rallied in the 1970s in support of freely available birth control, which included abortion were driven by the same needs and aspirations that motivate many of us today: a desire to exert "self-control" and live the way we want to, taking responsibility for ourselves, our families and our future families. This is a responsible and sociable ambition. We know that not everything will go according to plan—indeed, more often than not, very little goes according to plan, because not everything can be controlled.

Fertility is one of the things that we cannot control entirely. Even today, it is not possible to plan to become pregnant on schedule. For many women, it is impossible to get pregnant at all despite the greater availability of, and advances in, assisted reproductive technologies. Others who become pregnant are not able to carry a pregnancy to term. On the other hand, birth prevention is almost always possible—at least technically. Abortion, at least in the earlier weeks, is not a complicated procedure. The medications increasingly used to end pregnancy safely, simply need to be made available for a woman to take. Even in the days when women died from "backstreet" or "back-alley" abortions, the cause of harm was more likely to be the absence of antibiotics than botched procedures.

When a woman is denied the opportunity to end her pregnancy, it is not because there is a problem that doctors *cannot* solve; rather, it is because either they *may* not solve it (because they are prevented by laws or policies), or they *will* not solve it (because they think it is wrong). When it comes to pregnancy, the medical means to the end is no mystery; women's freedom to make their own personal reproductive choice is constrained by the will of society, not the ability of science.

This means that when we discuss reproductive rights, the right to abortion is significantly different from the right to have a child, or even the right to control fertility. A woman *can* have an abortion; she *can* exercise birth control. The issue is whether she *may* have an abortion. The means are available if the laws and means of access allow her to do so. That is not true of control over fertility more broadly. No matter how much society wants to assist conception, some women *cannot* conceive, or carry a pregnancy to term because, while it is in doctors' power to end a pregnancy, infertility treatment is not yet sufficiently advanced to grant the power to start one.

Despite the intensely personal nature of pregnancy from a woman's perspective, her decisions about it are almost invariably seen as matter of public interest. It is hard to see how it can entirely be otherwise since the futures of our families shape the future of society. The decisions we make about pregnancy as individuals have a population impact since our children are, quite literally, society's future. Added to that is what our acceptance, or rejection, of childbearing says about us as individuals, about society in general and about women in particular.

Abortion manifests itself as a woman's right; part of her claim to equality with men is the ability she has to plan and exert control over her life. But it simultaneously presents itself as a personal, individual and clinical solution to the problems a woman faces when she is unwilling to be pregnant. The discourse about women's right to abortion is political, but every woman's reason for seeking an abortion is deeply personal. Women have abortions for many reasons, but never as a demonstration of support for the political principle of a reproductive freedom. Paradoxically, many women turn to abortions to solve their own problem while firmly believing that abortion is wrong as a matter of principle

Every society has a public policy that controls when an individual woman can make a personal decision about the contents of her womb, even if, as in Canada, it is not expressed directly in legislation. This is because no society is indifferent towards the role of women and the welfare of families, and thus no society is indifferent to women's reproductive decisions.

Society's attitude to abortion speaks to its attitude towards women. Where the publicly accepted role for women emphasises their role as mothers and homemakers, access to abortion tends to be more constrained and restrained. This does not necessarily lead to a tendency to restrict abortion altogether. Sometimes concern about the family can lead to more liberal laws if they are seen to strengthen the family unit and make mothering easier.

The British law is a good example of this. Britain[7] was one of a wave of European countries to liberalise its abortion law in the 1960s, and the Abortion Act, which still regulates abortion today, was approved by Parliament in 1967 at a time when laws and social attitudes were becoming more permissive. Divorce was made easier; "homosexual acts" in private between men over the age of 21 were decriminalised and some laws on censorship changed. But a movement for women's liberation was yet to emerge—and it would be some years before Parliament agreed to limited equal pay legislation.

At the time, the Labour Government, under the premiership of Harold Wilson, was concerned with urban poverty and poor housing, especially in overcrowded post-war slums. Among the wealthier sections of society there was a view that the "poor" brought disadvantage on themselves. The debate throughout the early 1960s, which eventually

---

[7] See Audrey Simpson (1998). Abortion in Northern Ireland: A Problem Exported. In E. Lee (Ed.), *Abortion Law and Politics Today*. London: Palgrave Macmillan.

led to abortion law reform in 1967, reflected the way that politicians at that time saw abortion as a way of dealing with problem women and problem categories of family. In general, it was thought abortion might be a solution for women who were deemed medically unfit, psychologically disturbed, from "deprived" or "demoralised" backgrounds; whose families were "too big"; or who were too young to raise a family. Abortion was seen as means both to reduce the number of "delinquents, inadequates and deprived individuals," and to reinforce socially responsible family structures. The question of women having abortions because they simply did not want to have a baby never arose in the formal records of the parliamentary debates, because these women were not recognised as being a social problem.[8]

While the royal medical colleges had a healthy distrust of politicians poking their noses into medical matters, the medical press of the time revealed a particular enthusiasm for the part abortion might play in relieving society of the burden of care for the poor and feckless. One London family doctor complained that all doctors were familiar "with the large problem families with inadequate parents. Those endless children all looking alike, whose names one confuses … catarrhal, undernourished and badly clothed. These children are often unhappy and become delinquent … known to the local welfare workers." The problem according to this doctor was that his patients, who were "incapable of using contraceptives properly," did not even want abortion or sterilisation, and indeed often failed to even understand there was a problem at all. "Perhaps," he suggested, "a panel of social and medical authorities could decide whether in such cases, the existing children would seriously suffer by allowing the pregnancy to continue."[9]

Modern democratic societies are based on an assumption about women's equality that acknowledges that we should enjoy full participation in public life but requires that we combine this with our duties and responsibilities as parents. And most of us share this view. We do not want to choose between the external public world and the private

---

[8] See Keith Hindell and Madeleine Simms (1971). *Abortion Law Reformed.* London: Peter Owen.

[9] Cecil Gill (1966). And How Should I Decide? *Medical World*, January p. 23.

cocoon of our families. We want to be able to manage both, side by side. A society where we are not responsible for the children that we bear, but hand them over to the state to raise, seems dystopian because we want our parenting to be supported but not outsourced. Part of the joy of motherhood is raising children in a way that introduces them to our values and beliefs: we want to "grow them up" in our way of life.

A woman's life today involves both the work of mothering and the work that both earns an income and contributes to society beyond the home. This is a significant reason why there is no bright line dividing women who are full-time carers at home and women who work, or between women who have abortions and women who have babies. They are not different types of women who are committed to different ways of life. Rather, the priorities of an individual woman change. A pregnancy may be absolutely right for a woman this year, whereas last year she felt it was absolutely wrong.

Women want to be able to plan their families pragmatically, according to their own ideas and principles. This matters when it comes to decisions about if and when to have a child (or a second or a third). It also matters when it comes to decisions about how to raise the children they already have.[10] Abortion is one of the decisions that rightly belong to that private, personal world.

Generally, modern democratic governments also prefer pragmatic solutions. Regarding the management of problem pregnancy, for many governments this means a scenario where abortion is available, but still stigmatised. The state wants to maintain the idea that motherhood is the default setting for women, but with an override when that will cause problems.

In Britain the abortion law has endured almost unchanged for nearly fifty years because it does exactly this: it allows abortion on grounds when it would be hard for a woman to be a good mother. This satisfies the needs of the state, although not those of individuals whose reasons for wanting a pregnancy to end are as complex as their own lives.

---

[10] Rachel K. Jones, Lori F. Frohwirth and Ann M. Moore (2008, January). 'I Would Want to Give My Child, Like, Everything in the World': How Issues of Motherhood Influence Women Who Have Abortions. *Journal of Family Issues*, 29, 79–99.

In countries where abortion is provided on request in early pregnancy, the intention (and effect) is the same. Abortion of unwanted pregnancy is permitted because it is generally accepted that if a woman does not want a baby, she will be less inclined to give her child the attention and stable family environment that policy-makers believe children need. It is assumed that these women will take advantage of abortion as soon as they discover they are pregnant and so "the offer" of abortion on request is less important later in pregnancy.

Parental responsibility for the family is a value that remains a key tenet of modern society, even though in many countries there is an observable tendency for the state to intervene more and more in family life.[11]

The private nature of life within the family, as opposed to the public dimension of life in wider society, was more clearly demarcated in the past. It used to be said that "an Englishman's home is his castle," a folk saying that conveyed the reality of paternal sovereignty in the home. It also spoke to a broader notion that the home was a place for families to make private decisions for themselves and where they could "pull up the drawbridge" against outside interference.

The notion of "home" as "castle," in Britain and most of Europe, has crumbled as the state has extended its influence into the family home. Aspects of family life that for most of the twentieth century were seen as matters for parents[12] (such as how to discipline children, what to feed them, at what age they should be left alone) and even for couples to negotiate (the organisation of finances, what constitutes an abusive relationship) have increasingly become subject to government advice and guidance, and in some cases legislation.[13] Despite this development, there is a strong underlying commitment to the principle that parents should take responsibility for their children and raise them in a proper manner—or at least keep them under control.

For most people, particularly among the educated middle classes, it seems obvious and responsible to limit family size to what is individually

---

[11] Frank Furedi (2004). *Therapy Culture: Cultivating Vulnerability in an Uncertain Age*. London: Routledge.

[12] Jennie Bristow (2009). *Standing Up to Supernanny*. Exeter: Societas Imprint Academic.

[13] Frank Furedi (2008). *Paranoid Parenting: Why Ignoring the Experts May Be Best for Your Child*. London: Bloomsbury.

manageable emotionally, economically or even socially. Planned pregnancy is seen as responsible; it is regarded as the "right thing to do" practically and morally.

Women expect to be able to plan whether their pregnancies should be close together so that that the children are of similar age, or to space them several years apart. Women working outside the home expect to consider when to take a "career break" or when they will be entitled to advantageous maternity benefits. Women engaged in academic study are unlikely to want to prepare for childbirth as they prepare for exams.

First Lady, Hillary Rodham Clinton famously once reminded the USA that "it takes a village to raise a child"[14]—and so it might. But in practice, most modern Western societies expect parents, or guardians, to do the raising. It is ironic that often those who are morally censorious about abortion are the fastest to complain about "feral" children, who roam free of parental discipline, and large families supported by state welfare benefits.

Disadvantaged adolescents, with few aspirations for their future, less hope of a decent job and no interest in education are seen as both a risk to themselves and a threat to society. The middle-class fear of the feral children of the poor often expresses itself in protests that parents should be "made to take responsibility" for their children, or "should not be allowed to have them."

Governments, too, share the concerns about the cost and the social stability of the poor. But clearly, however much democratic governments might wish to control the way families live, the options are limited in societies that uphold principles of individual freedoms. Compulsory birth control for the poor is (at least for now) happily outside the boundaries of the acceptable political imagination in most parts of the world, although the temptations of "incentivising" birth control are never far from some of the more extreme fringes of conservative policy.

A combination of individual enthusiasm for child-free sex and governmental interest in promoting "suitable" families has lent itself to the promotion of "family planning" and "family planning methods." Social

---

[14] Hillary Rodham Clinton (1996). *It Takes a Village: And Other Lessons Children Teach Us.* New York: Simon & Schuster.

policies that compel women to have children they neither want, nor believe they can care for, do not sit well alongside a social desire to encourage greater parental responsibility. This provides a compelling "conservative" case for birth control for many of those who are otherwise indifferent to women's liberation.

Just as in Britain in the 1960s, support for legal abortion was built on concerns about large, poverty-stricken families unable to control their existing offspring, now much conservative support for abortion is based on the perceived need for "control" on births when families can't control themselves. Consequently, any number of social policies "nudge" those seen as unsuitable mothers away from pregnancy.[15] For example, in 2017, the British Government placed a two-child limit on the number of children entitled to state benefit support, presumably under the impression that poor parents could limit their family size if they were sufficiently motivated.

The most striking example of this has been governmental concern during the last thirty years or so to address the perceived problem of teenage pregnancy. In Europe, particularly Britain, and the USA, teenage sex and pregnancy have been a focus of social concern and policy intervention. The rationale is that pregnancy at a young age is bad for a young woman, because it takes her out of the educational system and limits her future options. This is believed to perpetuate a cycle of deprivation since, typically, it is girls from disadvantaged backgrounds that become pregnant. A supporting concern is that the public health outcomes of teenage pregnancies are worse than those for older women; because these babies tend to have a lower birth-weight, their mothers are less likely to have complied with ante-natal advice, less inclined to breastfeed and more inclined to smoke.

In Britain, health policy targets from the mid 1990s designed to reduce teenage pregnancies officially drew a distinction between lowering the number of births to teenagers and reducing the number of conceptions. The latter led to increased availability of contraceptive services directed at young people and targeted promotion of the more effective

---

[15] Simon Duncan, Rosalind Edwards and Claire Alexander (2010). *Teenage Parenthood: What's the Problem?* London: Tufnell Press.

long-acting contraceptives (intra-uterine devices [IUDs], injections and implants). These are administered by health professionals and thus not dependent on "user- compliance." Also because implants and IUDs must be removed by a clinician, which in itself requires planning, they do not a allow for a spontaneous decision that a baby might not be such a bad idea after all.

Although government officials stressed their initiatives were about the prevention of pregnancy, not the ending of pregnancy, the promotion of abortion services to young people also became more acceptable. After all, if teenage motherhood is "bad," then abortion—while not as "good" as "preventing the pregnancy" in the first place—is maybe "not so bad" as an unwanted birth.

The notion that children should be "planned and wanted" is shared by people of almost every background. This is partly due to the belief that babies should have the best start in life, which requires the prospective mother to comply with increasing amounts of pre-conception care behavioural advice, including what she should, and should not, eat and drink, and which unhealthy habits she should break. The focus on the need to "prepare for pregnancy" has created a neurotic environment where women who are happy to become pregnant unexpectedly need reassurance that their baby is unlikely to have been harmed by wine consumed and cigarettes smoked before the mother-to-be knew the baby was on the way.[16]

To subject one's future child to conditions in the womb that are less than ideal seems anathema in societies that insist that the rights of children are paramount once they are born. To those who think abortion is the equivalent of murder, it must seem bizarrely paradoxical that women sometimes request the abortion of an unplanned pregnancy because they fear they have undermined their baby's future by some episode of "bad behaviour"—perhaps an evening of binge drinking or dope-smoking— but some women do.

Society's views about the position of women in social life, the nature of family life and the importance of family planning, and the modern

---

[16] E. Lee, J. Bristow, C. Faircloth and J. Macvarish (2014). *Parenting Culture Studies*. London: Palgrave Macmillan.

social tolerance of abortion are also linked to our changed view of sex and what it means in the context of our personal, intimate relationships. Today, we no longer feel obliged to even pay homage to the procreative purpose of sex. We do not invariably see conception as being its natural function as much as something to be, depending on circumstances, potentially avoided or at least contained. In modern Western democracies at least, sex is accepted as an expression of love and intimacy, but also of fun and lust. This is as true among married couples as it is among teenagers. As long as both partners consent, pretty much anything goes. In a strange ironic twist for the twenty-first century, sex seems to be increasingly fetishised through everyday pornography, but decreasingly stigmatised in everyday life. We live in an age of long-term, fuck-buddy friends and apps that introduce us to strangers in search of a sexual encounter with no strings attached. We no longer worry if our adolescent children are having sex; we worry if they are not. If they are sexually active, our concern is that the sex is "safe" in the sense that they are protected against sexually transmitted infections and pregnancy. Fears of the untreatable and deadly HIV infection threw cold water on the fires of passion for a while, but the infection's relative containment within certain higher-risk populations, combined with improved treatments and outcomes, has eased much of the heterosexual angst.

Abortion Is Birth Control

Many people see abortion as simply a "harm-reduction" measure that reduces maternal mortality, especially in countries that are resource poor and where women have little access to the means to prevent pregnancy, and little support when they deliver the child. Around the world, abortion is used as a method of birth control even if it is not accepted officially as such. And the simple fact is that politicians and policy-makers have no option but to accept this or turn a blind eye.

When the anti-abortion Reagan administration in the USA passed measures in 1984 to deny US funding to foreign non-governmental organisations (NGOs) that provided or promoted abortion as a method of family planning, other donors, including government bodies, stepped in to address the deficit. What became known as the "Global Gag Rule" (also referred to as the Mexican City Policy), forbade US-funded organisations to fund abortion in cases other than rape, incest or a threat to a woman's life. It banned counselling and referrals for abortion and prohibited lobbying to make abortion legal or extend its availability.

This was a triumph of ideology over realpolitik for a conservative Republican US head of state. Other world leaders understood that the services Reagan deplored were necessary and helped to establish "workarounds" that would allow previously US-funded programmes to continue. While ideologues still feel the need to draw a clear line between preventing pregnancy and ending it, this is becoming increasingly problematic as scientific research leads to family planning methods that might do both.[17]

In practice, if societies want "family planning" through birth control, contraception and abortion *must* be accepted together. A society built on foundational values of parental responsibility needs a back-up plan when contraception fails. The notion that better use of contraception can prevent abortion is simply a myth. Better use of contraception may lessen the need for abortion, and there is much evidence to demonstrate that women prefer prevention of pregnancies to their termination.[18] Under the Obama administration in the USA, increased access to insurance plans that include contraception may have been a significant factor in the lowering of the abortion rate.

Similarly in the UK, abortion rates, specifically among teenagers, have dropped at a time when it has been government policy to promote the use of highly effective, non-user dependent contraceptive implants. But the UK may also be an example of where the limits lie. Outside of this specifically targeted age group, attempts to lower the abortion rate have noticeably failed, particularly among older women where abortion rates have been increasing.

---

[17] Elizabeth G. Raymond, Francine Coeytaux, Kristina Gemsell-Danielsson, Kirsten Moore, James Trussell and Beverly Winikoff (2013). Embracing Post-Fertilisation Methods of Family Planning: A Call to Action. *Journal of Family Planning and Reproductive Health*, 39, 244–246.

[18] John Bongaarts and Charles F. Westoff (2000). The Potential Role of Contraception in Reducing Abortion. *Studies in Family Planning*, 31(3), 193–202 and Cicely Marston and John Cleland (2003). Relationships Between Abortion and Contraception: A Review of the Evidence. *International Family Planning Perspectives*, 29(1), 6–13.

We might even speculate that promoting contraception may increase the number of abortions, because it legitimises and normalises the principle that we should plan our families. In 2020, the rate of abortions for residents of England was the highest since the Abortion Act was introduced, with one in four pregnancies ending in abortion. In the prior ten years it had decreased for girls under 18 but increased for older women. Whereas in 2010, 50% of women having abortions had a previous child, in 2020, 58% were already mothers.[19]

The argument that increased contraception and increased abortion use sit together is usually vehemently denied by some abortion supporters who insist that the availability of abortion does not affect contraceptive use. But what if it does? Why should it be a problem if a woman prefers to use a less-effective method of contraception (such as a condom) knowing that if it fails, she has abortion as a back-up option? It seems reasonable to assume that when women have expectations of preventing pregnancy, they may be to end one if prevention fails.

People who plan for sex, but do not want to plan for a family, can choose from birth control options that range from permanent sterilisation, long-term but removable implants and intrauterine devices, and injections that last for months before wearing off. Short-term contraceptive hormones can be taken by pill or patch or vaginal ring. Barriers can be used to keep ejaculate out of the vagina (condoms) or passing through the cervix (diaphragms and caps). Even after sex has occurred, it is possible to prevent conception with post-coital pills or an intrauterine device. In truth, even the so-called natural family planning methods, which predict the time in a woman's menstrual cycle when she is fertile, are reasonably effective.

No contraceptive method is infallible—although some fail more than others. Nor are we infallible when we use them. Typically, the less a person has to do with their chosen method, and the greater the separation between the decision to use it and the act of sex, the more effective it is likely to be.[20]

[19] Office of National Statistics: Abortion Statistics, England and Wales: 2020.

[20] James Trussell (2009). Understanding Contraceptive Failure. *Best Practice & Research Clinical Obstetrics & Gynaecology*, 23(2), 199–209.

Sex is complicated. People get "carried away"; they get embarrassed; they don't want to "break the spell." Probably most condom failures are a failure to get one out of the packet. The same principle of "user failure" applies to other methods, which is why it is not just the inherent method-efficacy of long-acting methods, but also the lack of user-dependence that affords them greater reliability.[21] However, the underlying point is simple: contraceptives fail. And it is incidental regardless of whether they fail because of an implicit fault or because we use them poorly. The result is the same.

Of course, there is another form of contraceptive failure—the failure to supply contraceptives to those who need them. The ability to use contraception at all is the privilege of the privileged. In social circumstances where contraceptive choice is limited, where cultural norms mean that men are reluctant (or resistant) to use available methods because their fertility desires do not accord with those of women, or where supplies are disrupted, it is even more difficult to prevent pregnancy. Women in the Global South and in the less-developed areas of the North, particularly in those countries that were formerly part of the Eastern bloc, bear a particular burden.

It makes no sense to separate abortion from other methods of fertility control. Instead of asking: "Why abortion?" Perhaps we should ask: "Why not abortion?" We need to establish what the significant differences are between (1) preventing the attachment of an early embryo to the uterine lining, *allowing* it to be lost as happens with some forms of contraception and (2) disrupting the attachment of the embryo, *causing* it to be lost as happens with early abortion. As we will discuss in the following chapters, the difference is hugely significant for people who believe that life is sacred from conception. For them, any deliberate destruction of embryos is wrong. But most people do not feel this way.

Abortion's opponents have laboured hard to separate (acceptable) contraception from (unacceptable) abortion, alleging that various contraceptive methods are, or have the potential to be, abortifacient. Contraceptive pills that do not contain oestrogen (and so allow ovulation),

---

[21] James Trussell (2011). Contraceptive Failure. In R. A. Hatcher, J. Trussell, A. L. Nelson, W. Cates, D. Kowal & M. Policar (Eds.), *Contraceptive Technology: Twentieth Revised Edition*. New York: Ardent Media, pp. 779–863.

intrauterine devices and post-coital pills have all been subject to challenge. The research and debate is welcome; it may be important to some women to be reassured (as they can be) that these methods cannot end an established pregnancy. And more knowledge is always better than less. But the way policy-makers apply the knowledge is far from helpful since, typically, it is used as a plank in a framework that distinguishes between "good" contraception and "bad" abortion: a bifurcation that is especially relevant to the Global South because it directly affects the way development aid can be spent.

Some country donors, such as the USA, and private donors, such as the Melinda Gates Foundation, prohibit their funds being used for abortion. Sometimes this is because the donors are explicitly opposed to abortion. Melinda Gates is quite open that her Catholic beliefs predispose her against investment in abortion—and her fund is her personal wealth to use as she chooses. But it is important to be clear that these restrictions have an effect. Research into methods of birth control that "blur the line" between abortion and contraception have been abandoned, not because they are ineffective or unsafe, but because they do not meet the political preferences of donors who are prejudiced against abortion.[22]

Often, contraception is promoted, particularly by agencies working in the Global South, as a means of *preventing* abortion. Strategies to promote international family planning projects are frequently linked to initiatives to improve maternal and child health; this is, in part, because it is claimed that extended use of contraceptives will reduce maternal death and morbidity from unsafe abortions.

Of course, this begs the question of why the agencies don't put more effort into replacing "unsafe" with "safe" abortions. This is how policy-makers usually approach a problem with medical care. Of course, all clinical interventions have risks, and we may aim to reduce the need for them. Dental surgery, for example, carries risks and we would prefer preventative oral care to tooth extraction. But we do not promote better oral hygiene as a means of eliminating unsafe dental surgery. We expect

---

22 Beverly Winikoff (2014). Is One of These Things Not Just Like the Other? Why Abortion Can't Be Separated from Contraception. *Conscience*, XXXV, 27–29.

to promote oral hygiene and safe dental surgery *when it is required*. When it comes to teeth, we are more honest and realistic than we are with birth control: in the dental world we accept that prevention is preferable, but we openly admit that it doesn't always deliver the required result.

With birth control, policy-makers, donors, international aid agencies and (sometimes) the medical profession collude in the blatant falsehood: contraception can prevent abortion. In truth, contraception does not and *cannot* prevent abortion. The experience of Europe shows this to be the case.

Despite doctors' best intentions, contraception has never replaced abortion. It may *lessen* the need for abortions and thus reduce the abortion rate. But the inconvenient truth remains: contraception sometimes fails and people sometimes fail to use it. If families are to be planned and births spaced, to give mothers a chance to recover between one pregnancy and the next, and if children are to be wanted, abortion must be accepted as a fact of life.

A strategy to legitimise abortion and make it safe would sit comfortably alongside a strategy to legitimise and improve access to contraception. A comprehensive birth control strategy that allows women to make reproductive choices for themselves would be as good for women in the Global South as it would be for women in the Global North. So why not simply package up abortion and contraception together as birth control?

If the intention is to reduce the number of abortions, then the simplest and most honest way is to make it illegal and/or unobtainable. This was the approach pursued by opponents of abortion during the US presidency of Donald Trump who was honest about his view that pro-choice women were "nasty" and abortion was wrong.

In the USA, regulations targeted specifically at abortion providers have made clinics more costly and difficult to run. As a result, abortion access is undermined as clinics close or reorientate their services. In 2021 National Public Radio reported that Mississippi had just one abortion clinic in the entire state of 1.3 million people. While Catholicism is often associated with attacks on abortion, in the American South the growth of the Evangelical movement has provided an expanding base of hostility to women's choice.

The Guttmacher Institute[23] reported that from January to June 2021, 561 abortion restrictions were introduced across forty-seven states as state policy-makers tested the limits of what the Supreme Court would allow. Developments in Texas were particularly bizarre with the Governor signing legislation to ban abortions at six weeks of gestation. The law came with a particularly intrusive twist that would allow anyone opposed to abortion—regardless of their relationship to a patient—to sue an abortion provider or anyone who helps a woman obtain an abortion in ways that include providing a financial loan, or giving a lift to the clinic.

State laws often fail to be enacted. But regardless, they have a chilling effect on providers and on women.

Abortion may be a safe and simple procedure—but it draws meaning, not from what it is, but what it represents.

Throughout modernity, the control of reproduction, including the control of abortion, has concerned the control of women's lives, their life choices and who should exercise that control—the woman, her doctor, her husband, politicians and policy-makers, or other social agencies.

Since the 1970s, the gradual acceptance, and respectability, of family planning, contraception and abortion, but especially abortion, has come to be seen as a *symbol* of women's emancipation from traditional motherhood and of women's participation in the modern world. The feminist academic and activist Rosalind Pollack Petchesky describes the importance of abortion in this manner:

> To feminists and anti-feminists alike, it came to represent the image of the "emancipated woman" in her contemporary identity, focused on her education and work more than on marriage and childbearing; sexual activity outside the disciplinary boundaries of the parental family; independently supporting herself and her children; and consciously espousing feminist ideas.[24]

---

[23] https://www.guttmacher.org/article/2021/04/2021-track-become-most-devastating-antiabortion-state-legislative-session-decades.

[24] Rosalind Pollack Petchesky (1986). *Abortion and Woman's Choice: The State, Sexuality and Reproductive Freedom*, UK edn. London: Verso, p. 241.

Petchesky was writing in the early 1980s, when the typical abortion patient in the USA and much of Europe was white, middle class, young and unmarried and probably quite radical in her political views. Today, that is not so much the case. Today, the typical abortion patient is every-woman. In Britain, one woman in three will, at some time, have an abortion despite easy access to free contraception from a state funded family doctor, or a local specialist clinic. The numbers change little from year to year. Most of these women are in their twenties and, as we have already discussed, about half are already mothers. In so far as there has been an increase in the UK abortion rate in recent years it has been to older women, who are not ignorant of, nor unable to obtain contraception.

Individual women do not see abortion as a political statement—they see it as a basic healthcare need, a solution to a problem, a way to right something that has gone wrong in their lives, and a means to take back control of a life that has spun out of control.

But that is not the way abortion is viewed by society. Abortion as a moral issue exists in an uneasy relationship with the pragmatic decisions that women make. Abortion seems to contradict the image of what motherhood should be, especially when it is presented as something counterposed to motherhood and not as decision that a mother might make.

Modern liberal society has yet to resolve how to deal with abortion and resolves this quandary in a duplicitous way. Society wants abortion to be legal and safe, but rare; used when needed, but not needed; available, but stigmatised; right to provide, but wrong to use.

This places a burden on the women who need abortion services and those who provide these services. What should be accepted and promoted as an integral part of reproductive healthcare services—as normal and necessary as smear tests and breast exams—is treated as a dirty secret. A country with a "good" abortion rate is one with a low abortion rate. A clinic to which women return for a second abortion is a clinic that failed to provide her with the knowledge and means to prevent it.

How does what people think about abortion accord with what we know about abortion, since what we know is that abortion is necessary for women, necessary for society, has been tried and tested for millennia and, when properly provided, is less risky than the drive a woman makes to get to the clinic? How do we establish that abortion is not just a right for women, but it can be right in itself and not a cause of apology or social concern? These are the questions that the following chapters attempt to answer.

Abortion, qualified by circumstances that meet someone else's agenda, fails to provide reproductive freedom that women need, and to which we have a claim. To seize the agenda for ourselves requires a different attitude to abortion, and a change in the way we think about ourselves, our choices, our relation to society and the standing of a safe medical procedure.

3

The Case Against Abortion

If abortion is a necessary part of modern life, then modern life needs to change, because abortion involves killing one person for the convenience of others.

This is a common and not unreasonable response to the argument in our first chapter. Consider how we would respond to this argument: "elderly people are a problem for society, and especially for women; so it should be legal for their lives to be terminated at the request of their carer?" For some people—admittedly a small minority—abortion is no different; it involves taking the life of one innocent human being for the convenience of another.

The Christian evangelist Gregory P. Koukl argues that: "if the unborn is not a human person, no justification is necessary. However if the unborn is a human person, no justification is adequate."[1] Koukl's approach to abortion is extended to embryo research by a professor

---

[1] Cited in Frances J. Beckwith (2007). *Defending Life: A Moral and Legal Case Against Abortion Choice.* Cambridge: Cambridge University Press, p. 129.

A. Furedi, *The Moral Case for Abortion,*
https://doi.org/10.1007/978-3-030-90189-9_3

of philosophy and Church–State studies at Baylor University in Texas, Frances J. Beckwith, who writes:

> If human persons ought not to be either subjects of research or killed without justification, and if the unborn from conception is a fully-fledged member of the human community, then killing embryos is *prima facie* morally wrong.[2]

The logic is hard to fault, but we need to bear in mind that the operative word is "*if*".

If, like Koukl and Beckwith, we accept that the embryo is deserving of every form of protection and every claim that we associate with members of our human community, truly there can be no defence of abortion. From this perspective, abortion involves the taking of a human life in a way that is not just tantamount to murder—it is murder.

Viewed in this way, the argument that women have a right to choose abortion as a personal private matter makes no sense at all. If a foetus has the moral status of a person, surely it would follow that there should be no greater scope for personal choice in "foeticide" than there is scope for personal choice in "parenticide." Society has very clear prohibitions about killing people and even advocates of personal autonomy in private matters accept that individual freedom has limits. Normally, we understand the limits of our own freedoms to be the point at which they impinge on the freedoms of others. This leads us to not only refrain from harming others, but to have a strong preference for tolerating others' opinions, as long as they do not harm us.

In this spirit, many people in modern liberal societies adopt a "live and let live" approach to abortion that supports the right of each woman to make a decision according to her own views. It is not uncommon for people who think abortion is wrong to prefer it to be safe, legal and left to the decision of the pregnant woman.

To Beckwith, this approach is not so much "live and let live" as "live and let die." He argues that believing that opposition to abortion should be limited to one's own actions ("if you don't agree with abortion

---

2 Frances J. Beckwith (2007). *Defending Life: A Moral and Legal Case Against Abortion Choice.* Cambridge: Cambridge University Press, p. xiv.

then don't have one—but let others decide for themselves too") reduces the abortion debate to a preference claim. To his ears, it sounds "as if the abortion-choicer is saying, 'Don't like murder, then don't kill any innocent persons'."[3]

For abortion's opponents, the claim that they have an absolute belief in the sanctity of human life, which is founded on principles and core beliefs, has allowed them to stake out their camp on the moral high ground—pushing those advocating for abortion as a necessary "fact of life" into an unprincipled quagmire. For thinkers such as David Oderberg, the deontological perspective that abortion is wrong in itself is superior to the teleological thinking of moral ethicists[4] who judge acts according to the results they achieve. Oderberg presents consequentialist thinking as a form of philosophy of convenience.[5]

This dismissal of modern utilitarianism is shallow and caricatured, but there is something that is, at the same time, satisfying and safe about the certainty of deontological absolutism. The notion that there can be no abortion because human life at every stage is sacred has an attractive certainty. It seems to represent a clear foundational pillar of a principle against which to lean. That it allows for no doubt, nuance or compromise seems reassuring, and it seems likely that this is why, in a world of swirling uncertainties and competing moral claims, a stance that presents itself as fundamentally "Pro Life" seems attractive. There are no namby-pamby "ifs" and "buts" to consider, only the basic principle: abortion is always wrong.

However, much as abortion's opponents would like to present themselves as having an uncompromising standard of pro-life values, the modern world, with modern values and aspirations, has undermined their moral foundations, leading them to make greater and greater compromises to their "no, no, never" position on abortion. As a result,

---

[3] Francis J. Beckwith (2007). *Defending Life: A Legal and Moral Case Against Abortion Choice.* Cambridge: Cambridge University Press, p. 5.

[4] Such as Professors John Harris and Peter Singer, leading ethicists (in Britain and the USA respectively) who consider abortion to be permissible on a broadly utilitarian and morally unproblematic basis.

[5] See David S. Oderberg (2000). *Moral Theory: A Non-Consequentialist Approach.* Oxford: Blackwell, pp. 66–76.

their authority to level criticisms at abortion's supporters for lacking in principles rings hollow.

However, today very few opponents of abortion claim to oppose it under any and every circumstance.

Pragmatism sits more easily than fundamentalism with today's zeitgeist and it seems increasingly difficult to maintain support for the principle that it is *never* acceptable to terminate life in the womb. Most people accept the need for some kind of compromise in the law and practice to accommodate the views of others.

This was illustrated by the successful overturning of the ban on abortion in the Republic of Ireland, a nation that still identifies as culturally Catholic. In 2018, in a national referendum, a two-thirds majority voted to change the constitutional ban on abortion by striking down Article 40.3.3 of the Constitution. What had become known in the Republic of Ireland as the "Eighth Amendment" was adopted in 1983 and gave the life of the foetus equal protection to that of the woman. Paradoxically, the balance of opinion reflected in the 1983 vote was a mirror image of that in 2018; then two-thirds had voted for it to be adopted. Public opinion had reversed.

This constitutional change paved the way for a law which provides abortion on request in early pregnancy. Much of the support for constitutional reform was based on the need to move from restrictions so rigid that they had demonstrably undermined maternal care. In 2012, a 31-year-old woman, Savita Halappanavar, died in an Irish hospital from a septic miscarriage. In almost any other country in the world, her condition would have been managed by emptying her uterus. Her condition required that the pregnancy was ended. Here, staff felt unable to terminate the pregnancy until they could detect no foetal heartbeat. The consequences—the needless death of a young woman, were beyond tragic. Savita Halappanavar's death exposed that the arcane abortion law had consequences even for women with wanted pregnancies.

It was also increasingly evident to residents of Ireland that, regardless of the directions of the Church and State, women continued to avail themselves of abortion through illegally buying medication online or, by the more traditional route, travelling to other European jurisdictions where the procedure was legal.

The change in the Irish law made a significant international impression. Prior to the referendum it had become a "showcase state" for the international anti-abortion movement.

The last decade has seen progressive changes to the abortion law made in countries as different as Argentina and the Isle of Man. Fundamental opposition to abortion in all circumstances seems increasingly hard to maintain against both arguments for the tolerance of pluralism in political opinion and for pregnant women to be trusted to make decisions about their lives. A growing narrative that individuals know their own lives, are best placed to draw on their experience and make decisions accordingly has created a growing challenge for those who oppose abortion on the basis of principle.

Once the principle of equal protection for the life of the woman and foetus is ruptured, it is hard to maintain firm foundations for total opposition to abortion based the equality of human life at all its stages. This is why the 2018 Irish referendum was so bitterly contested. If the life of the woman is paramount over that of the embryo in some cases, this begs the question, why not in others?

This chapter looks at the how abortion opponents have struggled to stay "on message."

The status of the embryo is at the heart of the abortion debate. This has been contested by scholars in philosophy, science and religion for centuries and is still unresolved. For some ethicists it speaks to far more than the nature of a cluster of cells but the essence of what makes us human and what makes humans special and deserving of our "sanctity of life." Is it our species membership? Our capacities? Our potential? Or, are we not special at all—or at least no more than other living creatures?

Traditionally, arguments against abortion have centred exclusively on the moral status and value of the foetus and have made no attempt to take into consideration any rights or claims of the pregnant woman on whom the unborn life depends. And their proponents make no apology for this. In the scale of wrongs, what can be more wrong than the taking of an innocent life? And what can be more innocent than a baby that has not taken its first breath? Is it such a big ask for a woman to carry her pregnancy to term and be delivered of a baby and all that it represents?

The conflict over abortion is seen to be a contest between the interests of a mother-to-be and her child-to-be: to put it another way, between the interests of the woman and the foetus *in utero*. How this is resolved and, just as crucially, *who* resolves it, lies at the heart of the abortion contest.

Opposition to abortion is sometimes viewed as being based on religious belief—Catholicism, in particular. But, essentially, this is not the case. There are fascinating debates between scholars about the evolution of the different religious claims about the start of life, even within Catholicism. *A Brief Liberal Catholic Defense of Abortion* is a particularly rich account of the nuanced development of Catholic thinking, its consideration of different theories of "ensoulment" and the requirement that engagement in sexual intercourse is predicated by commitment to the possible life resulting from an act celebrating love.[6]

Many Catholics, however (even those who practice and are active in their church) reject Vatican prohibitions of birth control, and claim that in modern Western society Catholics use birth control at the same rate as non-Catholics.[7] Population data support this. For example, the fertility rate in Italy is one of the lowest in Europe, and contraceptive use in Ireland is comparable to the UK.[8]

It is simply incorrect to associate modern opposition to abortion with Catholicism, or any other faith-based belief. It may be that conservative individuals who are opposed to the values associated with modern birth control (sexual freedom, women's equality and self-determination) are also more likely to be church members, but that is not always the case.

There is a rationale to abortion opposition that stands apart from faith and belief. The logical framework that underpins much opposition to abortion thinking is as follows:

i. From the moment conception takes place, the embryo is a full member of the human community;

---

[6] Daniel A. Dombrowski and Robert Deltete (2000). *A Brief, Liberal, Catholic Defense of Abortion*. Urbana: University of Illinois Press.

[7] Rachel K. Jones and Joerg Dreweke (2011). *Countering Conventional Wisdom: New Evidence on Religion and Contraceptive Use*. Washington, DC: Guttmacher Institute.

[8] Nargund G. (2009). Declining Birth Rate in Developed Countries: A Radical Policy Re-think Is Required. *Facts, Views & Vision in ObGyn*, 1(3), 191–193.

ii. In principle, it is wrong to kill any member of the human community;
iii. Every abortion procedure kills such a person;
iv. Therefore, every abortion is wrong.

If this is your framework of values, it is hard to see how abortion is allowable. And according to that viewpoint, one opponent of abortion notes, "it is a serious wrong that is committed on a scale that is hard to grasp. In the USA, around 1.4 million abortions are carried out every year. In Britain it is 180,000. In Australia, the figure is 80,000. In Russia, some 3.5 million abortions occur annually, and in China … the figure (though hard to verify) is over 10 million.[9]

For anti-abortion fundamentalists this represents a scale of horror unprecedented in history.

The Move from Morals

During recent decades, however, opponents of abortion have moved away from this foundational anchor of moral principle, seemingly in an attempt to connect with contemporary values.

It may be that anti-abortion advocates have shifted tactically because they believe modern Western society to be more secular, more "consequentialist" and less attracted to foundational moral principles. Or perhaps they themselves have been affected by the lure of pragmatism and moral relativism for which, in the past, they have condemned liberals. However, the focus of the argument against abortion has shifted from the absolute objection that abortion is morally wrong in itself to claims based on its detrimental impact on women and society, as well as to the foetus.

Today, opponents of abortion are more likely to try to claim legitimacy from science than from moral certitude, and to represent themselves as being as "pro" the lives of women as much they are pro-life in the

---

[9] David S. Oderberg (2000). *Applied Ethics: A Non-Consequentialist Approach*. Oxford: Blackwell, p. 2.

womb. Instead of polarising discussion along a dividing line of what is "right" and what is "wrong" they are paying more attention to issues that will allow those individuals who are unconvinced and unideological to move closer to their way of thinking. They target people whom the feminist writer Katha Pollitt[10] has described as "the muddled middle" with a strategy that aims both at their heads, through appeals to scientific evidence, and their hearts, through appeals for compassion.

It is always helpful for advocates of any persuasion to claim support from changes in scientific thought. Not only does evidence appear to give a claim of objective credibility, but *new* evidence invites a change of mind. Abortion opponents claim that their case for the foetus's right to life is stronger than it has ever been because more is factually known about the foetus than ever before. And it is true that medical science has increased our understanding of certain aspects of foetal development, especially regarding how it is affected by the life of the pregnant woman. The moral impact of this increased knowledge, however, remains open to debate.

Just five decades ago it was assumed that the uterus contained the foetus like a diving bell, preserving it in the environment necessary to sustain it. Since the 1960s, we have grown increasingly aware that a pregnant woman's behaviour can impact on the developing foetus. We know that poor diet, excessive alcohol consumption and smoking can compromise foetal health; we know that certain vitamins can be beneficial. Women are not only advised on antenatal care during pregnancy, but also on pre-conception care to prepare their bodies to provide the most healthy nurturing environment for a planned pregnancy.

Pregnancy tests are now able to confirm the hormonal changes of early pregnancy even before its symptoms appear; thus women's knowledge of their condition is possible from very early stages of pregnancy.

Abortion's opponents are correct to assume that these developments may give "being pregnant" a greater "meaning" to some women, particularly those who want to be pregnant. Early clinical diagnosis and social assumptions about early pregnancy care may suggest to some women that they already have a role and responsibility to the "unborn child,"

---

[10] Katha Pollitt (2014). *Pro: Reclaiming Abortion Rights*. New York: Picador.

even before it has drawn a breath. Antenatal ultrasound scans, and tests to detect abnormalities, allow us to be relatively confident that the baby is developing healthily, which also encourages an emotional investment from early on in the pregnancy.

A woman at twenty weeks' gestation with a wanted pregnancy may well have named her "unborn child," and already started to stock the nursery and be presenting her pregnant belly in the maternity fashion of the moment. She will anticipate the first glimmers of foetal movement with excitement. Her partner, even the wider family and friends, may be planning how they will welcome their new family member. The loss of the pregnancy through a miscarriage, even during the early weeks of pregnancy, may be as devastating as the loss of an infant.

Society's encouragement of a culture of pre-birth motherhood may seem to encourage abortion's opponents. But the concerns of women who want to be pregnant are not necessarily applicable to women who see their pregnancy as a problem. Abortion's opponents have a tunnel vision focused only on the foetus, and because the woman's perspective is not manifested in the foetal form, it is invisible.

This may create some genuine confusion. How can it be permissible that while one foetus be is protected and nurtured, the other is destroyed and disposed of? The only possible answers seem to be that those requesting abortion are either ignorant, or in denial that they are carrying a "pre-born" child.

This reasoning has resulted in the production of a gallery of materials for public education. Posters, leaflets, postcards, videos, plastic foetuses, and jewellery in the shape of tiny feet are designed to illustrate a simple message: this is the start of human life and this is what abortion destroys. Abortion clinics are criticised for not showing women the scans of their pregnancies and accused of concealing what a woman's foetus truly looks like. The protesters justify their presence by claiming that if women "knew the truth" it would change their decision because, they ask: "who could knowingly stop the beating heart of their baby-in-waiting?"

In some US states, claims that women need information specific to their individual pregnancy, to provide properly informed consent to abortion, have led to requirements that the mother of the unborn child view her ultrasound scan, or listen to the foetal heartbeat. The information provided may have an emotional impact at some level, but there is no evidence that shows it changes minds.

Women do not seek abortion because they are ignorant that the foetus is a potential child—they seek abortion precisely *because* they know it.[11] In truth, abortion providers, like all good doctors, are keen to provide any information a patient wishes to receive. They, more than anyone, are motivated to ensure their patients' consent to clinical intervention is obtained properly. Not to do so, in most countries, would lay them open to criminal prosecution and potentially costly private litigation.

A request for an abortion is a request to end, not just the condition of pregnancy, but the possibility of a live birth. That, after all, is the point of the procedure, and evidence that a foetus has a heartbeat is simply a fact, but is not an argument against an abortion.

Contemporary foetal imaging techniques have improved the diagnostic capabilities within foetal medicine, but to the untrained eye, they do not come close to being as affecting as the photographic images of the foetus taken by the Swedish photographer Lennart Nilsson in the early 1960s. His iconic photographic feature, "The Drama of Life before Birth," which first appeared in *Life* magazine in 1965, and later as a book,[11] still sets the standard for the presentation of embryonic/foetal development as a personal path of evolution. As many feminist critics have pointed out, Nilsson's photography employs all manner of deliberate technical presentation and descriptive techniques to evoke "foetal personhood." And yet, if it was the photographer's intent to dramatise life before birth to turn opinion against abortion, he failed: just two years later in Britain, and nine years later in the US, abortion was legalised.[12]

For more than a century, people have known that from early in pregnancy, foetuses look like miniature babies, and yet they have continued to make legal, moral and public policy decisions related to abortion regardless.[13]

---

[11] Lennart Nilsson (1990). *A Child Is Born*. London: Doubleday.

[12] Karen Newman (1996). *Fetal Positions. Individualism, Science and Visuality*. Stanford: Stanford University Press.

[13] Sara Dubow (2011). *Ourselves Unborn: A History of the Fetus in Modern America*. Oxford: Oxford University Press. Dubow provides a thorough account of how in the USA in the 1930s

Nevertheless, as Rosalind Pollack Petchesky observed, taking metaphysical and moral ideas and presenting them as "arresting visual images that are utterly physiological and often just plain morbid" achieves "a propagandistic *tour de force*."[14] It shifts the debate from the abstract to the specific. It makes the foetus seem real, equating its existence to that of the woman, thus helping abortion's opponents build the case that there truly are two people to consider.

By juxtaposing images of well-developed but "defenceless" foetuses with dismembered remains following abortions, anti-abortion advocates manage to manipulate maternal feelings of protection towards the unborn "baby" into gut-wrenching horror at its destruction.

From any metaphysical or moral perspective, the notion that either policy on abortion, or women's attitudes to their pregnancy, should be shaped by what the foetus *looks* like seems unbelievably shallow. If one holds a principled belief that abortion is murder, then surely it is wrong regardless of whether the foetus looks like a child or a frog.

Nonetheless, development of ultrasound scanning technologies, which are often said to have "created a window into the womb," have considerable emotional power. Much media attention has been given to the development of "4D" ultrasound in the 1990s, which provided a sharper image of the foetus (in the fourth dimension of "real time"). These computer-constructed images were far more like photographs than the fuzzy outlines of "something-in-a-snow-storm-that-might-look-like-a-baby-if-you-try-hard-to-see-one." They are still nowhere near as evocative as Nilsson's photographs, but they have become popular with women who think of themselves as expectant mothers and are impatient to see if the baby has dad's nose.

In the USA and Europe, opponents of abortion have embraced the technology to argue for a reduction in the legal abortion time limit, claiming the scans show that "unborn babies" can stretch, kick and leap around at twelve weeks, make intricate finger movements at fifteen weeks and yawn at twenty weeks. However, there are significant questions as

---

preserved fetal specimens were displayed as educational specimens, and how they became an emblem of the American family.

[14] Rosalind Pollack Petchesky (1986). *Abortion and Women's Choice: The State, Sexuality, and Reproductive Freedom*. London: Verso, p. 334.

to what "meaning" can truly be attributed to physical movement in the womb, which has been dismissed as a form of anthropomorphism by some concerned with foetal responsiveness, especially with regard to pain.[15]

The shallow anthropomorphism of today's anti-abortion obsession with foetal appearance is a pitiful parody of the concern that scholars once had about how the appearance of the foetus affected its status.

The appearance of the embryo was a matter of great significance to medieval scholars because it related to theological discussions about the soul. Whether the embryo had a "human" body was directly related to Catholic prohibition on abortion since an important principle of the Thomistic school—after the thirteenth-century Dominican scholar Thomas Aquinas—was that there could be no "personhood" without the presence of a rational or spiritual soul that had been "infused" into the body by God.[16] If there was no human body, there could be no human soul, because the two were intractably and inseparably linked. For Aquinas, the relationship between the human soul and the human body was dialectical; each relied upon the other to be what it was. Unless the *body* was human, it could not receive a human *soul*; unless a human soul was instilled, there could be no humanness. Aquinas, viewed by many scholars as one of the most significant contributors to Western thought,[17] sought to reconcile the principles of the Catholic Church with the philosophical principles of reason, assuming that revelation could guide reason and reason could demystify faith.

Catholic scholarly fascination with embryonic form prompted similar concerns after the development of early microscopes in the seventeenth century which allowed what was thought to be human life to be seen in semen.[18]

---

[15] Stuart W. G. Derbyshire (2001). Fetal Pain: An Infantile Debate. *Bioethics,* 15(1), 77–84.

[16] Daniel Dombrowski and Robert Deltete (2000). *A Brief, Liberal, Catholic Defense of Abortion.* Urbana: Illinois University Press, pp. 26–31.

[17] Bertrand Russell (1946). *The History of Western Philosophy and Its Connection with Political and Social Circumstances from the Earliest Times to the Present Day.* London: George Allen and Unwin, pp. 372–386.

[18] Karen Newman (1996). *Fetal Positions: Individualism, Science, and Visuality.* Stanford: Stanford University Press, p. 33.

Interest in what the foetus feels and knows may be longstanding, but it has never been as embedded in the zeitgeist as it is now. It is easy to see how, once the idea that the only difference between a baby and a foetus is its geographical relationship to the uterus, society starts to think about how to treat the foetus more like a baby.

One big step down from the moral high ground was made when opponents of abortion linked their right-to-life claims for the foetus to its appearance and another was when they started to raise concerns about specific abortion methods. The impact of the abortion on the foetus has moved from being an objection to a general wrong (its death) to a more focussed assault on specific procedures, or even aspects of procedures (the way the death of the foetus is brought about).

Abortion horror stories focussing on evil doctors, torturous techniques and the callous discarding of remains represent the revival of a long-standing feature of anti-abortion advocacy. The intention, presumably, is to demonise providers, turn the stomach of public opinion and terrify potential patients.

Various inventive techniques have been used to place images in the public domain. Billboards, social media sites, leafleting in areas where clinics are situated are routine.

In the 1997 UK general election one anti-abortion group established itself as a specific "Pro-Life" party. It ran the number of candidates that would entitle it to include five minutes' worth of footage alleged to represent the products of abortion within a party political broadcast. The high cost of election expenses was deemed worth it: if the PPB was broadcast, millions of people would find themselves viewing "the truth about abortion" on primetime TV; if it were banned, it would serve as evidence that "the truth" of abortion is genuinely too offensive to be seen. The presentations of abortion in the broadcast were dishonest in a number of ways. The images of late gestation procedures are unrepresentative of most abortions. In the UK, more than 80% of abortions take place before ten weeks of pregnancy, most being in the form of a medication-induced miscarriage when the appearance of the foetus is more like a partially sprouted mung bean than the "pre-born" baby of the campaign material. In most other countries, the proportion of late-second trimester abortions is just as small; in many cases, legal time limits prohibit them altogether.

Images of the foetus following abortion places a focus on its destruction that is utterly fetishised. The impact on the foetus is all that is shown, with no consideration as to the causes and consequences the abortion has for the woman. It is also true that this revelling in the gore, broken bodies, severed limbs and crushed heads has a pornographic quality. Considering the outcome of a procedure in terms of the byproduct, what is technically regarded as "the clinical waste," is a perversion of the way we consider other surgical interventions. The bloody, excised tumour is not perceived as the outcome of an operation to treat breast cancer; the outcome is the tumour-free breast and the cancer-free woman who can now continue her life as lived before her diagnosis. If we followed the same approach, we would see the outcome of the abortion as the empty uterus and the woman freed from the burden of her unwanted pregnancy. But these "indisputable truths" seem to have only limited impact on what has come to be described as abortion's "yuk factor." Images of foetuses after abortion and detailed descriptions of what happens during an abortion procedure have proven to be a powerful weapon in the anti-choice armoury.

A particularly successful campaign that centred on the horror of abortion was waged in the USA against a procedure known to doctors as intact dilatation and extraction (D&X) and to its non-medical opponents as "partial birth abortion." The Supreme Court confirmed a ban by Congress of the procedure in 2007 following a controversy that had dominated and shaped the discussion about later-term abortions since the late 1990s.

Congress described D&X as "a gruesome and inhuman procedure that is never medically necessary and should be prohibited." The majority opinion of the Supreme Court mirrored this, noting that "a foetus is a living organism within the womb, whether or not it is viable outside the womb" and that "choosing not to prohibit [a brutal and inhumane procedure] will further coarsen society to the humanity of not only new-borns, but all vulnerable and innocent human life, making it increasingly difficult to protect such life."[19]

Admittedly, descriptions of a D&X abortion make for grim reading—even without the emotive language and cartoons that embellish the descriptions used by the procedure's opponents. But as a description of foetal destruction relatively late in pregnancy, how could it be otherwise? D&X, as described in an article defending the procedure in the *New England Journal of Medicine* (*NEJM*) "involves dilating the cervix, partially extracting the foetus, puncturing the skull while it remains in the uterus, and removing the brain tissue through suction, thus allowing for easy removal of the otherwise intact foetus through the birth canal."[20]

The *NEJM* notes that D&X procedures were rare: reportedly performed by just thirty-one providers in 2000 and accounted for 0.17% of all abortions each year. A far more common procedure was dilatation & evacuation (D&E). Paradoxically, D&E is arguably no less "gruesome" than D&X, and it is the results of D&E that are most commonly used in anti-choice literature. In D&E, rather than puncturing and decompressing the skull of the foetus to allow intact removal through the dilated cervix, the foetus is dismembered in the uterus and removed in parts. One aspect of D&X that was given little attention by the US Congress or Court was that the procedure was developed because, in the view of those who practised it, it reduced the small but existing risk to the woman of uterine damage or perforation from surgical instruments and sharp remnants of foetal bone.

The campaign against, and ban on, D&X has been a significant strategic success for abortion's opponents. The public campaign shaped how the American public thought about abortion for more than a decade. Although just a tiny proportion of abortions were carried out beyond the first trimester, and a fraction of these involved D&X, these procedures came to represent "the truth about abortion." Under pressure, and on the defensive as a result of the increasingly lurid descriptions of

---

[19] Cited and discussed in R. Alta Charo (2007). The Partial Death of Abortion Rights. *New England Journal of Medicine*, 356, 2125–2128.
[20] Ibid.

D&X, much of the pro-choice movement adopted a strategy of down-playing the extent to which it was used. This tactic seriously damaged their credibility when it became evident that the procedure was used more extensively than reported and led to unwarranted speculation about how truthfully facts had been presented.

But most concerning is that Members of Congress and Supreme Court judges have inserted themselves between doctors and patients, substituting their emotional responses to the description of a surgical intervention for medical learned opinion about the best clinical practice. Dr. Michael F. Greene, Professor of Obstetrics, Gynecology and Repro-ductive Biology at Harvard Medical School and Director of Obstetrics at Massachusetts General Hospital, is one of many doctors who has argued that the banning of the procedure represents "the intimidation of Amer-ican physicians"[21] causing them to be constantly anxious about whether their performance on the operating table can be justified in court.

Both the scrutiny of clinical practice, and the "horribilising" of tech-niques used, are now well established as preferred ways to undermine abortion practice. In March 2015, the Kansas House of Representa-tives passed a bill to ban D&E abortions with one member referencing medical experiments in World War II by Nazi doctor Josef Mengele: "This procedure we discuss today is the ultimate evil. You're literally ripping apart a live human being."

The increasing political regulation of abortion clinical practice accel-erated under the Trump administration and became a successful way to shut down abortion services without a head-on debate about abor-tion morals. The Guttmacher Institute, which tracks abortion statistics and supports abortion rights in the USA, claims that the 2021 legisla-tive season saw more abortion restrictions signed into law across the States than in any other single year. A report in *The New York Times* illustrates the terms of the debate in its report of a legal ban on an abortion technique in Texas. For the American College of Obstetri-cians & Gynecologists, the procedure was, "the safest and medically preferred abortion procedure ... [which] ... results in fewer medical

---

[21] Michael F. Greene (2007). The Intimidation of American Physicians—Banning Partial-Birth Abortion. *The New England Journal of Medicine*, 356, 2128–2129.

complications." Abortion opponents referred to the technique used for second-trimester abortions as "dismemberment abortion" and called it "barbaric."[22]

A similar focus on the "horror of abortion," in recent decades, has been whether the foetus feels "pain"; this has been an area of particular interest and anti-abortion advocacy.

The claim of foetal pain in abortion has been an effective tactic for those seeking to persuade legislators to ban it, induce maximum guilt in those undergoing it, and encourage public revulsion against it. In the USA, in 2021, twenty states had laws that curtail abortion on grounds of pain and a "Pain-Capable Unborn Child Protection Act'" (S.160) has been sitting with the Senate for some years. In the UK, references to foetal pain are made frequently in parliamentary discussions on abortion and have been examined by the Parliamentary Science & Technology Committee. The issue has been sufficiently important to have caused the Royal College of Obstetricians & Gynaecologists to produce a "Review of Research and Recommendations for Practice" on "Foetal Awareness" (which were included in recent national guidelines on abortion.

The debate has had substantial international impact. In 2007, the UK Parliament tasked its Science and Technology Committee to examine the issue, which it did and rejected proposals that the time limit for abortion be reduced. However, as a consequence of continued lobbying from members of parliament opposed to abortion, government officials requested that the Royal College of Obstetricians and Gynaecologists (RCOG) review the issue, which it had studied ten years earlier. It did so and concluded that the foetus was not sufficiently developed physiologically to feel pain before twenty-four weeks' gestation:

> Connections from the periphery to the cortex are not intact before twenty-four weeks of gestation. Most pain neuroscientists believe that the cortex is necessary for pain perception; cortical activation correlates strongly with pain experience and an absence of cortical activity generally indicates an absence of pain experience. Furthermore, there is good

---

[22] Texas Can Ban Common Form of Second-Trimester Abortion, Appeals Court Rules. *New York Times* 18 August 2021.

evidence that the foetus is sedated by the physical environment of the womb and usually does not awaken before birth.[23]

This advice was reviewed again before inclusion in the 2019 UK National Institute of Clinical Excellence *Guideline: Evidence-Based Recommendations for Abortion Care (Termination of Pregnancy)*.

Almost all pain specialists address the problem in a way that considers pain experience to be more than a physiological response, but is, instead, based upon a complex mix of neuroanatomical responses with learned associations and interpretations that are only possible once an individual is sufficiently developed mentally to process experience in a conscious sense that relies on an awareness of its body and itself. This forms the basis of an argument that suggests how foetal responses *in utero* demonstrate just how *un*like a conscious individual the foetus is. Dr. Stuart W. G. Derbyshire is a scientist who is personally pro-choice but has professionally sought to bring balanced and nuanced interventions to the debate, reviewing his approach as new evidence has come to light.[24]

The importance attributed to the discussion on foetal pain by anti-abortion advocates seems extraordinary since they would presumably be just as opposed to abortion if it were to be demonstrated conclusively that the foetus was numb and unresponsive to all sensation (which no one claims). People who believe abortion should be legal do not hold that view because they are convinced the foetus is insensate, but because they are convinced that the procedure is necessary for the woman. *If* the foetus were found to experience pain, it may prompt changes in practice. to reduce "unnecessary suffering"—perhaps some kind of pre-procedure foetal anaethesthesia—but not a ban on abortion.

[23] Royal College of Obstetricians and Gynaecologists (2010). *Foetal Awareness: Review of Research and Recommendations for Practice. Report of a Working Party.* London: RCOG, p. 11. NICE (2019). *Guideline: Evidence-Based Recommendations for Abortion Care (Termination of Pregnancy).* London: National Institute of Clinical Excellence.

[24] See Stuart W. G. Derbyshire and A. Raja (2011). On the Development of Painful Experience. *Journal of Consciousness Studies,* 18(9–10), 233–256; Sullivan Mark D., Derbyshire, Stuart W.G. (2015) Is There a Purely Biological Core to Pain Experience? *PAIN,* 156(11): 2119–2120; Stuart W. G. Derbyshire and John C. Bockmann (2020). Reconsidering Foetal Pain *Journal of Medical Ethics* 46, 3–6.

For anti-abortion advocates, the discussion about foetal pain has served as a vehicle to create public unease about later gestation procedures, to encourage feelings of guilt in women who request an abortion in later pregnancy and to generally encourage the misconception that the foetus has feelings and emotions and suffers—"just like us."

In truth, the way that we "suffer" or "endure" pain is a complicated mash-up of physical, psychological, emotional and even philosophical elements. One crucial element for us in thinking about lived pain is context. Each of us knows what pain means for ourselves and how it expresses itself in associated suffering. We know what different pains signify: that the "ouchiness" of a stubbed toe is different to a nagging toothache, which is different to spasmodic menstrual cramps. Sudden pain feels different to anticipated pain. For us, pain has context, associations and meaning; it is something we associate with a cause or reason not just something that happens to us. Even the stubbed-toe "ouch" is an "ouch" because the human experience of pain is not as a matrix of neurons but a matrix of meanings in which something hurts because of a cause, and because of a hurt there may be a consequence. Pain is not a stand-alone event that can be isolated from the kind of life that we live, rather it is an experience, a part of "feeling" something as part of our life.

Before we assume the foetus feels things in the same way that we do, it is worth considering several things that are as important as the neuroscience that is usually considered. For example, what is pain for? And, what would be the purpose of pain for the foetus?

For us, pain is a signal of injury that induces action and commands our attention to our lived-in world. It signals that something is harmful. In the uterus, what would it be for? Do we consider that a foetus has other feelings (whether emotions or sensations)? Does the foetus feel hunger, thirst, anxiety, impatience to be born, dread of being born? Considering the physical trauma that the foetus must experience as it is pushed through the birth canal during a woman's labour, one might consider that there might be great evolutionary benefit in the development of pain mechanisms and sensation only after birth.

No one can say with absolute certainty that they know beyond doubt what the foetus experiences in the womb. There is a huge literature on pain experience in animals as well as humans that considers life experience and is quite as politically charged as that which concerns the foetus. The danger is that that our desire to be certain can sometimes lead us to refuse to consider true answers to a question *that has been asked* and instead we answer with answers based on the evidence of what we can uncover.

While there is much we cannot *prove* about the presence or absence of pain experience, especially when we might not even agree on the definition of pain, the motivation of abortion doctors to avoid pain—just like any other doctor—should be beyond question. This is, however, not the case. Just as abortion techniques are presented as devilish activities, so the doctors who provide them are cast as demons.

As the foetus has been humanised, so abortion doctors have been *de*humanised and their integrity is increasingly called into question. While abortion providers see themselves as helping women by providing essential care that allows them to implement their reproductive decisions, abortion opponents portray providers as either profiteers who exploit women, or (at best) misguided and lacking moral perspective.

The behaviour of abortion providers is scrutinised far more intensely than that of their colleagues in other areas of medicine. Their actions are held to a far higher standard. Wherever abortion care is legally provided, there are almost always special laws and regulations to "police" the practice, spelling out in detail how clinical services must be run, as though legislators lack confidence that abortion providers share the integrity and competence of other clinical practices.

This creates an atmosphere of distrust that their opponents can easily exploit. Allegations of impropriety and misdeeds of abortion providers make the headlines and fuel the climate of suspicion regardless of their truth. For abortion opponents, it does not matter whether doctors are prosecuted successfully. An atmosphere of intensified legal scrutiny has a chilling effect regardless.

Attempts by UK abortion opponents to uncover evidence of unlawful abortion practices fail repeatedly but create a chilling climate of suspicion. In 2005, the Secretary of State for Health required the Chief

Medical Officer to conduct a full-scale investigation into a charitable not-for-profit abortion provider following allegations of unlawful conduct. The official report, published after a year-long examination, concluded that no illegal activity had taken place.[25] More recently, attempts to entrap UK providers into providing abortions that failed to meet the legal grounds led to a swoop of inspections by the regulatory agencies. Over a three-day period all clinics and hospitals registered as abortion providers in the country were visited unannounced. Once again, no evidence of illegal abortion was turned up—although administrative irregularities with abortion-related paperwork in NHS hospitals led to some abortion doctors facing a threat of prosecution for almost two years before all charges against them were dropped.

In the USA, abortion providers have been the subjects of undercover filming which is then edited for dramatic effect. Planned Parenthood Federation of America (PPFA), a not-for-profit women's health service that provides abortion, has been subject to a persistent campaign of misrepresentation which led to serious debates as to whether the organisation should be stripped of government funding. In 2016 opponents of PPFA constructed "evidence" that purported to show that the clinics traded foetal tissue for profit, in a bizarre echo of allegations against abortion providers in the 1970s, when UK clinics were accused of selling aborted foetuses for soap.[26]

Probably, exploitative charlatans (and even criminals) do exist among the ranks of clinic owners. In countries where abortion is unlawful or severely restricted, women do fall prey to unscrupulous providers. If a service is driven underground, or into the shadows of questionable legality, the darker the motives of those involved are likely to be. The arrest and prosecution of Kermit Gosnell in 2011,[27] for the murder

---

[25] Chief Medical Officer (2005). *An Investigation into the British Pregnancy Advisory Service Response to Requests for Late Abortions—A Report by the Chief Medical* . London: Department of Health (Gateway ref: 5463).

[26] Michael Litchfield and Susan Kentish (1974). *Babies for Burning.* London: Serpentine Press.

[27] See e.g. Sabrina Tavernisen (2011, January 22). Squalid Abortion Clinic Escaped State Oversight. *New York Times.*

of infants in the course of running and operating a clinic in Philadelphia that was a caricature of every fantasy of a nightmare "abortuary," is evidence that "abortion butchers" can exist.

Regardless of their clinical competence, legal compliance or beneficence, abortion providers have always been, and will always be, subject to caricature as immoral by those who believe that they are (literally) carrying out the devil's work.

The focus on abortion practice, the procedures, and the experience of the foetus, has successfully generated a broad concern and unease based on the "yuk factor" in abortion—those parts of the practice that unsettle, discomfort and concern people at a visceral level. But this is not a successful strategy to challenge the legitimacy of abortion *qua* abortion. Rather, it provokes demands for abortions to be carried out earlier, or to be regulated more tightly, and invites suggestions for how abortion could be performed in ways that seem more acceptable and more humane. Ultimately, these are technical and medical questions that might speak to the ethics of medical practice, but not directly to the morality of abortion.

If abortion is fundamentally wrong, how it can it be more wrong because the foetus looks like a baby? Would a late gestation abortion be less wrong if it were performed using another technique? Would a foetal anaesthetic to eliminate the possibility of foetal pain make a difference?

It is evident that abortion's opponents see these issues as tactical battles in the context of their total war. A successful campaign against a particular abortion technique, such as D&X, may set a precedent for action against others, enabling abortion procedures to be criminalised one by one.

But there is, nevertheless, a huge gulf between a principled argument that abortion is wrong and the argument that a specific procedure is wrong. There is even more of a gulf between the argument that abortion is wrong because it is murderous, and abortion is cruel because it kills the foetus painfully.

The case against abortion—having moved from a principled objection to the taking of foetal life to attempts to underscore its supposed "horror" and cruelty to the foetus now pays more attention to the woman.

It may be that abortion's opponents have realised that focussing on the foetus and ignoring the woman risked marginalising women because now the movement that once was self-righteously anti-abortion regardless of the consequences, has started to present itself as self-consciously pro-women.[28]

Protesters at clinics frequently claim to be there to counsel women and "tell them the truth" (to offset the lies that they insist providers provide). They produce information leaflets detailing exaggerated and imagined risks of abortion in an attempt to build a case that it is bad for women. Spinning round feminist rhetoric about abortion being a means of regaining control, anti-abortion literature increasingly insists that motherhood is the mature, strong choice when a woman faces pregnancy.

Of course, in reality, no one has a greater interest in clearly explaining the risks and benefits of a procedure than the doctor who performs it. A woman cannot make her own decision to consent to abortion unless she is able to assess the risks and benefits of the choices available to her. Cynics might even suggest that abortion providers are especially motivated to ensure that women are provided with information and time to reflect on it, because society is increasingly litigious. No doctor wants to face future allegations of malpractice from a woman who regrets her decision.

Even if moral standards are set aside, modern medicine is built upon the principles of informed consent. A doctor's defence against assault is that his patient willingly consented to the intervention with full knowledge of the true risks and benefits. Modern societies typically have intricate policies and procedures to safeguard patients deemed not competent to provide this consent on their own behalf. Usually these are based on the principle that a doctor's first obligation is to do no harm. Even without reference to personal ethics, this is what the law requires.

Nevertheless, abortion's opponents insist that the risks of abortion have been underestimated, and protesters at clinics still claim that their presence is essential to provide information that providers deny women.

---

[28] Ellie Lee (2003). *Abortion, Motherhood and Mental Health: Medicalizing Reproduction in the United States and Great Britain*. New York: Aldine de Gruyter, pp 19–41.

Abortion is one of the most studied of all medical procedures and the substantial body of evidence available to those who wish to delve into the risks is colossal. Resources produced by medical colleges that include obstetricians and gynaecologists[29] (in the USA, the American College of Obstetricians and Gynecologists [ACOG] and in the UK the Royal College of Obstetricians and Gynaecologists [RCOG]) carry particular authority, because their members are as concerned with birth and babies as they are with abortion.

The claim that abortion damages fertility is particularly worrying to younger women who, while wanting to end *this* pregnancy, may have plans for future motherhood. One might think that sensationalist media accounts about the number of women who "repeatedly" have abortions would put this false allegation to bed, but the myth persists to the point where some of these "repeat" abortions are the consequence of young women mistakenly believing they are less fertile after an abortion.

Two especially contested areas have been the relationship between abortion and an increased risk of breast cancer, and the long-term psychological impact from abortion. These have been rich areas of anxiety for abortion's opponents to mine since these conditions have increased among women at the same time that the incidence of abortion has increased. The fact that figures of abortion rates, breast cancer rates and depression rates have increased in the last ten years does not however mean that one thing causes the other. *Correlation* (when two things happen at the same time) and *causality* (when one thing brings about another) are different. It has been widely reported that during the 2020 COVID epidemic dog ownership increased in Britain and North America. This does not mean dog ownership is related to respiratory infection.

Demonstrating, beyond doubt, that abortion *does not* cause breast cancer is far more difficult than sowing the seeds of doubt that it might cause it. When we face the diagnosis of a serious illness, we examine the entrails of our lives to find something to blame, and, in such moments,

---

[29] In the USA, the ACOG and in the UK the RCOG produce detailed guidelines containing information that their members should communicate to patients and how relative risks should be explained. In the UK, the National Institute for Health and Care Excellence work with professional bodies to provide evidence-based guidance.

we especially consider those things that some people consider to be morally wrong.

In every area of scientific inquiry, it is far harder (and sometimes impossible) to demonstrate conclusively that something has no impact; it is far easier to find examples of possible evidence that suggests possible cause—especially when you believe it must exist, and you are highly motivated to find it.

For many people there seems to be an intuitive "common-sense" element to claims that harm to a woman might result from the sudden, deliberate interruption of a pregnancy. Pregnancy is a natural state of being, and it seems reasonable to assume that it is best that the processes that are triggered by pregnancy should be allowed to run their course as nature intended. To bring a pregnancy to a sudden, "unnatural" end seems to be an invitation to some kind of problem arising, since even if the products of conception are removed successfully, the woman's body will need to readjust. Pregnancy involves significant changes in the hormones that specifically affect the woman's body, often in ways that are obvious to her. Swollen breasts, tender nipples, and a heightened emotional state are often the first hints to a woman that she has conceived. It begs the question of what happens when the cause of these changes is brought to a sudden, some would argue, "untimely" end.

Claims that abortion results in post-abortion psychosis and depression have continuing resonance, possibly because they seem to speak to "common sense," and especially so in an era when depression is defined so broadly as to include general unhappiness.[30] One of the few generalisations we can make about women seeking to end an unwanted pregnancy is that they are in a place they would rather not be. An abortion is no woman's ambition, and the unwanted pregnancy is often (although not always) a marker of a lot of other unwanted things in her life. Many women feel sad, angry, frustrated and even depressed following an abortion.

But this is not evidence that the abortion is the cause of these emotions; many studies show that a woman's emotional state after an

---

[30] Ellie Lee (2003). *Abortion, Motherhood and Mental Health: Medicalizing Reproduction in the United States and Great Britain.* New York: Aldine de Gruyter, pp. 46–54.

abortion is a continuation of how she felt before the procedure. Abortion does not end troubles beyond the pregnancy, and for many women, the pregnancy is not the only unwanted aspect of their lives. Regret is often expressed, not about the abortion itself, but the circumstances that made it necessary.

Nevertheless, the notion of a post-abortion syndrome, which is a variant of post-traumatic stress disorder, persists, supported by observations that it is under-reported, because doctors fail to look for it and because it is a politicised issue. Vincent Rue, an advisor to a former Surgeon General in the USA under President Reagan, is often credited with defining the syndrome. He claims that a medical profession that prefers to believe, for reasons of political correctness, that abortion brings relief, disregards it.[31] It is more likely that clinical psychologists disregarded the frequent claims for a post-abortion psychiatric syndrome, because of the loose, unspecific, catch-all nature of the condition. For example, Rue alleges that symptoms can include: "a variety of autonomic, dysphoric and cognitive symptoms; dissociative states lasting from a few minutes to several hours or even days during which components of the abortion are re-lived and the individual behaves as though experiencing the event at the moment; impulsive behavior, increased irritability, emotional liability, and depression and guilt resulting in self-defeating or suicidal behaviours." He then goes on to list the following symptoms that "may also be seen":

> Emotional distancing and numbing, feelings of helplessness, hopelessness, sadness, sorrow, lowered self-esteem, distrust, hostility towards oneself and others, regret, sleep disorders, recurring distressing dreams, nightmares, anniversary reactions, psycho-physiological symptoms, alcohol and/or chemical dependencies and abuse, sexual dysfunction, insecurity, painful unwanted re-experiencing of the abortion, relationship dysfunction, communication impairment and or/restriction, isolation, fetal fantasies, self-condemnation, flashbacks, uncontrollable weeping,

---

[31] Vincent M. Rue (1995). Post-abortion Syndrome: A Variant of Post-traumatic Stress Disorder. In Peter Doherty (Ed.), *Post-abortion Syndrome: Its Wide Ramifications*. Dublin: Four Courts Press, p. 20.

eating disorders, preoccupation, memory and/or concentration disruption, confused and/or distorted thinking, delusions, bitterness, an enduring sense of loss, survivor guilt with an inability to forgive oneself, psychological distress associated with physical complications and the corresponding need for psychotherapeutic and/or psychopharmacological treatment.[32]

Given the broad range of symptoms, it is easy to see why the condition can be dismissed—but also why it has been accepted. It is likely that almost every woman who has had an abortion has experienced a collection of these "symptoms" at some time in her life, and it is also likely that they have been experienced by those who have never ended a pregnancy—either because all of their pregnancies have been wanted, or because they have never conceived. Is there a woman anywhere who has not gone through "bad times"—whether or not she has experienced an abortion? Contrary to the assertions of anti-abortion activists, the majority of women granted an abortion report relief as their primary feeling, not depression.

Despite the absence of scientific support for the assertions of the anti-abortion movement, the myth persists. In a relatively recent move, some US states now require physicians to warn women seeking an abortion of the dangers to their mental health, in spite of the complete lack of scientific justification for doing so. In South Dakota, a 2005 state law not only mandated this perversion of informed consent, but also added a reprehensible smattering of emotional manipulation by insisting women be told they are terminating "a whole, separate, unique, living human being."

The arguments that abortion damages women have been quite successful in breaking down a barrier previously faced by opponents of abortion. Making a pro-woman case has made it easier to attract women to their cause.

The most important development in opposition to abortion is an apparent step back from the moral engagement and the clear absolute

---

[32] Vincent M. Rue (1995). Post-abortion Syndrome: A Variant of Post-traumatic Stress Disorder. In Peter Doherty (Ed.), *Post-abortion Syndrome: Its Wide Ramifications*. Dublin: Four Courts Press, p. 20.

opposition *based on principle*. Most of abortion's opponents are unlikely to focus their argument on a claim that abortion is wrong. Instead they concentrate on its risks to the woman, the cruelty to the foetus and the corrupt nature of its providers.

This may be an attempt to be sharper strategically, and to move away from the stereotypes and caricatures of their movement as religious, old-fashioned and indifferent to women. But an attempt to appear evidence-based and relevant and feminist brings its own dangers. The shift away from clear moral principles implicitly undermines the very principle of a moral principle.

For example, if your beliefs are contingent on medical claims that abortion damages women, what are the consequences when the evidence demonstrates otherwise?

It is curious that so much of the argument against abortion has come to focus on science and to uncover "evidence" of harm caused by abortion. Science may be useful in informing the decisions of policy-makers, but science cannot decide if abortion is right or wrong, or whether or not it should be legal. The moral status of abortion and its legality are questions that can only be addressed through moral and political debate. Our belief that the foetus does not feel pain does not negate objections to abortion any more than claims that it does stand as an argument for its prohibition. However, it would be wrong to conclude that the discussion is irrelevant or of concern only to doctors and scientists.

Today's anti-abortion movement is more nuanced and diverse in the arguments it employs. It is wrong to see it as Catholic, or traditionally conservative. Abortion's opponents are drawn from a far wider cross-section involving people who care about the protection of the "most vulnerable" and those "with no voice" (the foetus), and even some those who identify as feminist and see abortion as a medical means to manipulate and manage women to increase their availability to men.[33]

Of course, the notion that abortion is wrong and its providers are amoral, if not immoral, is always lurking behind the veil of other more pragmatic arguments. But to be successful, these claims need to connect

---

[33] Mary Krane Derr, Rachel MacNair and Linda Naranjo-Huebl (2005). *Prolife Feminism: Yesterday and Today*. Kansas City: Feminism and Non-Violent Studies Association.

with the concerns of the women they seek to convince. In the twenty-first century, appealing to morals is difficult when it is not always clear where a moral consensus lies, or even what the moral landscape is. It rather suggests the moral landscape of abortion needs to be redrawn—but in a rather different way.

4

The Case Against "The Case Against"

The case against abortion emerged from moral and theological principles and has adopted more secular and pragmatic arguments to win an audience. The case for legal abortion has been pragmatic from the start.

Supporters of legal abortion have never been a mirror image of their opponents. That abortion is wrong is not opposed by the argument that "abortion is good," but rather that women need abortion to preserve their health and well-being. It is certainly no woman's ambition to have an abortion, and most women, while not regretting their decision, regret the need to make it. Even those who see abortion as a political right do not see it as a right to be exercised, for example, like the right to vote or the right to free movement. Even in the political sphere, abortion is understood for what it is: simply a possible solution to the practical problem of an unwanted pregnancy.

Abortion seems to have no champions. Women would prefer not to need them; doctors would prefer not to need to perform them. When opponents of legal abortion say "abortion is bad," the counter-position is not "No, abortion is good," but often "Yes, but abortion is necessary."

This is not a matter of semantics or nuance. To support legal abortion is not to advocate that a woman *must* have one, but to support her

© The Author(s), under exclusive license to Springer Nature
Switzerland AG 2021
A. Furedi, *The Moral Case for Abortion*,
https://doi.org/10.1007/978-3-030-90189-9_4

choice of abortion if that is what she decides. This cannot be summed up as "abortion is always good" because, clearly, that is not what it means. If you believe that women have the right to make their own reproductive choices, then it follows that coercing or "conning" a woman into abortion is as wrong as denying her an abortion. The arguments against abortion and those for *freedom to choose* abortion are not different sides of the same coin. They express very different approaches to a moral quandary. One is prescriptive—saying what a woman cannot decide: the other is permissive—empowering a woman to make her own moral choice.

As Katha Pollitt says, "the term 'pro-choice' is an accurate term for those who support a woman's right to decide for herself whether to end a pregnancy or carry it to term."[1] "Pro-choice" is the way that most advocates of legal abortion would describe themselves—and so it is the term we will use, although their arguments have seldom been based on a woman's right to make reproductive choices, which is unfortunate, because the case for unrestricted access to legal abortion would have been clearer if this had been the case.

Making Abortion Reasonable

In our largely secular modern society, where extremism is regarded with suspicion, the pro-choice movement has been more comfortable leaving discussions of fundamental values and principles to their opponents and, instead, concentrating on abortion as a modern need (which, of course, it is). Consequently, their attention has been focussed on a way of explaining how abortion fits into women's lives.

Typically, the case put forward by even the most enthusiastic supporters of abortion choice is that there should be less of it—since no woman positively *wants* an abortion any more than someone wants a heart bypass operation or a skin graft. As providers argue, abortion is a solution to a problem pregnancy, and if there were fewer problem pregnancies, there would be fewer abortions. Thus, over the past few decades

---

[1] Katha Pollitt (2014). *Pro: Reclaiming Abortion Rights.* New York: Picador, p. 14.

there have been several initiatives to bring together coalitions of those who oppose abortion and those who do not, to reduce the number of procedures. Some saw this as an area of "common ground" on which they could work; others saw it as a marshy quagmire in which advocates of reproductive choice would sink.

Common Ground

On his first day in office as president in 1992, while reversing some of the anti-abortion policies of the Reagan–Bush administrations, Bill Clinton said his vision was of "an America where abortion is safe, legal and rare."[2] This is a vision that has been enthusiastically embraced by activists who wished to avoid accusations of extremism and appear reasonable. During the 1990s and into the twenty-first century campaigns originating in support for the choice of abortion increasingly adopted the language and goal of abortion prevention.[3] Campaigns for increased contraception and sex education were promoted in an attempt to demonstrate that abortion was no one's preferred end. This had the unintended effect of fuelling a discourse that presented abortion as a problem only for the young, the disadvantaged and the ignorant, and implied that it could be solved by prevention strategies. This approach ignored the inconvenient truth that the need for abortion, experienced by one woman in three, can arise for all manner of reasons at any time during her fertile life.[4]

The claim of reasonableness had become important to supporters of legal abortion in the first decade of the millennium, especially in the USA, where the controversies about "partial birth abortion" had left abortion's supporters feeling bruised, defensive and generally "on the back foot." By focussing attention on late procedures, this anti-abortion

---

[2] Robin Toner (1993, January 23). Settling in: Easing Abortion Policy. Clinton Orders Reversal of Abortion Policy Left by Reagan and Bush. *New York Times*.

[3] Tracy A. Weitz (2015). Rethinking the Mantra That Abortion Should Be "safe, legal, and rare". In Carole Joffe and Jennifer Reich (Eds.), *Reproduction and Society Interdisciplinary Readings*. New York: Routledge, pp. 67–75.

[4] Stanley Henshaw and Kathryn Kost (2008). *Trends in the Characteristics of Women Obtaining Abortions 1974–2004*. New York: Guttmacher Institute.

campaign had seemed to define *all* abortions in the public imagination as that procedure where a doctor sticks scissors in the back of the neck of a near-term "baby," and those who believed that abortion should be a woman's choice were bizarrely caricatured as wanting abortion "any time, any place, anywhere."

While the argument that abortion should be a rare occurrence seems to fit with women's desire to avoid it, it is also open to a number of interpretations. Indeed, abortion can be made rare in so many ways that the phrase becomes utterly meaningless. Abortion can certainly be made rare by restricting it to the point where it is barely legal, persecuting doctors and deterring women by misinformation and stigma.

The question left hanging in the air was: if abortion is safe and legal, then why should it be rare? Why *shouldn't* women use it? Arguing that abortion should be rare in the future implies that we think there are too many now. But what is the proper number, the *right* number of abortions for a society to have?

We all want heart surgery to be rare, because we want people *not to need it*, but we don't campaign or make speeches about the need to make heart surgery rare. We might campaign for initiatives to reduce heart disease and so lessen the need for surgery—but we don't advocate for fewer procedures. Nor would we judge a country's health service on the basis of the how many cardiac procedures are carried out—it may be that the country has no heart disease that requires the procedure or no cardiac surgeons to carry it out.

Most reproductive health professionals counsel a woman against relying on abortion for birth control because, like any clinical procedure, it carries risks; and while the risks of abortion are lower than the risks of childbirth, they are higher than modern methods of contraception. But typically we regard the relative risks of the various matters of birth control as essentially a matter for the user. Contraceptive pills carry greater risks to their users than condoms, but as the risks are relatively low, most women accept them. The risks of abortion might, quite reasonably, be viewed in the same way, particularly in countries where birth control's financial costs are born by the user.

So, why do we find it so difficult to accept when a woman relies on abortion for birth control? Why is it so difficult to simply say abortion is OK?

It is understandable that abortion's opponents claim that there are too many abortions, or that women choose abortion "too easily," or that too many women have two, three or more abortions. But why would that be an issue for those who think that abortion is a legitimate choice? Is a rising abortion rate not "a good thing" if it demonstrates that abortion is more accessible and acceptable? Is it a problem if a woman has unprotected sex and, knowing she has risked pregnancy but calculating her personal risk as low, decides to save herself the cost and hassle of acquiring the morning-after pill, because she can end the pregnancy easily enough by abortion?

In the UK, state-funded abortion providers have "key performance indicators" aimed at lowering the rate of "repeat abortions" (a phrase that brings to mind the language of the criminal justice system: the recidivism of "repeat offenders"). Clinical staff internalise this approach; it is not "good" when, having been a patient at an abortion clinic once, a patient returns a second time with an unwanted pregnancy. But why should we see it as a "negative indicator?" Maybe on her first visit, the woman found the procedure so *un*traumatic and straightforward, and maybe she discovered the staff were so kind and helpful that she felt able to switch to a preferable, but less effective contraceptive method and use abortion deliberately as a back-up.

Perhaps advocates of legal abortion spend too much time trying to convince opponents that women don't substitute abortion for contraception, or use it without "good reason."

We might claim that in earlier centuries there were good reasons to dissuade women from abortion. In the past, abortion was a risky business—and in some low resource settings it continues to be. But the risks of abortion are susceptible to exaggeration, both by advocates who oppose abortion, and those who believe strongly that contraception is a "better" means of birth control.

Historical studies of abortion in England[5] document the extent that abortion was used in the past. One hundred years ago, working-class women in London were extremely reluctant to adopt contraception, much to the chagrin of the medical profession. Even in 1920s London, it was quite normal for women to regard it as simpler and more convenient to "bring on" a missed monthly bleed, than to try to use costly and uncomfortable sheaths and "female devices."

It is ironic that the early twentieth-century birth control pioneers, Marie Stopes (in the UK) and Margaret Sanger (in the USA), are derided by today's opponents of abortion, as both were strongly motivated to *reduce* the number of abortions, especially among poor city dwellers. Marie Stopes' birth control clinics in the deprived areas of 1920s London tried to popularise use of her "cap" to wean working-class women off their long-established culture of abortifacient pills, potions, herbs, douches and interventions. In an account written in 1929 she observed:

> In three months I have had as many as twenty thousand requests for criminal abortion from women who did not apparently even *know* that it was criminal. In a given number of days, one of our travelling clinics received only thirteen applications for scientific instruction in the control of conception, but *eighty* demands for criminal abortion.[6] (Original emphasis)

Abortion was popular because it gave women a measure of control, when *coitus interruptus*, the main method of birth control, was a matter of male judgement, restraint and skill.

Stopes' motivation to shift women from abortion to contraception made sense at a time when folk remedies were often unreliable and sometimes dangerous, especially when they involved instrumentation.

---

[5] See Peter Fryer (1965). *The Birth Controllers.* London: Secker & Warburg; and John Keown (1988). *Abortion Doctors and the Law: Some Aspects of the Legal Regulation of Abortion in England for 1803 to 1982.* Cambridge: Cambridge University Press.

[6] M. C. Stopes (1929). *Mother England: A Contemporary History.* London: John Bale, Sons and Danielsson, p. 137 cited in Barbara Brookes (1988). *Abortion in England 1900–1967.* London: Croom Helm, p. 6.

Today, there is no need for the concerns that worried the early birth control pioneers, because abortion in early pregnancy can be delivered safely and easily. With modern treatments, instruments and techniques— some specifically developed for use in low-resource settings— abortion in the first months of pregnancy can be provided with relatively little risk. Disposable manual vacuum aspiration (MVA) equipment, which allows an early pregnancy to be sucked out through a tube that has been passed through the cervix requires no electricity, because the vacuum is created by a syringe, and is relatively simple to use. The "abortion pill"— comprising two drugs, mifepristone and misoprostol—is now commonly used in almost all countries with modern health services. The medication temporarily blocks the production of those hormones that maintain the pregnancy and induces cramping and bleeding. In effect, the abortion pill causes a miscarriage much the same as the loss through "natural" spontaneous miscarriages experienced by millions of women around the world. As we described earlier, abortion's opponents claim that the risks of abortion are underestimated, but their claims call into question the integrity of every leading body of professional clinical opinion that the establishment holds in high regard. The World Health Organisation (WHO), international and national medical associations and colleges of obstetricians and gynaecologists produce authoritative assessments of the risks and complications of abortion—just as they do for other clinical interventions.[7] None of them agree with accounts of abortion-harm generated by the anti-choice advocates. These bodies guard their reputations for evidence-based opinions that are not swayed by vested interests. If there are criticisms made of them, it is typically that they are conservative, risk-averse and reluctant to step into areas of controversy. Thus it seems unlikely that, when it comes to abortion, their conclusions are biased by feminist influence.

---

[7] WHO Department of Reproductive Health and Research (2012). *Safe Abortion: Technical and Policy Guidance for Health Systems*. Geneva: WHO.

Responding to the "Pro-Life" Challenge

It is difficult to see how supporters and opponents of a woman's right to choose can find common ground, however carefully the messaging is managed and massaged, because no common ground exists. Supporters and opponents of legal abortion are divided by a dispute about values.

As sociologist Kristin Luker explains in her influential book on unplanned pregnancy, "Each side of the abortion debate has an internally coherent and mutually shared view of the world" that is "completely at odds with the world view held by their opponents." The consequence of this, she notes, is that "the two sides share almost no common premises."[8]

Abortion's opponents really do speak a different language. They focus on morals and values and stress our duties to the embryo. Those who campaign for legal abortion tend to focus on "rights" rather than "what is right." The argument for abortion choice leans towards a non- judgemental approach that is agnostic when it comes to the rightness or wrongness of the abortion as a specific act, and instead, focusses on the context of abortion as a necessary and unpreventable fact of life in modern society. It is not so much whether abortion is "right" or "wrong," but that it just "is"; and the application of a moral value is seen as redundant, at least as it applies to life in the womb.

For the two movements, both the philosophical starting point and the locus of concern diverge in a way that can make intellectual engagement challenging.

Essentially, both sides are concerned about "the meaning of life"—but the "meaning of life" means something different to both sides, even to the point of dispute as to whose life is meaningful. For abortion's opponents it is the life of the *foetus* that matters, while supporters of abortion focus on the lives of the women seeking to have an abortion. Many of abortion's opponents hold a view of what is important about human life that is profoundly different to those who find abortion acceptable. The opponents of abortion claim that abortion is wrong because "it ends the

---

[8] Kristin Luker (1984). *Abortion and the Politics of Motherhood.* Berkeley: University of California Press, p. 156.

life of the unborn child" whereas for abortion's supporters ending life in the womb is precisely its point.

At the heart of any decision about abortion is the question: which life matters more? Both the life of the woman and the life of the foetus may be valued—but for those on either side of the issue, the value of one life is weighed in relation to the value of the other. For some of us, abortion causes us to consider the "relative value" of human embryonic or foetal life in relation to the life that the woman chooses to live. This weighing of lives according to a balance of "worth" seems appalling to those who believe in the equivalence of all human life from conception. The moral equivalence of a woman with rights and responsibilities with a biologically undeveloped and unconscious entity is equally appalling to those who don't.

For abortion's opponents, the central matter is the nature of the foetus and its membership in our human community, with the full rights and claims that come with its membership in that community. In contrast, abortion's supporters start with the needs of the woman, believing that whatever status we grant to the foetus, it *must* be less than hers.

This question—which life takes priority?—is at the centre of every abortion debate from the most simple to the most sophisticated.

Those opponents of abortion who sit in the world of academic philosophy often dismiss pro-choice thinking as "consequentialism," a form of utilitarian thinking that does not start from an essential philosophical principle, but from considering the consequences of a premise. In the case of abortion, both Beckwith and Oderberg suggest that the pro-choice moral argument *starts* with the assumption that banning abortion would cause harm to women; and from this premise they build an argument to justify preventing this harm. In short, they view the pro-choice moral argument as a philosophy of convenience.

This philosophical one-upmanship has never seriously bothered those who advocate for abortion; in some ways it has even been helpful in drawing a clear line between the two sides of the argument. On one side of that line is a woman whose life is impacted in some way by being pregnant; on the other is an abstract and academic discussion of when life begins. In these circumstances, weighing the extent of the relative harm caused by prohibiting abortion when compared with the consequences of allowing the procedure seems to be a sensible way of proceeding, even if it doesn't meet the approval of philosophy professors. Life is, after all, so much more complicated than philosophy.

Many abortion supporters have deliberately avoided the language of morality, seeing it as the preserve of the conservative right and the Church. To make a *moral* argument could be seen to imply a prescriptive code of living that is at odds with liberal "non-judgementalism." To make a moral judgement about other peoples' lives seems out of kilter with the beliefs of those inclined towards a worldview of feminism and lifestyle liberalism.

Moral judgements about family life acquired a bad name and an association with the conservative right during the last decades of the twentieth century. Throughout the 1980s and 1990s, conservative politicians in the USA and the UK placed great emphasis on the traditional nuclear family, as they tried to garner support based on their defence of middle-class traditional values.

One of Margaret Thatcher's main initiatives when she became British Prime Minister in 1979 was to set up a Family Policy Group to examine how mothers could be encouraged to stay at home; parents could be made more accountable for the anti-social behaviour of their children; and an education curriculum with "a clear moral basis" could be delivered. In today's society, with its emphasis on diversity, pluralism and equality, this seems archaic. But the 1980s was the decade of AIDS, which was a powerful curb on the 1970s sexual liberalism; and concern about AIDS was quickly packaged as a moralist campaign to discourage heterosexual promiscuity as well as gay sex.

Conservative messages and traditional morality were explicitly linked in a way that would seem arcane in the twenty-first century when the influence of the Church is much reduced. But in the 1980s, conservative politics and Christian moral values were bound together in battle against feminists, left-wing activists and radical academics. The invective employed by the director of the government-sponsored Social Affairs Unit, writing in *The Times*, would never be used today in mainstream British politics. However, at this time, when the Prime Minister was consciously promoting moral values, it was unremarkable for a respected writer to describe the dangers facing society as:

AIDS, linked to promiscuous homosexuality; herpes and gonorrhea both connected with increased promiscuity; breast and cervical cancer possibly caused by the long term use of the contraceptive pill, the latter also possibly linked to sexual activity; and the growing problem highlighted recently … of the sexual abuse of children.

And the cause of this cataclysmic situation? The abandonment of tradition.

> The old wisdom, displaced by progressive gospel, no longer looks quite so passé. Its adherents did not question everything but followed religion and social conventions even when those appeared arbitrary and senseless … Desires were repressed by inculcated habit and deterrence. Repression was not then viewed as a bad thing. And a necessary corollary of the rules was the guilt, fear, scandal and stigma so denounced and derided by "rational" progressives. They do not appear so ridiculous today.[9]

This writer called openly for society to be subjected to an "injection of intolerance," which was delivered. Thatcher's Britain became associated with a decade of moral panics and the promotion of Victorian values. The blanket claim to restore moral values covered several attempts to restrict the abortion law and included: restricting contraception access for teenagers; increased censorship of "video-nasties," pornography and sex on television; limits on assisted conception, research using embryos and surrogacy; and the closing of sex shops and restricting sex education in schools.

The conservative worldview saw the traditional family as being under threat from a generation with liberal attitudes that prized women's involvement in public life outside the home. A breakdown in family values was seen as both a cause and a consequence of social problems. Even those conservatives with no religious basis for their thinking considered abortion from this perspective. Abortion was a marker that a woman had "done something to be ashamed of." Like pregnancy, abortion was

---

[9] *The Times* 24 October 1984 and 5 December 1984 cited in Kate Marshall (1985). *Moral Panics and Victorian Values: Women and the Family in Thatcher's Britain*. London: Junius, pp. 4–5.

evidence of sex—but while the proud mother-to-be in a maternity frock was emblematic of family values, an abortion patient was a symbol of the "badness" of sex outside marriage and of a woman rejecting her supposedly natural role as a mother.

The Thatcher government's moral crusade resulted in very few significant lasting changes to legislation or social policy. However, it did serve to discredit pro-family values and consolidate a reaction against the "M" word among non-conservatives.

Supporters of abortion reacted against this *moralisation* of abortion and constructed an alternative narrative that avoided moral claims. They eschewed judgementalism altogether and emphasised that because only the woman facing an unwanted pregnancy was in a position to understand her circumstances, no one was in a position to judge her.

While abortion's opponents clearly advocate the "wrongness" of abortion, abortion supporters counter this with an argument for the "need" for the choice to be there, often conceding that abortion is "a wrong, but the right thing to do" in certain circumstances. This has the advantage of reflecting popular opinion and mirrors the views of many women who request abortion.

Abortion providers observe that many patients want to explain that they "don't agree with abortion at all," but in their own circumstances, "it's really different." These women may simply be saying what they think is expected of them and trying to conform to their own preconception that a woman in need of abortion should be contrite. Perhaps it is also true that many women base their opinions on abortion on the stories about feckless teenagers and abuse victims presented by the media, and genuinely view their unplanned pregnancy as "different." Of course, when a 26-year-old married mother arrives at a clinic to end her unwanted pregnancy, she is very different; at least she is different from the stereotypes, but not to the other women in the waiting room.

The allegations that women who have abortions are acting selfishly, are self-centred, and unwilling to make the sacrifices that a "good woman" would make, impact on women and leave many wondering if they should have been "better."

Abortion is seldom promoted as a morally good choice that demonstrates women's rational, responsible decision-making. It is unusual for abortion's supporters to make moral claims about its "rightness" as the feminist commentator, Katha Pollitt, does in *Pro: Reclaiming Abortion Rights* when she argues: "abortion is an urgent practical decision that is just as moral as the decision to have a child." Abortion is not the antithesis of motherhood but "part of being a mother and caring for children, because part of caring for children is knowing when it's not a good idea to bring them into the world."[10]

It could be argued that the absence of moral claims in favour of abortion has been advantageous in Britain, since the discussion has not been polarised along principled lines to the extent that it might otherwise have been. Some arguments seem attractive to people who do not hold strong value-based positions. They can more easily agree that abortion should exist as a back-up (but not a substitute for) contraception; that it is preferable to unwanted children who may be subject to abuse and brutality and increased family deprivation; that it should be available for the needy, but not the feckless. For these people, Bill Clinton's view of a society where abortion is safe, legal and rare seems fair and reasonable, because they wish for abortion to be available, but exceptional.

Public opinion has been able to find a middle space in the debate, which *seems* to accommodate both sides. Abortion has been problematised by the moral discussion, which frames it as a wrongful act that should be minimised. However, the pragmatic-practical discussion accepts the reality of unwanted pregnancy and allows that abortion is a sensible resolution for at least some of these pregnancies. Abortion can be seen as a "lesser evil"; wrong in principle, but necessary in practice. It has been easier to build support for abortion in this way than to engage in a contest for the moral high ground.

The narrative of abortion-exceptionalism suits most people. "I believe abortion is wrong except when [insert reason according to subjective preference]" both problematises and permits the procedure. It seems to accommodate both sides of the divide with a workable compromise and most national legal frameworks have found a way to accommodate this: the more successfully the accommodation has been made, the more stable the law has been. The British law, which has only incorporated one

---

[10] Katha Pollitt (2014). *Pro: Reclaiming Abortion Rights*. New York: Picador, p. 16.

minor change over half a century, stands as an example of the stability that can be achieved with abortion exceptionalism.

On paper, in Britain, abortion remains illegal unless two doctors certify that a woman meets certain medical criteria. If the gestation is later than twenty-four weeks, unless there is a serious risk of damage to the woman's health, abortion is permitted only when there is substantial risk that the baby would be born with "a serious handicap."[11] Before twenty-four weeks' gestation, it is sufficient that there be greater risk to the woman's physical or mental health than continuing the pregnancy. In practice, this means that the law can be interpreted very liberally, since most doctors will concede that abortion is generally safer than labour, and that the damage caused to mental health from an unwanted pregnancy is greater than granting an abortion request.

This has created a framework where abortion is: (1) medicalised (in that it is only available on medical approval, and can only be carried out by a registered doctor in registered premises); (2) set aside as a special practice (in that it is subject to a specific regulations that are different to other clinical procedures); and (3) stigmatised (it is illegal except in certain circumstances and doctors may opt out of providing the service if they object on grounds of conscience). While the law allows abortion, it reinforces that the normal end to a pregnancy is birth and motherhood. This goes some way towards ameliorating concerns that abortion is treated casually and used as a regular means of birth control, but it also provides some succour for legal abortion supporters, since the law is interpreted liberally, and abortion is almost fully state-funded. Both supporters and opponents of abortion have been wary of parliamentary debate on the issue since they both stand to lose as well as gain. When the law was last amended in 1990 it reduced the upper gestational limits for most abortions to twenty-four weeks (from twenty-eight weeks), but removed the time limit in cases of foetal anomaly altogether—maintaining a balanced scorecard.

Most countries have found their own ways of achieving a compromise between stigmatising abortion, in general, and allowing it under specific circumstances. Often different time limits are imposed for different

[11] To use the original term of the less sensitive 1960s.

reasons. Throughout Europe and North America, abortion is typically available to any woman who requests one in the first months of pregnancy but restricted to specific reasons as the pregnancy progresses. This balances the perceived advantages to society from allowing women to end unwanted pregnancies, with the widely held view that the foetus acquires increasing status and value as it grows and develops.

Roe v Wade, the US Supreme Court ruling that framed the abortion law in 1973, is a clear example of this thinking. The court attempted to resolve three conflicting principles: the individual right to privacy (which is implied by the Constitution); the right of the state to protect maternal health; and the right of the state to protect developing human life.[12] It did this by dividing pregnancy into three gestational stages. During the first trimester of pregnancy the woman had the right to determine her own future privately, without state interference, and this took priority over the right of the state to intervene. Thus during this time, the state conceded a virtually unconditional legal right to abortion. In the second trimester, when it was thought that the risks of abortion were relatively greater than in the first trimester, the right of the state to regulate and protect women's health became "compelling," but only insofar as it would insist on reasonable standards of medical care and not so much as to deny a woman an abortion.

Only in the third trimester did the state's right to protect the developing life in the womb come to the fore. In making this decision, the court placed great emphasis on its understanding of "viability," which it understood as that point at which the foetus could live by itself, outside the uterine environment, albeit with substantial medical support. The judgement has been described as a "masterly compromise, especially for such a pluralistic society, and a valuable effort to depoliticise the abortion issue."[13]

These laws may seem like a reasonable compromise, and, from a functional point of view, they are certainly better than no abortion at all. However, from a moral standpoint, they satisfy no one and so abortion,

---

[12] See C. J. Mohr (1978). *Abortion in America: The Origins and Evolution of National Policy.* Oxford: Oxford University Press.

[13] Edwin Kenyon (1986). *The Dilemma of Abortion.* London: Faber & Faber, p. 226.

despite the "masterly compromise," has remained at the centre of the continuing culture war in the USA.

There are two serious problems with "abortion exceptionalism": it maintains and reinforces stigma, because it accepts that "abortion is not permissible *unless* … ," and it fails to place the choice about an abortion where it needs to be: in the hands of the pregnant woman. Laws and restrictions introduce a third party to the decision-making process who is not directly affected by the outcome and overlooks one very important matter.

When all else is stripped away, abortion affects only two people *directly*: the woman who wishes it and the clinician who will perform it. Clearly, the man who "fathered" the pregnancy has an interest in its outcome, and may have a strong opinion on whether it ends with a baby or an abortion. But pregnancy itself is not a sex-neutral condition. It is a female who is pregnant; it is a clinician who will terminate the pregnancy. The man may have a view and may be very invested in the decision since the baby expresses his genetic future too, but as to the pregnancy itself, and any decisions related to it, he is a bystander.

Any laws and regulations that insist on grounds, or specific reasons, that limit when a woman can choose abortion, or when a doctor can perform one, underscore that a woman's decision is not sufficient. And when mandatory regulations insist on a certain level of medical care, it implies that abortion is risky, and that abortion doctors cannot be trusted to base the level of care on their knowledge and ethics. No special laws or regulations govern when a doctor can repair a hernia, or set a fractured arm; the existence of special laws for abortion begs the question: "why is abortion different?"

Of course, the difference with abortion is not solely its impact on the woman, but on the foetus. For the woman, abortion is a simple, straightforward and safe clinical intervention, which is far less complicated than many others procedures she may undergo. For the foetus, abortion is fatal.

This is an uncomfortable truism, which no one celebrates—least of all the doctors or patients who undergo an abortion. Support for legal abortion clearly manifests a judgement that foetal life does not have the moral standing of a woman's life. It privileges a woman's "choice" over the life of the foetus. Arguing that restrictions on abortion are wrong, and that it should be seen as an acceptable, legitimate means of birth control seems to trivialise abortion. It casts advocates of abortion liberalisation as coarsened, immoral and indifferent to the future of human life. None of this is true, but the emotive impact of pictures of aborted late-gestation foetuses is not easily balanced by accounts of the compassion and empathy of the abortion doctor, nor why the doctor believed it was for the good of the woman.

The difficulty of making a positive case for abortion is a key reason why abortion supporters have put aside the *moral* argument and redirected the discussion towards the *circumstantial*—namely why women need abortions and how the number of abortions can be reduced—with a particular focus on reducing the number of women who need abortions.

Thus over the years only a small number of advocates[14] have argued that, as a matter of principle, abortion should be subject only to those same restrictions that would be imposed by other clinical interventions that share the same risks.

Campaigns for the liberalisation of abortion throughout Europe have tended to set the bar low. Where there have been campaigns for abortion to be made available to women solely on their request, this has usually been limited to the first trimester.

Although the tactical reasons for this seem like a reasonable compromise (allowing some women have legal abortions and protecting some foetuses from it), it is unsatisfactory. It accepts and reinforces the notion that "something changes" in the status of a pregnancy between one week and another that changes the locus of concern from the woman to the foetus. If abortion should be acceptable at twenty-four weeks, why should it not be acceptable at twenty-four weeks and one day? It lays a brittle foundation for the defence of abortion as a clinical practice and is not a sound foundation on which to base advocacy for a woman's right to make her own decision.

Further to this, hard time limits which set a guillotine at a particular day are a particularly cruel form of legal fiction. An embryo does

---

[14] A notable voice in opposition to this trend has been Marge Berer, editor of *Reproductive Health Matters*. See M. Berer (2002). Making Abortion a Woman's Right Worldwide. *Reproductive Health Matters*, 10(19), 1–8.

not implant in an identifiable instant. In reality and in real-time, it is a process that does not fit easily into the time-framework that a law court requires. The medical profession gets around the lack of real precision by inventing a measurable proxy. So, for the purposes of law and medical practice, pregnancy starts on the first day of the last menstrual bleed when, in the real lived-in world, that is a day when she may not even have met the man with whom she would have sex. Most women ovulate at mid-cycle. Even scans that date later pregnancies have a margin of error and so fail to provide the accuracy one might think necessary for a legal judgment.

A common argument for liberalising restrictions in early abortion is that it reduces the need for later abortion. Aside from the fact that this is not necessarily true, it has the effect of increasing the stigma attached to later procedures, because it implies that the need for a later abortion is the "woman's fault" for delaying treatment that should have been sought sooner. Abortion on request in the first trimester may also sit more comfortably with public opinion, because early abortion seems to be "less than" a "proper abortion" since there is no baby-like foetus. Increasing the use of medication to induce what is, in effect, a miscarriage, has underlined how an early abortion can be like an early pregnancy loss. And, since early abortion is so common,[15] people often have personal experiences to draw on—if not their own, then that of a family member or friend.

Abortion's opponents may not have conceded that they have lost the battle against early abortions, but on the ropes of public debates, speakers will almost always acknowledge that an early abortion may be acceptable and is always preferable to a later abortion.[16] In a mirror image, many of abortion's supporters will accept that certain restrictions on later abortions may be needed.

"Abortion: as early as possible and as late as necessary" was a neatly nuanced demand developed in the 1980s by activists in Britain, which has come to carry particular weight, because it captures the principle that

---

[15] Almost 90% of abortions take place within the first ten weeks of pregnancy; less than 3% take place after twenty weeks.

[16] Ann Furedi (1988). Wrong but the Right Thing To Do: Public Opinion and Abortion. In Ellie Lee (Ed.), *Abortion Law and Politics Today*. London: Macmillan, p. 162.

abortion should be available without restriction *and* the sentiment that early abortion is preferable. It is unfortunate that while much attention has been paid to the first part, little focus has been given to the "as late as necessary" component.

Later abortion has been an easy target for abortion's opponents. The foetus undeniably has the appearance of a baby. It moves and we attribute significance and interpretation, just as we anthropomorphise our pets. It's difficult *not* to believe that a foetus feels pain and responds to stress like a baby, because it looks so much like one.

There is no broad constituency to be mobilised in support of later abortions on the basis of their personal experience, because few women have had that experience. On the other hand, many people have known the joy and excitement that comes with a wanted pregnancy in its later months. Most women eager for their delivery will be reassured by kicks and squirms, which may help them to identify strongly with their child-to-be. Often, women who have borne a child of their own say they simply "can't understand" how women can choose abortion; often, that is because they are recalling how they felt.

The claim that early abortion can prevent later abortions is widely believed, but it is a convenient *un*truth since, most often, later abortions are requested for reasons that are not connected to early abortion access. Most women request later abortions for reasons too varied and complex to be eliminated by early abortion care. Sometimes they may have wanted an earlier abortion and been delayed (or obstructed) somewhere along their clinical journey; sometimes it takes a while to raise the necessary fees (where fees must be paid); sometimes women do not know where to go to get help. These are issues that can be addressed by improving services. In Britain, where access to early abortion is relatively straightforward and free of cost, most late abortions today are for women who discovered they are pregnant late, had been ambivalent about their pregnancy and needed time to make up their mind. Or, they found that their lives have changed such that a wanted pregnancy became unwanted. Demographically, these women are very similar to women who have early abortions; there are few differences in their lives—perhaps there is a little more drug use and a higher proportion of teenagers. However, women having later abortions are broadly similar to those having them earlier.

From the woman's point of view, it matters little whether she is thirteen weeks, twenty-three weeks or twenty-five weeks when her home is repossessed … or her workplace goes bankrupt … or her husband leaves, or her existing child is diagnosed with severe autism … or her boyfriend is found to be abusing her existing daughter… or her mother has a stroke and has to move in with her. The thinking that informed her decision remains as sound at twenty-five weeks as it did two weeks earlier. But now her decision whether to have an abortion has been removed because society views an abortion as wrong.

Abortion exceptionalism through time limits gives an unequivocal message that some abortions (in this case, those in the first trimester) are acceptable and some (later) abortions are wrong. The application of specific "grounds" or "approved" reasons has the same effect as when women have to demonstrate their reason is "good enough" to qualify them.

A further consequence of the "good reason" reasoning attached to exceptional cases is that it raises the challenge of the "bad reason" reasoning. If abortion should be available because women have good reasons—what happens when their reason is not so "good?" And what happens when the public at large, or liberal society, thinks the reason is downright bad?

One might think that supporting a woman's choice of abortion implies support for her choice regardless of whether *you* think it is a choice you might make for yourself, or even whether you approve of it. However, as we discuss later, some abortion reasons have challenged the binary "yes/ no" response to the question: do you support a woman's right to decide? Just as anti-abortion advocates have found it hard to maintain their commitment to foetal life in some circumstances, so abortion's supporters have sometimes found it difficult to maintain respect for a woman's right to decide. Many of those who are "broadly pro-life" find themselves dissenting when challenged with examples of women denied abortion following rape, or incest—especially when a girl as young as nine is pregnant, or when a woman is carrying a foetus so damaged it could not be born alive, or when the pregnancy may result in death. Similarly, many people who regard themselves as pro-choice balk when abortion is requested because the foetus is female, or it has a disabling condition, because they believe the requests reinforce sexism or anti-disability sentiment in society.

When the UK Parliament in 2015 faced a proposal that would have banned abortion for gender-based reasons, the pro-choice lobby was far from united in its response. At the first vote, only one single member of the House of Commons[17] was prepared to oppose the Bill as an attack on a woman's right to decide. The measure was eventually defeated after an effective campaign that demonstrated that the law already effectively prevented such abortions and there was no evidence that significant numbers of sex-selective abortions took place. The notion that such abortions, if they were to take place, would be "bad abortions" remains largely unchallenged.

A similar erosion of principle has taken place in relation to support for a woman's choice of abortion when a disability is diagnosed. The defence of disability-linked abortion is most commonly that these are wanted pregnancies and the prognosis is severe. This may be the case for the significant majority, but again it begs the question of where we stand when we personally view the disability in a different way from the potential parents. The diagnosis of Down Syndrome, caused by a chromosomal abnormality Trisomy 21 has become a specific cause of contention. The number of children born with the condition—associated with delayed and limited physical growth, a range of intellectual disabilities, characteristic facial features, and often other health impairments—has decreased significantly as increasingly women access screening to identify their risk with the intention of abortion if there is a problem. Some see a choice to terminate affected pregnancies as an expression of prejudice against people with disabilities. Others argue there is no connection between social attitudes towards born people with a condition and the choice to terminate a pregnancy. Who is right? A more pertinent question might be: does it matter who is right? Should society prevent a woman from exercising her judgement in relation to her own pregnancy because it disagrees with her decision? Would it not be inconsistent and fickle to support any choice a woman makes, except the one we disagree with?

---

[17] Glenda Jackson was Labour MP for Hampstead and Kilburn before she left Parliament in 2015.

In Europe particularly, abortion associated with disability has become a major issue as it presented as a matter of competing human rights; the rights of the disabled as pitched against the rights of women. Many European countries now offer all women screening tests in early pregnancy to detect increased risk of the chromosomal abnormality resulting in Down Syndrome. Despite increasingly liberal and inclusive attitudes towards disability, nearly all women take the test and more than 90% end the pregnancy if there is a diagnosis or high probability of Down Syndrome. In 2020, *The Atlantic* magazine reported that in Denmark in 2019, just eighteen children with the condition were born in the entire country. The decline in the number of children with Down Syndrome has led to a massive international campaign bringing together disability rights activists and opponents of all abortions, under the banner of "Don't Screen Us Out." The concern is that women's choice to abort will lead to elimination of "people like us." Down Syndrome is presented not as an abnormal condition to be avoided, but a difference to be embraced.

Ironically the campaign to problematise screening stresses that screening is eugenic in that it aims to manipulate the make-up osf society to eliminate people like them. The campaigners miss the point that the same allegation might be made about their campaign. Traditional eugenicists argued that social interventions to create the right type of society, populated by the right type of people, should be privileged over the personal decisions of individual people. In previous centuries that meant encouraging the birth of children free from the conditions that cause disabilities.

Now these campaigns, fearing women's individual choices will lead to the elimination of "difference," unwittingly mirror their arguments. While traditional eugenicists thought too many "disabled" children were born, today's modern eugenicists think that in countries such as Denmark and the UK, there are too few. They aim to confound that preference by limiting access to screening programmes and preventing abortion. The underlying assumption is that that there is a correct number of children affected by a condition that should be born. A world without infirmity, which was once a goal is now presented as a dystopia.

The problem with trying to influence the type of babies born to fit a social vision is that it assumes that would-be mothers share that social vision and wish it to shape their own personal family life. That is not always the case and if the decision to continue or terminate a pregnancy is to be a woman's choice, then the decision will always be subjective, based on what that woman wants at that time in her life. A woman who chooses to terminate a pregnancy affected by Down Syndrome is no more making a statement about the condition, that an economically disadvantaged women is making a statement about deprivation. She is saying the choice to have that child is not right for her.

Of course, society as a whole is made up of a multitude of personal decisions, which politicians try to shape for what they regard as the social interest. We have become increasingly accustomed to the influence of social engineering in which governments openly talk about "nudging" people into "good decisions," and the boundary between personal decisions and political statement is increasingly eroded.[18]

But campaigns such as BirthStrike, established in 2019 in the UK to unite people who have decided not to have children due to climate consciousness have—at least to date—made little impact. We do not generally see a decision about pregnancy as an expressivist act made as an example of how we think other people should behave. It is important that this remains the case, since a society where the decision to have a child ceases to be a private, intimate and personal decision is one where reproductive freedom has been lost.

Not Pro-Abortion or Anti-Life but Pro-Choice

Support for abortion, as we discuss it here, is a matter of support for a woman's *choice* to have an abortion. To be "pro" abortion, abstractly, would be bizarre; no woman has an ambition to have an abortion. At best, termination of pregnancy is inconvenient and uncomfortable. When contraceptives were primitive and unreliable, abortion may have been a rational choice of birth control since it was simpler to "bring

---

[18] See Richard H. Thaler and Cass R. Sunstein (2021). *Nudge: the Final Edition.* Harmondsworth: Penguin; and Frank Furedi (2020). *Why Borders Matter: Why Humanity Must Relearn the Art of Drawing Boundaries.* Routledge: London.

on" an occasionally late "monthly" than to obtain and use uncomfortable, intrusive and unreliable sheaths and caps. But today, it is rare for women to think their pregnancy is better ended than prevented, because easier methods of birth control exist. Abortion supporters are not trying to change this by "promoting" abortion as *better* than contraception. Abortion rights campaigns are not the birth control equivalent of the Campaign for Real Ale, which measures success in the number of people who switch from lager to authentic ale. But nor do we see abortion as a "bad" thing in itself.

Abortion supporters identify themselves as "pro-choice," and not "pro-abortion," because they are "pro" whatever the woman chooses for herself. It is her right to decide about her future that is valued. The outcome of the decision is irrelevant to pro-choice advocates. What matters is that the decision to continue, or end, her pregnancy should be made by her in full knowledge of the consequences that it will have for her life as a woman and for the life she carries in her womb.

This is why the "pro-choice" movement quite properly insists that it is not a mirror image of the campaigns that oppose abortion. If you are against abortion, it is very clear that you think a woman *should not* have one. To be pro-abortion might imply that you think that you think she *should*. To be pro-choice is to be unequivocal that you *support the decision being hers.*

The difference is expressed well in advocates' approach when they provide pregnancy counselling services. In the UK, for example, pregnancy counselling services are provided by charities that support (indeed provide) abortions, and charities that oppose them. Life, a significant opponent of abortion, provides counselling centres claiming to promote "a positive alternative to abortion." Clients who attend Life centres who are considering abortion are dissuaded from making that choice. Alternatively, the charities that provide abortions describe themselves as "supporting women's choices." Records from the British Pregnancy Advisory Service (BPAS), which I ran for seventeen years, show that, although most women attend pregnancy counselling have already decided to access the abortion services they provide, 16% of patients choose to have their baby. A successful outcome of pro-choice counselling is that women feel they have reached a good decision, no matter what that decision is.

The distinction between being pro-choice and pro-abortion is not pedantic wordplay and we will return to consider this in Chapter 8. Indeed, to be pro-choice may on occasion involve *opposing* abortion as when abortion is promoted as a preferred option for certain women in certain situations, and sometimes to be pro-choice in these situations might involve a defence of a woman's right to continue her pregnancy. There are many people who will support abortion, because they do not think certain women should be mothers, or that certain children should be born.

The eugenic origins of the birth control movements are well documented,[19] and were not limited to explicit drives to reduce national populations, or to the racial purity campaigns that drew wide support across Europe and North America in the 1920s and 1930s.[20] Campaigns to promote abortion (or other birth control measures) for the public good are the flip side of campaigns to *prevent* it for the public good.

The tension between tolerating individual decisions about child-bearing and promoting what is good for society is still very much present in the framing of social policy and popular discussion. It underlies many of the initiatives against teenage pregnancy in Europe and North America, where policy-makers hold the view that young women who choose to become mothers in their early teens should be "nudged" or incentivised to make a different (read "better") choice. Initiatives to provide "long-acting" contraceptives and rewards to stay in school may be justified as being best for the girls themselves, but they are underpinned by strong views about what is best for society.

Concern about the size and make-up of national populations also continues to influence international development policies for the Global South. Even when a powerful international body such as the UNFPA (United Nations Population Fund) acknowledges, as it has for more than twenty years, that there is "no evidence that population growth

---

[19] See Daniel Jo Kevles (1985). *In the Name of Eugenics: Genetics and the Uses of Human Heredity.* Penguin: Harmondsworth.

[20] See Richard Overy (2009). *The Morbid Age: Britain between the Wars.* London: Allen Lane, chapter 3; and William H. Schneider (1990). *Quality and Quantity: The Quest for Biological Regeneration in Twentieth-Century France.* Cambridge: Cambridge University Press.

is the *cause* of poverty,"[21] concern about family size and the "timing and spacing" of children dominates discussions about international aid. The narrative is concerned with women's health equality, education and progression, along with infant mortality, and the solution is seen as family assistance to enable women's choices. But it is very clear from Western donors that the "correct choice" for women is fewer children,[22] and this is what the aid organisations encourage. High maternal morbidity rates generate initiatives to help women have fewer births, not to have more children safely. Those who believe that constraints on fertility are necessary to create a population that matches the availability of resources, display a woefully sad view of the value of human life and human potential. It also suggests that a woman's right to make the personal reproductive choice that is right for her should be set aside for the good of society, or—as some environmentalists would argue—for the good of the planet.

The notion that a woman's personal reproductive choices should be put aside for the greater good of society, or the planet, is not so very different to the notion that it should be put aside for the greater good of the foetus. The consequence of demanding that a woman terminate her pregnancy for the sake of the planet's future children is not so very different from the demand that she maintain her pregnancy for the sake of the child in her womb. Both calls place the personal preference of the woman to one side. To uphold a "woman's choice" in the context of her reproductive rights means supporting her choice not just to have an abortion, but also her choice to *not* have an abortion. It means supporting her right to use contraception or to *not* use contraception. Support for reproductive choice is based on the principle that regardless of her reasons, her circumstances or the outcome—she gets to decide.

Sometimes this is seen as an expression of non-judgementalism—as though those of us who stand outside the decision should have no opinion and adopt a position of informed indifference to what women decide. But that is not the point at all. Deciding to be "pro-choice"

---

[21] See L. S. Ashford (1995). New Perspectives on Population: Cairo. *Population Bulletin,* 50(1), 31.

[22] See Frank Furedi (1997). *Population and Development: A Critical Introduction.* Cambridge: Polity Press, chapter 7.

involves a judgement—one that stipulates that the right to make one's own choice should be valued in its own right and judged to be important in itself.

Support for the access to abortion, as early as possible and as late as necessary, can only be defended consistently, from an intellectual and a practical perspective, if we understand and appreciate three things: the true value of what it is to be human; the meaning of personal autonomy; and what this signifies when it comes to control of our bodies.

Making these arguments involves an uncomfortable departure from the familiar terrain we have explored so far.

5

It Is Human? Do We Care?

The status of the foetus cannot be easily set aside however much we prefer to focus on the woman. Arguments that the foetus has its own claim to life, even its own rights, chip away at support for women's reproductive choice. They unsettle many politicians and policy-makers and make some doctors—even those who are willing to provide abortion to the limits of the law—feel uneasy.

Sometimes women who request abortion services struggle with what might be described as a conflict between their head and their heart. In their head, they know they need an abortion; in their heart they feel they are doing something wrong.

Once again that bifurcation in moral reasoning emerges: the "wrongness" of killing the foetus is mitigated by pragmatism. We are back to where we started; in society's eyes abortion is a "necessary evil," "wrong but sometimes the right thing to do."

It does not have to be like this. Support for a woman's right to end her pregnancy does not mean that we accord *no* value or respect to the life of the foetus. However, it does indicate that any value we attribute is less.

© The Author(s), under exclusive license to Springer Nature
Switzerland AG 2021
A. Furedi, *The Moral Case for Abortion*,
https://doi.org/10.1007/978-3-030-90189-9_5

There is a clear difference between the life of a woman—a conscious, knowing creature who is self-aware, who has hopes, ambitions, cares and responsibilities of her own—and the life of a foetus that does not even know that it is alive. This difference is not something that is conjured up to provide support for a woman's right to choose abortion.

The puzzle of what makes us truly human has tasked philosophers since the ancient Greeks. The question of what makes *our* lives "sacred," and what makes life valuable to ourselves and others, hangs over humanity. Some thinkers might even claim that the answer lies in the fact that we even ask the question.

The notion that human life is defined by the foetus's beating heart and DNA, a claim made by many who believe abortion is wrong, is a narrow, constricted and limiting way of looking at what life is. Human life is so much more. When we consider the full richness of human life as we *know* it, the difference in the fully human life of the woman and the biologically human life of the foetus cannot but strike us. Ronald Dworkin points out that the ancient Greeks had two distinct words for life[1]: *zoë* meant biological life in the sense of "aliveness"; *bios* meant the personal life-course of an individual, the life that we as individuals live, the life that we "know." Traditions that claim we are fully human "from the moment of our conception" are espousing just one way of looking at the nature of humanity. This belief was reinforced in the past by deference to religious notions of human life being created in the womb by God. Today, it is reinforced by deference to scientific notions that we are defined by genetics. Both of these approaches overlook a vital claim of humanity: that we are what we make of ourselves. Our ability to be aware of ourselves and our self-interest, to make decisions, to take responsibility for ourselves and others, to write the story of our lives—these are the things that define us as human in a way that is as important as our DNA.

These personal attributes are what make it possible for a woman to seek an abortion. These personal attributes are what the foetus does not,

---

[1] Ronald Dworkin (1993). *Life's Dominion: An Argument about Abortion, Euthanasia, and Individual Freedom*. London: HarperCollins, p. 82.

and cannot, have. And that is what makes their lives different. The presence of these qualities makes one life worthy of a secular sanctity, and their absence subjects one life to the determinations of others. This does not mean that its absence of sense-of-self makes human life in the womb worthless. But this inherent difference suggests we might, perhaps even *should,* consider it differently and in a way that is contingent in relation to the life of the woman. The foetus is quite literally wrapped in her in a way that no other human form can be by another.

This and the following chapters make the case for the value of life as lived and why such a life takes priority over life in the womb.

The experience of "being pregnant" is unique—and it feels unique. Pregnancy may be wonderful if you want a baby, utterly disturbing if you don't, and as the baby's movements become more pronounced, it is difficult to avoid recognising that being pregnant is more like being "occupied," as distinct from just "getting bigger."

Women experience the changes of pregnancy differently and, usually, what makes the difference is their expectations, and anticipations, of what the pregnancy will mean for them. A woman's life changes from the moment she knows she is pregnant. She now needs to make decisions, choices that are different from those of her non-pregnant friends, and different from those of the unknowingly pregnant self that she was yesterday.

When women make the choice between a baby and an abortion, it is a choice made according to their feelings about themselves and how they understand their *own* life and, indeed, the matter of life itself. Humans are creatures with a conscience; we make decisions based on how to think about what is right and wrong.

No woman has an abortion because she believes in the destruction of human embryos, or because she wants to exercise her right to abortion in the way she might exercise her right to vote. She chooses abortion because she believes it is right for her, not because it is 'a cause' she supports.

She may come to that decision in the time it takes her to draw her next breath, or she may struggle to find a way through a maze of confusion. She may seek advice and counselling, or she may tell no one. She may never deviate from her first instinctual reaction, or her attitude to the pregnancy may change over time. But however her conclusion is reached, almost invariably it is a decision primarily about what *she* wants and needs and can cope with. Perhaps it is to be a mother (again); perhaps it is to keep her life as it is. And so, when a woman chooses to end her pregnancy, it is not out of hatred or indifference to the foetus. It is also unlikely to be out of ignorance about what the foetus has the potential to become. It is far more likely that the time is not right for her to bring a child into being. Perhaps she feels the right time will be next year or perhaps she feels it will never be right. Perhaps it would have been right if her circumstances were different. Perhaps it would have been right if the "father" had been different.

Whatever the reason for the abortion, everyone involved wants the procedure to be carried out as humanely as possible. Of course, the primary concern is the woman, but for many women and their doctors, the foetus seems to matter too. This is why the pictures of dismembered foetuses from later abortions are so cruel; they don't inform women, but taunt them.

It seems counterintuitive to suggest that respect might be due to the embryo or the foetus, while allowing its destruction. And yet, why should we not acknowledge that it has a certain specialness? We can accord a particular moral status to the embryo (by virtue of species membership) and acknowledge that it is worthy of respect (by virtue of its potentiality), while at the same time unconditionally supporting a woman's right to choose to end its life.

This may seem to be a huge step into the quagmire of moral thinking that many abortion advocates prefer to avoid. But we can acknowledge that the embryo is special, that the coming into existence of a biologically unique entity is awe-inspiring even if we believe its life can be ended.

To do other than this seems to devalue and degrade the meaning of human personhood. Species membership, a beating heart and human DNA may not mean that an embryo is a person, with all the rights and claims that people have. But it has the potential to be a person—which is more than can be said for a cat, a horse or an eagle at their prime. If we value what people are, it makes sense to give some value to what they come from.

Most advocacy that supports abortion does not simply avoid the "status-of-foetal-life" minefield—it surrounds it with "danger" signs and cautions everyone to stay away. From a pragmatic, instrumental point of view, it is a bleak and hopeless area of exploration, because there are only two outcomes for a pregnancy, regardless of how the debate is nuanced. Either the pregnancy ends or remains viable. The woman either has a baby or she doesn't.

When all is said and done, it seems simpler to leave the philosophy to philosophers, politics to politicians and the law to lawyers. This way, doctors can carry on doctoring and women can get on with the lives they want to live. But there is something unsatisfying about taking a route around these issues instead of working out a sound route through them. More importantly, it leaves the terrain of argument concerning foetal life unexplored, except by those who have their own instrumentalist concern: to build a case against abortion, and a woman's ability to make her own decision about her pregnancy. A consequence of our failure to contest the territory of foetal life is that it has allowed opponents of abortion to present it as their very own "moral high ground." They have cast themselves as defenders of principle, moral standards and human worth, while advocates of legal abortion are seen as compromisers without moral courage, bowing to the need to be pragmatic.

Support for clear moral principles is attractive in a world where so much seems to be compromised. One of the reasons why "Pro-Life" societies have grown in strength in UK universities over the last decade is because of their appeal to moral standing and human worth. Ironically, in the past, feminists associated the abortion decision with strength, courage and self-worth; now anti-abortion activists argue that young pregnant women are strong enough and capable enough to raise a child and deserve better than abortion. In the USA, campaigns aimed at pregnant teenagers, calling for them to "Stand Up, Girl" and show their moral power, strength and independence by continuing their pregnancy, have become a feature of today's advocacy.

Discussions about the rights and wrongs of abortion can seem irritating to people who prefer to concern themselves simply with providing the service as part of their commitment to public health. And those solely focussed on the rights of women find attempts to bring the foetus into the frame of debate unsettling, inconvenient and irrelevant since, a focus on foetal life almost invariably takes some attention away from the pregnant woman.

How we look at life in the womb is far from simple to begin with, and made more difficult, because the abortion debate has turned it into a politically loaded issue. Both sides of the debate have, on occasion, taken their own tours down absurd paths of argument. To demonstrate that life in the womb is baby-life as we know it, some opponents of abortion have, at times, attributed qualities to the early foetus that are perfectly ridiculous and biologically implausible, while supporters of abortion have at times attempted to deny the foetus any human attributes at all, likening it to a tumorous growth.

An understanding of life in the womb is unlikely to change the minds of advocates on either side of the abortion debate. Would a woman desperate for an abortion change her mind if it were proved that the foetus could appreciate Mozart, smile and preferred her to eat chocolate than chillies? Probably not, because nothing about that would change the reasons why she needs to end her pregnancy. We can take a similar view on the vexing question of what the foetus feels during abortion. Conclusive evidence that the foetus experiences suffering as we suffer would be more likely to provoke a discussion about how to minimise it during the procedure, rather than result in an end to the practice of abortion.

Even if we are inclined to dismiss claims that "the unborn from conception is a fully-fledged member of the human community," these claims are worth considering because they tell us a great deal; not just about how abortion's opponents understand the status of the embryo, but about how they see human life, what it is to be a person, and to what living entities a truly civilised, humanitarian community should accord moral respect.

When someone presents an embryo or foetus as morally equivalent to "one of us" they assume that it raises its status to that of a born person. Looked at in another way, does it not equally lower the status of "us" to that of the embryo? Does it not reduce the unique and fabulous nature of our human life to our genetic material? Do they really believe that all that is special about the human race is expressed in the form of an entity that has no sense that it is alive, or even what life is? Could there be a more empty and degraded sense of humanity than to reduce it to its biological components, when human life is truly so much more?

To value human life truly, we need to appreciate what it is and what makes it unique.

Normally, "being alive" is not enough for us to accord an entity significant moral standing even if we share a presumption in favour of life. Most of us accept that certain kinds of life may be taken in certain kinds of circumstances—although we may differ in where we may draw these lines.

We generally accept that human life is inviolable, but we make exceptions for "just wars," perhaps the execution of those who have committed heinous crimes, maybe even "mercy killing" to end suffering from which there is no hope of recovery. Most of us place a much lower bar on the killing of non-human animals, accepting their destruction for a good purpose—some of us would see that as security ("I'd kill a marauding bear"), others food ("I'd kill a lamb for its meat"), some sport ("I'd kill a boar bear for the thrill").

The status of embryonic life is complicated by its specific characteristics. In a biological "species" sense, it is human. It is certainly not a horse, or a rabbit or a cat. Its genetic material—the DNA present from the earliest cell divisions—identify it as a member of the species *Homo sapiens* but is does not (yet) possess any of the qualities that distinguish humans from animals. In fact, it does not even possess the qualities that cause us to balk at the wanton destruction of animal life. Even the most trenchant opponent of abortion would be hard-pressed to argue that an embryo without a developed nervous system is as sentient as the mouse we place traps for.

When we consider, however, the relative worth of the lives of horses, rabbits, cats and embryos, the parenthetic "yet" in the previous section is all-important. The embryo is special, because of what it has the *potential* to become. Even when there is no possibility that it *will* fulfil that potential, modern societies tend to accord the human embryo a certain reverence. An example of this is the way research that involves human embryos in the UK is regulated by codes that were developed, not only by scientists or doctors, but by a learned committee directed by a philosophy professor, Dame Mary Warnock, then Mistress of Girton College,

Cambridge University.[2] The Human Fertilisation and Embryology Act 1990 (amended in 2008) governs how human embryos can be used in research and treatment and the Human Fertilisation and Embryology Authority is dedicated to its enforcement.

Even after an abortion, in many countries, the foetal material is treated differently than other "clinical waste"; in many countries, special regulations and guidelines set down ways in which foetal material may, and may not, be stored and destroyed—typically separately from other material. In Britain, guidelines specify the permitted methods of "sensitive disposal." The special way in which the *human* embryo is treated implies that there is something distinct and important about the value of the embryo even when abortion is legally permitted. Usually this special value rests on its "potentiality."

When Does Life Begin ... to Matter?

An incremental approach, which values the life of the embryo just a little at first, but increasingly as it progresses to birth, makes sense to many—on both sides of the abortion debate. For a core of abortion opponents, however, it makes no sense at all to talk about the potentiality of the foetus, or to differentiate between an embryo at seventeen hours post-conception, a foetus at seventeen weeks' gestation, a baby seventeen days after birth and an adolescent at seventeen years of age.

For many Christian thinkers, "living beings come into existence all at once and then gradually unfold to themselves and to the world what they already, but only incipiently, *are*."[3] As David Oderberg explains, "Conception does not bring into existence a potential human being, but an *actual* human being with the potential to develop, given the right factors, into a mature human being."[4] In other words, human beings are

---

[2] See Robert Edwards (1989). *Life Before Birth*. London: Hutchinson, pp. 113–123.

[3] Robert E. Joyce (1978). Personhood and the Conception Event. *The New Scholasticism*, 52(Winter), 106, 113 cited in Frances J. Beckwith (2007). *Defending Life: A Moral and Legal Case Against Abortion Choice*. Cambridge: Cambridge University Press, p. 134.

[4] David S. Oderberg (2000). *Applied Ethics: A Non-Consequentialist Approach*. Oxford: Blackwell, p. 21.

ontologically prior to their parts. This means they maintain one consistent identity while they grow and develop, and furthermore, it is the organism's nature that causes the developments to occur.

The idea stems from the notion that God shapes our form to be what it needs to be to perform the functions we require at that specific stage of life. So the foetus is perfectly formed to exist in the womb, just as the child is perfectly formed to play and to learn, and the aged have the form they need to reflect. From this perspective, the embryo is no more pre-human than the elderly are post-human. We simply "are" what we are—and "we" includes those of us who are pre-born.

Although the idea that "we are what we are" from conception may be rooted in theories about ensoulment, there have been strenuous efforts to find a secular, "scientific" anchor to enable the claim that "We know from science what the embryo is ... a complete albeit developmentally immature human being."[5]

Science increasingly lends itself to this aim. Twenty-first-century secular thought has also directed its focus towards the womb to discover the origin of our personal selves, looking to genetic determinism to explain what makes us who we are as individuals. Our unique genetic coding, present in the earliest stages of our embryonic development, is now attributed with shaping far more than the physical features that concerned the Mendelians in the late nineteenth century. So many of our individual characteristics—personality traits, habits and addictions—are thought to be "laid down" in our genetic coding that there is a credible claim, for those who might wish to make it, that the essence of who we are is there from the earliest embryonic cell divisions. The respected Protestant theologian and opponent of abortion, Paul Ramsey, claims:

> Microgenetics seems to have discovered what religion never could, and biological science seems to have resolved an ancient theological dispute ... [With the exception of identical twins] no one else in the entire history of the human race ever will have exactly the same genotype. Thus it can be said that the individual is *whoever he is going to become from the moment*

---

5 Robert George and Christopher Tollesfen (2011). *Embryo: A Defense of Human Life*. Princeton: The Witherspoon Institute, p. 20.

of impregnation. Therefore his subsequent development may be described as a process of becoming the one he already is.[6] (Emphasis in original)

Obviously, today's genetic science has evolved from being the product of confused imagination and wishful thinking that led early scientists to imagine sperm as little men. And it is true that there are aspects of ourselves that are determined by our personal genetic make-up; all manner of characteristics, ranging from those that affect our appearance to those that may determine the nature of our death, are inherited.

We can, however, accept that DNA denotes species membership and an individual genetic code, and still believe our humanity is more than the sum of our biological parts. You do not have to be a Christian, with a belief in ensoulment, to believe that we are more than a beating heart and whatever is encoded on the double-helix of our DNA.

That the embryo is alive must be beyond doubt—but what is the meaning of this *Home sapiens* livingness?

Frances Beckwith, throughout his comprehensive argument against abortion, repeatedly asserts that every argument that permits abortion assumes that the entity in the womb "is not fully human."[7] He sees this point as important because, to him, it demonstrates that those who permit abortion are either ignorant of biological fact, psychologically "in denial" about the human status of the foetus, or socially disposed to redraw definitions of humanness in a way that excludes "inconvenient" types (much as Hitler's followers in the 1930s instrumentally defined Jews, Roma, homosexuals, the disabled and many others as "non-human" or "sub-human").

In truth, claims that fundamentally deny the human basis of the embryo have been rarely made. In the 1970s, some feminists argued that the foetus is akin to a tumour—simply human tissue that has been triggered into development much like a cancer with no moral significance—but this view was never commonly held. Sometimes, people with a scientific bent like to joust against the arguments for continuous linear development by pointing out that a fertilised egg can develop

---

6 Paul Ramsey (1968). The Morality of Abortion. In Edward Shils et al. (Eds.), *Life or Death: Ethics and Options*. Portland: Reed College, pp. 61–62.

7 He repeats this dismissal on pp. 95, 97, 99, 100, 101, 103, 104 and 106.

into something that is not a single embryo, which they say proves the error in assuming than an early embryo is an embryonic person. It may, for example, develop into a hydatidiform mole, an abnormal development where the placenta develops into a mass of cysts that can become cancerous.

Other claims that place the foetus outside humanity rely on a non-biological definition of humanity that sees "humanness" as linked to a definition that society bestows, much like the quality of "personhood" that we will discuss later in some detail. From this perspective, humanity is conferred not by any intrinsic quality of the embryo, but by membership of society. Accordingly, membership of the species *Homo sapiens* is insufficient to confer human status, because everything rests on how the status of the entity is determined by the pregnant woman herself, or by the society in which she lives. Social anthropologists observe that, globally, the value of born infants, especially in traditional societies, varies according to the availability of resources required to keep them alive. Certain ceremonies, such as naming ceremonies that mark acceptance by the social group, may be delayed until the child's survival is probable.[8]

The social construction of "human status" that comes into play appears bizarre and inconsistent to Beckwith and others of like mind, but it does accord with how many women experience pregnancy. Women who want to be pregnant often identify their pregnancy as their baby, valued as a person and perhaps even named, as soon as a pregnancy test shows positive. When a pregnancy is wanted, miscarriage, even in the earliest weeks, may be mourned by the woman, her family and friends, while another woman, who is unaware of her pregnancy, might experience a loss at the same gestation as nothing more remarkable than a "heavy period." A third woman with an unwanted pregnancy may experience the loss (whether by a deliberately induced abortion or a spontaneous "miscarriage") as a profound relief. In all three pregnancies, the embryos will have the same physical form but the different way in which the pregnancies are regarded suggest that the status of the foetus is determined by something other than its physical form. How the pregnancy

[8] Helge Kuhse and Peter Singer (1985). *Should the Baby Live? The Problem of Handicapped Infants*. Oxford: Oxford University Press.

fits with the woman's life-story is significant in how that pregnancy is understood by her and others. The way that society frames pregnancy, and every type of discourse concerning embryos, foetuses and babies, has been the subject of many sociological and anthropological studies.[9] Put simply, they show that different societies view "life" differently. In a modern developed society, it is possible to see the foetus as an "unborn child" because the normal outcome of pregnancy is an uncomplicated birth. Typically, the foetus is seen quite differently in circumstances where labour is risky, infant survival rates are low and pregnancy has much less certain outcomes for mother and child.

It is hard to argue against the empirical observation that the value of human life is specific to the context in which it is born. Discussions about foetal viability (the gestation of pregnancy at which a baby can survive if born) clearly show this. In London, neonatologists debating whether the threshold is twenty-one or twenty-two weeks' gestation recognise that this is so dependent on expertise and technology that the chances of survival for a premature baby depend on whether or not it is born in a highly specialised unit. A tiny infant that might survive with heroic efforts in one hospital will stand no chance of survival in another. Where there is no chance of continued survival, attempts at resuscitation that might be the standard of care on a specialist neonatal unit, would seem a cruel and pointless prolonging of suffering for the baby and its parents. Paediatricians in deprived and struggling geographical environments view discussions about viability in London and New York as belonging to another world altogether. Throughout war-torn and underdeveloped Afghanistan, where almost one baby in five[10] born at term fails to survive, the attitude to infant life is somewhat different to that in a London teaching hospital, where teams of expert paediatricians, with

---

[9] See Roseanne Cecil (Ed.) (1996). *The Anthropology of Pregnancy Loss: Comparative Studies in Miscarriage, Stillbirth and Neonatal Death.* Oxford: Berg, pp. 1–11; and Jacqueline Vincent Prija (1992). *Birth Traditions and Modern Pregnancy Care.* Shaftesbury, Dorset: Element, Chaps. 3 and 4.

[10] US Central Intelligence Agency (Ed.) (2015). *World Fact Book.* Washington, DC: Potomac Books.

heroic efforts, succeed in saving the lives of almost one baby in five born at twenty-three weeks.[11]

We may accept that individual women have the right to decide about the future of their pregnancies, based on our respect for their capacity to make decisions and to have agency in their own lives, but there is something unsatisfactory in defining humanity in a manner that rests so much on an individual's subjective opinion. We might accept that that pregnancies and infants are regarded differently in societies where all claims on life are fragile—but that seems different from accepting that the value of *human life* may be defined on a case-by-case basis according to its "wantedness." This seems too subjective and random.

If the humanness of the foetus is detached entirely from its essential characteristics and relies solely on subjective definition, how is a reference of the "mother-to-be" to her "unborn baby" different to the crazy cat lady's claim that kittens are "her children"? Yet we know that it is different. There seems to be something about species-membership, something about a woman being pregnant with one of our kind that makes a difference and confers human pregnancy and the human foetus with a special value, even in countries with liberal abortion laws.

And yet, there is rather more truth and wisdom in the claim that the foetus "is not fully human" than Beckwith's rhetorical dismissal recognises. And it is indeed this absence of "fully-humanness" that allows some of us to dismiss any claim to "the right to life of the unborn child."

The Value of Life

So, what is it about "human life" that we value? And what value do we place on human life in relation to other values that we have, and in relation to other lives?

The claim made by opponents of abortion that the human embryo is as entitled to its "right to life" as we are to ours is the genuinely held

---

[11] K. L. Costeloe, E. M. Hennessy, S. Haider and F. Stacey (2012). Short Term Outcomes After Extreme Preterm Birth in England: Comparison of Two Birth Cohorts in 1995 and 2006: The EPIcure Studies. *British Medical Journal*, 345, e7976.

belief that the value of embryonic life is equivalent to ours and that it has what some ethicists refer to as "full moral status." But where does that leave the woman in whose womb the foetus grows? Does her moral status lessen as that of the foetus becomes greater? It is not easy to pin down exactly what is meant by full moral status—because, when it comes to philosophy, it sometimes seems that there are as many definitions for a term as there are philosophers who use it. For our purposes, let us accept in line with the *Stanford Encyclopedia of Philosophy* that: "an entity has moral status if and only if its interests morally matter to some degree for the entity's own sake, such that it can be wronged." Crucial to this definition is the limiting of moral status to entities that can be *wronged for their own sake*. This accepts that it may be immoral to destroy my antique vase, without assuming that the vase is a moral entity. I am the entity to whom the wrong is done, since the destruction of the vase is my loss.

As soon as one moves beyond inanimate objects into a living world, things become complicated, because we start to question what wronging something "for its own sake" means. Does it mean that the entity must be capable of feeling a sense of being wronged? Most of us can agree that, say, a tree cannot be wronged for its own sake; it is insensate, having no feelings or consciousness at all. The moral status of animals is contested to the point that there is no broad consensus and certainly no consistency across species. Do calves that are raised for veal have moral status? Do wolves that are killed to prevent them from killing deer have moral status? What about deer culled to prevent them killing saplings?

The term "full moral status" (the highest moral status) is usually reserved for beings that possess sophisticated cognitive functions; beings that have rational capability, beings that "know" or can work things out in a way that implies self-awareness. Traditionally, in modern developed societies, full moral status has been limited to humans—although recognition of the greater cognitive sophistication of certain species has raised questions about the moral status of certain animals, such as dolphins and great apes. The Australian bioethics Professor Peter Singer, currently at Princeton University, is one of the most well known and controversial writers on applied ethics. He has rejected a human-exclusive understanding of personhood, which he perceives as "speciesism." Singer is the author of "The Great Apes' Charter"[12] a case for full moral status for apes based on their capacities. He is also co-author of *Should the Baby Live?*[13] a controversial, but analytically logical, defence of infanticide based on the limited capacities of infants. For Singer, personhood is non-species specific and time-changeable. A chimpanzee's life has greater moral value than someone with a debilitating brain injury that has destroyed their mind.

Professor John Harris also lends his weight to the question of should we value "humans" above all in his challenge to us to answer the following question: In what context would we have an alien from outer space "for dinner"—would it be placed next to the host as a guest, or on the platter as the main course? How would we decide?[14]

A helpful allegory used by many writers concerns a father who hears his daughter call up from the garden, "Daddy, can I kill it?" How should the father respond? We are advised that the answer surely depends on what "it" is and whether the killing is justified. Clearly, it matters whether the "it" is a weed on the path, a cockroach, a marauding rabid dog, the pet rabbit, the girl's infant brother, a passerby or a homicidal maniac. It is easy to demonstrate that, even if we would be horrified by the wanton destruction of the pet rabbit, we regard people as special. The special-ness of "people" or "persons" begs the question of why we make this distinction and how we make this distinction.

In the second half of the seventeenth century, the philosopher John Locke considered how to distinguish persons from other creatures in a way that made sense of the value we place upon them. In his view a person was:

A thinking intelligent being, that has reason and reflection, and can consider itself as itself, the same thinking thing, in different times and places, which it does by that consciousness which is inseparable from

---

[12] Jessica Eisen (2010). Liberating Animal Law: Breaking Free from Human-Use Typologies. *Animal Law*, 59, 60–75; Peter Singer (1995). *Animal Liberation*, 2nd ed. London: Thorsons.

[13] Helga Kuhse and Peter Singer (1985). *Should the Baby Live? The Problem of Handicapped Infants*. Oxford: Oxford University Press.

[14] This is fully explored in John Harris (1985). *The Value of Life: An Introduction to Medical Ethics*. London: Routledge, Chap. 1.

thinking and seems to me essential to it; it being impossible for anyone to perceive without perceiving that he does perceive.[15]

In this explanation, he was following a line of thought that extends back to Aristotle, who accepted that humans had "nutritive" life that we share with plants and an instinctual life that we share with animals—but, most crucially, we have a rational character: we are able to carry out rationally formulated projects and to employ a deliberative imagination to do so.[16]

The aspect of rationality has been much discussed and debated,[17] with some critics objecting that a claim to include rationality as a criterion for personhood is elitist and excludes irrational individuals. Some feminists have criticised this formulation, claiming that rationality is a masculinist value. Even if one ascribes some merit to these claims, they are beside the point, because in this context, Locke clearly uses rationality to differentiate from instinctive, intuitive processes that result in action. A person selecting which chair to occupy may choose the same cushioned seat as a cat—but the cognitive process that results in the intention to sit in that place is different. The cat may be drawn by the warmth and soft qualities of the chair—as may we—but we consider in a different way. We have, what we might call an all-things-considered way of thinking. It is not just the seat but what the seat represents: comfort, yes, but also: near the front? in reach of the bar for the interval drink? out of sight of the co-worker we wish to avoid? All-things-considered we decide this is better than that. We decide that this is right and this is wrong in relation to practical detail as well as big-picture issues. Rational thinking may deals with the immediate but extends beyond it.

And to that we must add that Locke's notion of considering oneself in different times and places is every bit as important. Having a sense of the past and the future gives a special meaning to our presence in the "now." It suggests that maybe there are different futures according to different actions one might take—and if these futures depend on what we do, they are (at least in part) for us to decide. This kicks sand in the face

---

[15] John Locke (1689). *An Essay Concerning Human Understanding.*

[16] Aristotle. *Nicomachean Ethics.* I.13, *De anima* III 1.1.

[17] M. S. Komrad (1983). A defence of medical paternalism maximizing patient autonomy. *Journal of Medical Ethics,* 9, 38–44.

of claims that humans are just other animals with our destiny shaped by circumstance. We have a conscious sense and a power of will.

And this means that we are, in a significant sense, authors of our own biography. Our life story is not written by God, or by nature, but in great part by ourselves—through the decisions we make. The foetus possesses the life the Greeks called *zoë*—which is common to every being that possesses a beating heart and its own DNA (be it a cat, snake or horse)—but it has no *bios*; and it is bios that puts the "human" in human life.

Seeing these attributes as universal human features does not mean that every individual employs them, and no person uses them all the time. A sleeping person is as unaware of himself, or herself, as a sleeping dog is, but it would be absurd to suggest we surrender personhood at night. Except in bizarre circumstances, we wake up as the same thinking, knowing thing that were when we closed our eyes.

Similarly, it is tempting to balk at the description as ourselves as "rational" when we know that many of the decisions we take are impulsive, maybe even careless—anything but rationally considered. But that is beside the point. To talk about humans as rational means simply that we are capable of weighing the merits of situations and acting according to a thought-out, anticipated plan, which—even though it be ever so simple—is something no other species (nor, we might note here, the foetus of our species) can demonstrate. Harris suggests that for Locke, "The rationality required is of a fairly low order, just sufficient for an individual to 'consider itself the same thinking thing in different times and places'." Self-consciousness was simply the awareness of that reasoning process.

The Specialness of Humans

The special nature of human personhood is empirically evident in the way we live our lives, and in our history. Indeed, the very fact that we have "history" as individuals and as a species is key to our specialness. The way we live changes even during the course of a generation, and not by mere chance or circumstance, but because we are able to *imagine* how life might be improved, *identify* the obstacles to be overcome, and *invent* ways to bring about what we want. That we are able to do this is demonstrated by the evidence that we have done so in the past.

If you need to conceptualise just how humankind is different from other species, think about the way we have changed the world and have adapted what we have found around us to improve our lives.

Even within a generation, human life changes. There is no element of our lives that is unshaped by social developments and our specific individual hopes and ambitions that are both part of these developments and contribute to them.

Of course, "man is an animal," but there is something special about our kind of animal; our faculties are different. We can, and do, extend ourselves beyond instincts and basic intentionality. When we are hungry, we do not simply find food; we select and prepare our meal according to our preferred taste. Bees and ants may have complex social hierarchies and living arrangements—but not as a consequence of consideration. They don't *choose* to live the way they do; insects only make decisions in the anthropomorphic constructions of our human imaginations. Even the great apes and dolphins, which naturalists believe to have higher cognitive functions, such as the ability to learn and communicate, are substantially below the benchmark humanity has set for itself.

There is a reason why *human* moral philosophers constructed the great apes' charter; it was not a lack of access to a word processor that prevented gorillas from making their own demands. Similarly, no dolphin has protested against the tuna-fishing techniques that threaten them. Paradoxically, every campaign for "animal rights" is conceived of, articulated and organised by people—and with the intention of convincing other people. The point of the campaigns against the confinement of apes in zoos, or the use of other higher mammals in research, is to convince "us" that it is "wrong"—even those who claim moral equivalence for certain species have no aspiration to agitate among the animals themselves, and no one argues that, for example, the Cats Protection League should have feline leadership (or even representation).

Most of us believe all species should be treated humanely. When the little girl asks "may I kill it?" those of us who presume to favour life will tell her to leave "whatever it is" alive and unmolested unless there is a good reason not to, regardless of that it is. Wanton, unjustified destruction, especially of life, just seems wrong.

Even the cockroach's life has some value—even if just as bird food. We do not think it is right to kill something just because it is not human. Furthermore, we are quite able to respect, venerate and even love non-human lives at the same time as understanding and appreciating their difference. People may poke fun at those of us who adore our cats and claim they are "child substitutes," but it seems safe to assert that, for most of us, it is the very non-human "catness" of the cat that we find so adorable. A cat would be a poor child substitute, just as a child would be a poor cat substitute; each lacks the specific qualities of the other.

Lacking humanness, however, does not exclude a being from being the object of its expression, even if it cannot be its subject. Humaneness is characterised by compassion, tenderness and sympathy. We can, and do, apply these sentiments well beyond our own species. To be humane is part of our humanity; etymologically and conceptually they are linked.

Personhood

The concept of "personhood" is extremely helpful when we consider different types of lives and their moral value. In addressing the vexing matter of when human life begins, in an *organic* sense there is a convincing claim that life begins even before the sperm and egg combine into the conceptus since both the sperm and egg are living entities. In a philosophical sense the question is more open. A *Far Side* cartoon shows scientists in a lab peering down microscopes, with a caption that states: "while scientists debate about when life begins, they all agree it is after work."

Essentially, the point for us is not when life begins, but *when life begins to matter*. Trying to work out what lives are valuable seems meaningless (and impossible) from an objective point of view, because there are so many different ways to evaluate this and so many different subjective perspectives. The life of a cockroach may be valued by an etymologist as an object of study, and by a pest controller as a source of income, but the chef in whose kitchen it lives may value the destruction of its life even more.

One crucial distinction is made between those lives that are valuable in the eyes of others, and those that are valuable to themselves. The catchment of the first category (living things that we value) is so broad as to capture the broad diversity of organic matter. We value crops because we can eat them, trees because they give shade; flowers because they are beautiful. *We* value these things *because…*

A different category of life altogether is that which has value, not instrumentally, because we value it, but because *it values itself*. This is fundamentally different from the instrumental sense of value just described. What is important is not the content of an individual's account for why their life is valuable, but that the individual in question has the capacity to give such an account. For any individual entity to value itself, it must have a sense of itself—it must have an awareness that it exists.

For Harris, the point is this:

> [I]f we allow that the value of life consists simply in those reasons, *whatever they are* that each person has for finding their own life valuable and for wanting to go on living, then we do not need to know what the reasons are. All we need to know is that particular individuals have their own reasons, or rather, simply, that they value their own lives.[18]

There are all manner of complex and complicated discussions about personhood that examine the concept in relation to animals, beings from outer space, artificial intelligence, but this definition—that persons are capable of valuing their own lives—although alarmingly simple, neatly captures the essence of the matter.

It is important to be clear that it is the *capacity* to value one's own life that is important and not the actual value that one places on it. If someone with the capacity to value their life desires to end their life because it no longer has value, it does not make them any less

---

[18] John Harris (1985). *The Value of Life: An Introduction to Medical Ethics.* London: Routledge.

of a person—for only someone with the capacity to value life could "dis-value" it.

In order to value its own life, a being has to be aware that it has a life to value. Harris suggests that this would at least require Locke's conception of *self-consciousness*, which involves a being's ability to "consider itself as itself in different times and places." Self-consciousness is not just awareness—it is awareness of awareness. Additionally, to value its own life, a being has to be aware of itself as an independent centre of consciousness, with a future that it is capable of envisioning and wishes to experience. Only if a being can envisage a future could a being want its life to go on, and so value continued existence.

This is what makes human life special—that we have these capacities—that we are persons. Harris takes some care to emphasise that "persons" may not be limited to the *Homo sapiens* species. Perhaps other animals might have these qualities, as Peter Singer suggests, but if they do, they have surely kept them well hidden.

The discussion of how we value life and why, is important when we weigh the balance of the value of a woman's life against that of her embryo. It seems impossible not to conclude that in a woman we have a person who is self-conscious with a capacity to value her life and envisage her future, while the foetus, despite its human DNA and possibly even its human appearance, has no sense of itself at all. This makes the foetus human in a biological sense, but, perhaps, not in the sense that it's death carries the moral weight of the end to a life that knows life and values itself.

Abortion may be an act of killing—but it kills a being that has no sense of life or death, and no awareness of itself as distinct from others.

Because the foetus is not a person with full moral status, it does not follow that we should not regard abortion as a loss. Some of us may value the standing of personhood so much that if we were to draft a hierarchy of value, we would place embryonic human life directly under self-conscious persons, because of its potential to become what we value above all. So, we may believe an embryo has more moral value than a dog, even though the dog has greater sentience, independence and ability to express itself.

Ultimately, a hierarchy of respect is irrelevant, although probably we all have views on which lives matter more than others with that one important caveat: as self-conscious individuals, we all have the right to ours.

Perhaps the noise of the abortion battles has drowned out a quieter sadness about the destruction of embryonic or foetal life. Precisely because abortion pits that life in relation to a woman's, it provides less space for sadness about the end of a human life not yet lived.

Ronald Dworkin frequently refers in his writings to our sense of "cosmic awe," by which he means the awe that we all sometimes feel at the complexity and wondrousness of phenomena. Even if we have no belief in a god, or a religious faith, we are not immune from awe inspired by the vastness of a mountain range, the light from stars, or the constant crash of the waves on the shore.[19]

New life uplifts and inspires us with its promise for the future, and abortion may evoke a sense of sadness. If we presume that life is good in itself, the destroying of what is the result of aeons of natural selective evolution does, in some primal way, seem intrinsically pitiful. Infertile people sometimes talk about their sadness in feeling that they are the end of evolution for their own individual genetic line. They express their fear of "genetic death" with their own death, which is unsurprising when you consider how we think about "living on through our children."

While supporting a woman's right to decide on abortion, Ronald Dworkin displays a kind of secular sacredness in his consideration of the embryo and articulates beautifully how concern for the embryo can genuinely be detached from a desire to constrain women's decisions or prohibitions and restrictions that discourage abortion:

> The life of a single human organism commands respect and protection … because of the complex creative investment it represents and because of our wonder at the divine and or evolutionary processes that produce new lives from old ones, at the processes of nature and community and language through which a human being will come to absorb and continue hundreds of generations of cultures and forms of life and value,

---

[19] See Ronald Dworkin (2013). *Religion Without God.* Cambridge, MA: Harvard University Press.

and finally, when mental life has begun and flourishes, at the process of internal personal creation and judgment by which a person will remake himself, a mysterious, inescapable process in which we each participate ... The horror we feel in the wilful destruction of a human life reflects our shared inarticulate sense of the intrinsic importance of each of these dimensions of investment.[20]

Dworkin leads us to the place where thinking about abortion needs to sit in any society that values tolerance and freedom and personal autonomy. He explains that it is quite consistent to hold a "profound conviction that it is intrinsically wrong deliberately to end a human life" and yet "believe that a decision whether to end human life in early pregnancy must nevertheless be left to the pregnant woman whose conscience is most directly connected to the choice, and who has the greatest stake in it."[21]

This belief is consistent with the tradition of freedom of conscience, and it quite properly puts the responsibility for the decision about the future of a woman's pregnancy where it should be—with the woman in whose body the foetus resides. This does not devalue human life; rather, it demonstrates the value that we give to those aspects of life that are truly human and make us the people that we are.

[20] Ronald Dworkin (1993). *Life's Dominion: An Argument about Abortion, Euthanasia, and Individual Freedom*. London: HarperCollins, p. 84.
[21] Ronald Dworkin (1993). *Life's Dominion: An Argument about Abortion, Euthanasia, and Individual Freedom*. London: HarperCollins, p. 15.

6

Because Women Are People

With all our focus on whether a foetus is a person, it is easy to overlook something that is simple, straightforward and easy to verify. At no point in pregnancy does a woman *stop* being a person. She is living and has a life to live. She is self-conscious and self-aware: she *knows*! Her potential is not simply a matter of the genetic coding that is her species membership. Nor is she entirely dependent on either "nature" or the decisions of others. She shapes her own potential by the decisions she makes and the actions she takes. Every woman is the author of her own story even if she cannot always choose the settings and themes of her biography. Although we cannot always choose the circumstances in which we live, we are never completely passive objects to which things are done. We have hopes and dreams and ambitions.

The embryo's status in life may be uncertain, but its *position* in life is clear: it is *in utero*—contained in the womb of a woman. She is its life support in every way.

This should be a game changer. It is one thing to weigh the considerations of how society should consider an embryo *in vitro*— the embryo's life and status in the laboratory—but another to consider the embryo *in utero*. In neither situation can the embryo be described as having an

A. Furedi, *The Moral Case for Abortion*,
https://doi.org/10.1007/978-3-030-90189-9_6

independent existence. Both are utterly dependent on people for every aspect of their maintenance. But there is a freestanding quality about the embryo in the laboratory since anyone, with suitable training and competence, can supply what it needs, and the technician responsible for its creation can walk away—leaving someone else to continue the job.

The dependent relationship of the embryo *in utero* is more than just having requirements that must be met. This embryo is attached to the woman in whose womb it sits—and relies on her, and her alone, as a life support system. No one can substitute for her. There is no holiday substitute to allow her to take a day off.

The embryo *in utero* is not part of a woman's body; it has its own genetically distinct make-up (being half formed from the genetic material of a man)—but it is nonetheless "of" her since it is created from her and her interests are bound up with its future. Everything that impacts on that embryo has an impact on her and, likewise, nothing impacts on the embryo without impacting on her.

The difference in where the embryo is located has come to the fore as governments and scientific bodies have considered regulations concerning research on human embryos. Professor Mary Warnock was clearly considering this when, in the 1980s, she chaired the committee that would inform the regulations and laws that govern embryo research in the UK and have far-reaching influence around the world. The Warnock Committee set an upper time limit for embryo research at fourteen days after fertilisation, which seemed to jar with a much later abortion time limit of twenty-four weeks. Both limits still stand in the UK, which seems inconsistent if you think only of the embryo—but not when you think of their context. A time limit of fourteen days was determined to give scientists acceptable time for research; twenty-four weeks was understood to give time for a pregnancy to be terminated. At no time did the committee seriously entertain the notion that the embryo had any rights of its own.

During pregnancy it is impossible to accord any rights or status to the foetus as an entity in itself, without compromising and diminishing those of the woman in whose body it resides. When we think of women's rights, the right to ownership over their own bodies is not what comes to mind. And yet, this right is central to women's right to abortion.

The principle that our individual bodies are not a resource for others to use without our consent has obvious implications when we consider the relationship between a woman and her foetus. The use of a woman's body to nurture and develop her child-to-be is a willing encumbrance when the woman wants her baby. Her womb is occupied by consent. But can society really insist that she endure the assault required by pregnancy and birth against her will?

Abortion's opponents often insist that location cannot truly matter when we consider the status of the foetus. They argue that the value of life cannot simply rest on whether that life is situated in a womb or a cot. They compare the status of a foetus at twenty-three weeks that can be legally aborted, to that of a premature baby at twenty-three weeks, which paediatricians will strive to keep alive. It's the same baby, they argue, just in a different place. How can it possibly be, they ask, that a society that rejects the infanticide of a born infant allows the abortion of a foetus at the same stage of development?

The most straightforward and honest answer is that geography does, and should, matter, because it determines who maintains that life and how they do it. There can be no equivalence between the treatment of a baby and treatment of a foetus (even at the same "age"). No team of neonatal paediatricians can care for the twenty-three-week "life" *in utero*, yet no twenty-three-week life *ex utero* can survive without such a team. Because their physical and relational circumstances are different, it follows that the moral circumstances are different too.

No mystical transformation takes place in the foetus itself during birth, which means we consider its moral claims differently. However, that small journey, of just inches down the birth canal, has huge significance in the moral standing of the foetus and any claims that may follow from that. Once the woman has been "delivered," the baby is born into a life where it is no longer dependent on the maternal environment, but on the social environment. Now, for the first time, its interests can be considered independently of hers.

Born or unborn is the obvious marker that is relevant to the status of the foetus, and yet most legal frameworks impose an arbitrary upper time limit that defies rational explanation. If you accept that a woman should be able to have an abortion because the pregnancy resides within her—and our bodies are our own—then why should it matter if the pregnancy has been developing for three weeks, or twenty-three weeks, or thirty-three weeks?

The UK Parliament has historically used the point at which a baby might be born alive as an abortion time limit: twenty-eight weeks in 1967 was lowered to twenty-four weeks in 1991. For decades, the principle that viability is important has been largely accepted, and debate has focussed on where that line is drawn. Each media report of the survival of a supposedly "pre-viable" premature baby triggers a set-piece confrontation. Abortion opponents argue the gestational time limit should be lowered; abortion supporters insist that rare and exceptional cases are a poor basis for law; and neonatologists express concern about unrealistic expectations of premature survival.

The ethical weight placed on viability is bizarre when you consider that it is a concept that speaks to the development of society and not to the development of the foetus. Human foetuses develop their hearts and brains at the pace they have for millennia, but their survival outside the womb is dependent as much on the development of society as it is on the development of the foetus. The viability of premature babies depends on technical advances, economic resources and the social will to apply them. Viability, in reality, depends on the availability of a hospital with the equipment and skills for neonatal care.

The premature baby at twenty-three weeks is, indeed, no different from the foetus—except that its life is supported by a machine's system, not its mother's womb. Viability is as much a random determination as any other, and it has no significant part to play in the debate on abortion when the matter is considered from the woman's perspective.

Some women's feelings about their pregnancy do change as it advances. This is not always the case, however, and even when it is, this does not mean her circumstances change. Consider a woman who conceived a wanted pregnancy with a man she once thought loved her but has now left her. Now her pregnancy is unwanted; everything about her life is different. She had planned to be a mother as part of a happy couple; now she will raise her child alone. She thought she would enjoy the financial security and emotional security of her marriage; now she has lost all the future certainty she believed she had. She thought her child would represent her union with her soulmate; now the pregnancy seems proof of betrayal, lies and her foolishness. Are we really expected to believe that none of these things matter as much as the precise date of the conception?

Yet, if this woman requests an abortion at a clinic in Britain, the date of conception, as evidenced by an ultrasound scan, will determine everything. If she is twenty-three weeks and six days, she may end the pregnancy. Just one day later, and she assumes a non-negotiable obligation to give birth.

Legal time limits shift the focus for the pregnancy decision from issues concerning the life of the woman, in all their painful complexity, to the biological development of the foetus.

The obligation that society imposes on a woman to continue a pregnancy against her will, her judgement, her beliefs and her conscience is intolerable. It is a burden that that goes far beyond the responsibilities we expect her to assume for people that have been born, even our born children.

No one has addressed this point better than the American moral philosopher and metaphysician Judith Jarvis Thomson, in her 1971 essay "A Defense of Abortion." This sets aside all considerations of the nature and value at any gestation and bases an argument on a person's right to determine how their own body is used, regardless of its consequences for others.[1] Jarvis Thomson invites us to take part in a mind experiment which constructs a scenario whereby the foetus does have full moral status as a person. She explores how *even then* abortion might be permissible.

Jarvis Thomson presents what has become known as the case of the famous violinist. The scenario, which has been the subject of many philosophical debates and discussions, is this:

---

[1] Judith Jarvis Thomson (1971). A defense of abortion. *Philosophy & Public Affairs*, 1, republished in Louis Pojman and Francis J. Beckwith (1998). *The Abortion Controversy: 25 Years After Roe v. Wade, A Reader*, 2nd edn. Belmont: Wadsworth, pp. 117–132.

Suppose you are kidnapped by the Society of Music Lovers anxious to save the life of a famous violinist with a fatal kidney disease. Only your blood is of the right type to save him; your circulatory system is joined with his, cleansing his blood and allowing his kidneys to recover. You are, in effect, turned into a human dialysis machine. But only for nine months, because at the end of that time the violinist's kidneys will have returned to normal; he can be disconnected from you, and you can go your separate ways.

The questions Jarvis Thomson poses to us are these:

Is it morally incumbent on you to accede to this situation? No doubt it would be very nice of you if you did, a great kindness. But do you *have* to accede to it? What if it were not nine months, but nine years? Or longer still? What if the director of the hospital says, "Tough luck, I agree, but you've now got to stay in bed, with violinist plugged into you, for the rest of your life. Because remember this. All persons have a right to life and violinists are persons. Granted you have a right to life to decide what happens in and to your body, but a person's right to life outweighs your right to decide what happens in and to your body. So you cannot ever be unplugged from him."

Jarvis Thomson assumes we would find this outrageous, and most people do. She presents us with a person versus person conflict—a clash of one person's absolute right against another—and suggests that it is abhorrent to place an obligation on one person to save another.

One objection is that Jarvis Thomson's argument is compelling only because the individuals are strangers, who have no personal vested interested in each other. In *The Moral Question of Abortion*, Emeritus Professor of Philosophy Stephen D. Schwarz claims that "very thing that makes it plausible to say that the person in the bed with the violinist has no duty to sustain him; namely that he is a stranger unnaturally hooked up to him is precisely what is absent in the case of a mother and her child … [the mother] … does have an obligation to take care of her child, to sustain her and protect her, and especially, to let her live in the only place where she can now be protected, nourished, and allowed to grow, namely the womb."[2] This argument fails for two reasons. First, we can accept that the mother does have a greater moral obligation to her foetus that one adult stranger has to another, but it does not follow that because one is morally obliged to take a course of action, one can be compelled to do it.

Consider, for example, a mother with a five-year-old son with a rare blood type in need of a kidney transplant. After an extensive search for a donor, it is found that the only possible donor is the mother. But the mother refuses, even though the transplant will save her son's life and at little risk to her own health. Her *moral* obligation to agree is almost beyond doubt. But should the law compel her to give up her organ, perhaps by force? That no modern democratic society has laws that insist that someone submit to surgery for the benefit of another suggests the answer.

A mother simply cannot be required to donate bone marrow, or an organ, to existing children, and yet it is assumed that society needs laws prohibiting abortion. It seems bizarre that the imposition of an obligation to keep alive a foetus is greater than the obligation that society can impose on a mother when it comes to her living children. Intellectually inconsistent and irrational as it is, this is the legal framework that exists, almost without exception.

Arguments by analogy are always problematic. Some abortion opponents maintain that Jarvis Thomson's analogy breaks down, because it ignores the unique relationship that exists between a woman and her pregnancy, which places greater obligations on a woman when it comes to her pregnancy than she would have towards a stranger. Others dismiss the analogy, claiming that, unlike a woman who wakes up to find herself attached to someone against her will and through no fault of her own, a woman who becomes pregnant by consensual sex is responsible for her predicament. Her foetus is not a random person attached by an umbilical cord, but an entity that she helped to create.

But these are arguments against the analogy and not arguments against the point that the analogy illustrates. Jarvis Thomson demonstrates that even if we rank human life as the thing we value most, and we regard

[2] Stephen D. Schwarz (1990). *The Moral Question of Abortion*. Chicago: Loyola University Press.

it is as "sacred" and inviolable, the notion of "the right to life" is not unproblematic. Sometimes one person's right to life is pitched against that of another person. Sometimes one person's right to life is pitched against other rights that we regard as inviolable (in this case, the right to personal autonomy and bodily integrity). Philosophy textbooks are full of mind-experiments that explore how we weigh decisions about the value of life: would you shoot one person to save two? Is your obligation to victims of a tsunami equivalent to that of someone drowning just off the beach? Who do you throw out of the lifeboat? Call these conflicts what you will: incompatible decisions of principle; conflicting inviolable rights; clashes of deontological absolutes—they simply serve to illustrate that life is full of tough decisions. And also that the context in which they occur matters greatly.

A function of mind-experiments in philosophy is to strip an example of any extraneous factors that might sway a decision. A decision is distilled to what is seen as its fundamental essence, for example the value of one human life compared with two, or the choice to actively kill or to let die. Abortion is never abstract or distilled from the context of real life—and the decision whether to keep or end a pregnancy is contingent on things that are seemingly outside the scope of a choice to keep the embryo alive or not. In real life, abortion decisions are as much about relationships with others—children already born, husbands, lovers, parents and friends—as they are with the child that *would* be born.

One of the helpful aspects of Jarvis Thomson's violinist analogy is that it takes us outside of the abortion framework and reminds us that, in medicine, judgements about whose life matters—and whose life matters most—are made routinely. State-funded healthcare is typically structured on the basis of quality-of-life assessments, thus decisions about which medications doctors may prescribe are based on cost effectiveness as well as clinical effectiveness. Value judgements influence every decision about whether to fund an acute ward or a geriatric facility.

Even when cost is not an issue, choices are made between lives. Who, among a number of possible recipients should receive a donated organ? When should heroic efforts to save a life cease? We choose to save some human lives and not others—even outside situations where the differential value is apparent: in war (where the lives of combatants are viewed differently to those of civilians); or in capital punishment (where an individual's actions are deemed to have cancelled his or her claim to life). In reality, we accept that not all lives are valued in the same manner, and not all human lives are protected in every circumstance.

John Harris devised another mind-experiment,[3] shortly after the Jarvis Thomson violinist analogy, which, similarly, has been repeatedly cited, albeit outside the literature on abortion. Harris explores the assumption that the sacrifice of one person for the use of their organs could extend the lives of several, and the notion of a national lottery to determine who would be subjected to an "organ harvest" for the greater good. There is a neat utilitarian case to be made in favour of disposing of one man to use his heart, his lungs and his kidneys to save the lives of three or four persons, but, quite rightly, we consider this idea abhorrent, because it challenges the strongly held principles that modern democratic societies hold dear.

The principle that no person shall be used solely for the benefit of others because we have an intrinsic value in ourselves is at the heart of the notion of individual rights that is central to Western civilisation. The right to inherent respect for the integrity of one's own body follows from Immanuel Kant's categorical imperative that we should act in a way that we would wish to see generalised throughout society, and from this follows the coda that people should not be used instrumentally. Kant was one of the most important and influential thinkers of the European Enlightenment and his ideas about metaphysical enquiry and about the relations between reason, judgement and moral thinking are the foundation of many principles we take for granted. His construction of moral laws is what underpins our belief that people should be entitled to live for themselves and not as a means to others' ends. The acceptance of the inviolability of bodily integrity is what stops us from sacrificing persons for the public good.[4] From this two other key principles arise: (i) that it is wrong to violate the freedom of another to act according to their personal autonomous decisions (unless these would harm others); and

---

[3] John Harris (1975). The Survival Lottery. *Philosophy,* 50(191), 81–87.
[4] See H. J. Paton (1958) *Translation, Commentary and Analysis of Immanual Kant: The Moral Law—Groundwork of the Metaphysic of Morals.* London: Routledge.

(ii) that our bodies are our own and we have the right to live free from physical harm by others. This latter principle is sometimes referred to as "bodily integrity."

Some opponents of abortion, David Oderberg among them, simply hold that equivalence between the right to life and bodily integrity is wrong. These rights exist in a hierarchy in which the right to life reigns supreme. For him, "the general principle is clear: it is wrong to kill someone in order to escape physical inconvenience, whether that inconvenience lasts for a day or nine months."[5] This argument is expressed in a more basic and popular form by those who can't seem to understand why a woman cannot simply "just put up being pregnant for a while," as though the pregnancy is a temporary inconvenience like a dental brace.

This trivialisation of what pregnancy means for a woman is staggering, but equally so is the casual dismissal of the fundamental principle that competent adults should have the right to their own body.

The objection, "It's my body to do with what I want" sounds like (and often is) a teenage war cry, but the principle of bodily integrity is regarded as one of the most basic human rights.

The inviolability of our physical bodies underlines, and is an expression of, the importance of personal autonomy and our right of self-determination as a basic element of our rights as humans.

The notion that women's reproductive freedom is grounded in "a right to bodily self-determination" or "control over one's body" has been an important principle in the defence of abortion. Petchesky traces its roots back to the Puritan revolution in seventeenth-century England and a notion held by the Levellers:

> To every individual in nature is given an individual property by nature, not to be invaded or usurped by any: for everyone as he is himself, so he hath a selfe propriety, else could he not be himself, and on this no second may presume to deprive any of without manifest violation and

---

[5] David S. Oderberg (2000a). *Applied Ethics: A Non-Consequentialist Approach*. Oxford: Blackwell, pp. 22–31.

affront to the very principles of nature, and of the Rules of equity and justice between man and man ...[6]

As Petchesky puts it more simply, "A person to be a person must have control over himself or herself in body as well as mind." And, while it may have been expressed by the Levellers in masculine terms, their notion of individual selfhood has specific application to the conditions of women's lives in the seventeenth century, challenging the notion of women as property through laws against wife beating and the foundation of the Puritan marriage contract. It is this notion that "my body belongs to me" that lay behind the introduction of *habeas corpus* (that persons cannot be detained without cause) in 1628.

The principle of bodily integrity sits under all manner of modern judicial safeguards that range from the protection of prisoners from physical abuse to the protection of patients from involuntary treatment and medical experimentation. It is what stops John Harris's dystopian donor lottery from becoming government policy. It is what lies at the heart of laws on rape and other types of assault, kidnap, torture and pretty much everything that involves "consent." It even has some application after death, since organs may only be used posthumously when the person has opted to register as a donor and, even then, close relatives can object.

The irony of respecting the integrity of dead bodies, while failing to respect the bodily integrity of women, is noted wryly by law professor Emily Jackson:

It is clear that if a mother were to die suddenly having previously expressed an objection to her organs being used for transplantation, then even if the removal of an organ would save the life of her dying child, such an operation would be unlawful. If respect for corpses can trump the doctor's impulse to save a child's life, it seems absurd for the interests of an entity lacking legal personality to take priority over the bodily integrity of a pregnant woman.[7]

---

[6] Cited in Rosalind Pollack Petchesky (1986). *Abortion and Women's Choice: The State, Sexuality and Reproductive Freedom*. London: Verso, p. 3.

[7] Emily Jackson (2001). *Regulating Reproduction: Law, Technology and Autonomy*. Oxford: Hart.

Whatever one's view on abortion, there can be no doubt that it is only possible to protect a foetus against the choices made by its "mother" by suspending her right to make decisions about her own body. Resolving the conflict in favour of the foetus represents an extraordinary exception to the established principle that no individual can be *compelled* to use their body for any reason—even to save another's life.

Pro-choice advocates have argued for decades that "exceptionalising" pregnancy in this way would lead to expectations that pregnant women should behave, and be treated, differently. And so it has. Just as women with unwanted pregnancies are expected to suspend their rights and interests to maintain the pregnancy, so enthusiastically pregnant women have lost their status as autonomous individuals entitled to live in the way they choose. Pregnant women find themselves chastised for smoking, are refused alcohol in bars and are expected to comply with dietary and exercise advice.

In the USA, despite the constitutional commitment to the right to privacy,[8] respect for a woman's right to decide in matters where her pregnancy may be at risk seems even lower. There are many reports of pregnant women being compelled to accept HIV treatment, women being forcibly detained in hospital during advanced pregnancy and women being denied the ability to decide what treatment they will accept if suffering from chronic or potentially life-threatening illness.

Concern about women's behaviour in pregnancy has increased substantially throughout the early decades of the twenty-first century, focussing particularly on alcohol. A paper in the American *Journal of Health Politics, Policy and Law*[9] in 2013 documented more than 400 cases in which a woman's pregnancy was defined as a "necessary factor" leading to "attempted and actual deprivations of a woman's physical liberty." By 2021, the principle that women drinking alcohol in pregnancy was a matter of state interest had been generalised to the point

---

[8] Ellie Lee, Jennie Bristow, Charlotte Faircloth and Jan Macvarish (2014). *Parenting Culture Studies*. London: Palgrave Macmillan.

[9] Lynn M. Paltrow and Jeanne Flavin (2013). The Policy and Politics of Reproductive Health Arrests of and Forced Interventions on Pregnant Women in the United States, 1973–2005: Implications for Women's Legal Status and Public Health. *Journal of Health Politics, Policy and Law*, 38(2), 299–343.

that the World Health Organisation, in the middle of a global pandemic, found the time to issue a 37-page Global Alcohol Action Plan (2022–2030) calling for "appropriate attention" to be given to the "prevention of drinking among pregnant women and women of childbearing age." The document claimed that prenatal exposure of a foetus to alcohol as a result of drinking in pregnancy was "one of the most dramatic manifestations of harm to persons other than drinkers." In effect, the WHO defined women's interests as subject to the health of children they might bear, even before these children were conceived.[10]

Control over one's body is an essential part of being an individual with needs and rights. It is one of the most important legacies of our political traditions and, however one feels about the status and value of the foetus, it seems bizarre that this fundamental right should be withdrawn from women during pregnancy. Even if one accepts that the rights of the foetus increase over time, it is a big jump to suggest that the rights of the woman lessen. Even those who think the foetus becomes more of a person as pregnancy advances do not go as far to argue that the woman becomes less of a person. That makes no sense at all.

Aside from a woman's bodily integrity, but connected to her sense of self and personhood, is the matter of decision-making. When it comes to abortion and other decisions about pregnancy, *who* makes the decision is as important as the decision itself.

There is a world of difference between a woman deciding that an abortion is her best option, and someone else making that decision on her behalf. With choice comes responsibility, in a real and not just rhetorical way. A decision that we have made freely for ourselves is a decision that we must own for ourselves. It maybe that the outcome of the decision may not lead to everything we want; it may even be that we make a choice that we come to regret—but the decision was ours.

The choice about the future of a pregnancy properly belongs to the pregnant woman, because she is the person who is affected most by the decision. She will, quite literally, live with this decision for the rest of her life. If she continues her pregnancy, she will, of course, live with

---

[10] WHO Alcohol, Drugs and Addictive Behaviours Unit (2021) *Global Strategy to Reduce the Harmful Use of Alcohol*. WHO: Geneva.

responsibility for that future child; if she opts for abortion, she lives with the knowledge of that decision.

One of the problems with discussing abortion as an abstract philosophical "conundrum" is that it fails to recognise the real physical impact that pregnancy, and its end, has on the woman herself. Once a woman is pregnant, she cannot become "unpregnant" except by the termination of that pregnancy in abortion or the delivery of her baby. Neither procedure is entirely without risk and both have physical, and possibly emotional, impact. Someone must decide, and the most obvious person is the one who will be most affected by the decision. That is, the pregnant women. Of course, she does not make the decision in isolation. Others may claim an interest in the outcome and may want to be involved. Typically, women make their decision with others who are significant to them, on whom the pregnancy impacts—but not always. Sometimes women feel that it is a private, personal matter for them alone: her body, her life, her right to decide.

Once again, the sense of this depends on the perspective from which this issue is considered. Centring on the foetus alone, as if it were an independent entity, it may seem reasonable for others to claim an interest. Genetically, of course, the foetus is as much related to its father as to its mother, and the "paternal" right to a role in abortion decisions has been, and continues to be, tested and contested in different legal jurisdictions around the world.

Paradoxically, the case against paternal intervention has been most successfully dismissed where abortion is seen as a medical matter on which doctors have the final say. In the UK, for example, where two doctors must certify that a woman meets grounds that determine an abortion's legality, interventions by men have been kicked out of court. A landmark legal case in the 1970s[11] established that a husband could not obtain an injunction to prevent his wife from having an abortion or stop a medical practitioner from performing an abortion. The main influence on the court, however, had nothing to do with a woman's right to decide, rather, the ruling rested on the court's refusal to override the

---

[11] Paton v. Trustees of British Pregnancy Advisory Service [1978] 2 All 987 and Paton v. UK [1980] ECHR 408 discussed in S. Sheldon (1997). *Beyond Control: Medical Power and Abortion Law*. London: Pluto Press, pp. 87–90.

decision of the *doctors*. Having failed in the UK, the aggrieved husband took the case as far as the European Court of Human Rights, following a different line of argument: that a father's right to intervene should be allowed under that Court's commitment to "respect for family life." This case also failed. One very significant, obvious objection to paternal intervention is, of course, establishing who the father is. Some abortions are requested because a woman believes herself to be pregnant by "the wrong man"—a lover instead of a husband, or a husband instead of a lover. If a married woman is seeking an abortion because she thinks she is pregnant by her lover, which man has the right to intervene? What steps are to be taken when a woman does not know who the father is? It takes a very unwise judge to rummage in this particular Pandora's box of complications.

Traditionally, a woman's ability *to act* to preserve her bodily integrity, in the case of abortion, has relied on the assistance of others. Ending a pregnancy safely has required the help of a doctor, a nurse, a midwife or some other knowledgeable person experienced in abortion practice, and this has raised difficult issues of contested moral standpoints. It is one thing for a woman to assert that she has the right to end her pregnancy, but does she have the right to insist that a medical practitioner assist her? And what happens when that medical practitioner has an equally strong compulsion that it would be wrong for him to do so?

The medical-legal framework of many countries contains a provision for conscientious objection to involvement in abortion care, which is intended to provide protection for people who hold faiths that forbid their involvement.[12] There is growing unease, however, that in some countries, conscientious objection has become a means to undermine the framework of abortion services. Where a majority of doctors claim conscientious objection, services may be impossible to obtain, regardless of whether they are legal and even state-funded. There is an ongoing debate about where the boundaries of those services covered by conscientious objection lie. Should nurses who provide preparation for, and care after, abortion be able to excuse themselves on grounds of conscience?

---

[12] Mark Wicclair (2011). *Conscientious Objection in Health Care: An Ethical Analysis*. Cambridge: Cambridge University Press.

What about receptionists? Administrators who send correspondence about treatment? Those who organise theatre lists, or staff rotas? Those who clean operating theatres?

Often the impact of conscientious objection is made worse because the law, or medical regulations, restrict abortion treatment to doctors, thus excluding other clinical professionals, such as nurses and midwives who would welcome the opportunity to be involved in abortion care. There is also a deep suspicion that, when medical students and trainees are under pressure, "conscientious objection" becomes less an expression of faith and more an expression of a desire to cut down on their workload or involvement in what they see as an unpleasant task.

There is a strong lobby among those who support legal abortion to make these lines clearer by declaring that medical professionals who conscientiously object to abortion should be excluded from involvement in women's reproductive health care[13] as they are inevitably an impediment to good quality care. Arguments range from the technical administrative problems they cause with work scheduling to those that are concerned with whether a doctor who cannot empathise with a woman's desire to end her pregnancy, or at least respect her right to decide what happens to her body, is unsuited to this area of work.

It is understandable that doctors who believe they have a duty to provide abortion services feel put upon in these circumstances, and that women who request abortions experience stigmatisation and rejection when faced with a doctor who rejects their abortion choice for moral reasons. Health services have attempted to minimise the practical problems of conscientious objection though medical codes of practice and guidelines that insist that patients are quickly referred to other colleagues who will help.[14] But these measures cannot mitigate the stigma that is brought to abortion when a doctor claims that abortion is unacceptable.

---

[13] Christian Fiala and Joyce H. Arthur (2014). "Dishonourable disobedience"—Why Refusal to Treat in Reproductive Healthcare Is Not Conscientious Objection. *Woman– Psychosomatic Gynaecology and Obstetrics*, 1, 12–23.

[14] For example the British Medical Association provides conscientious objection guidance for doctors and medical students and the General Medical Council has clear rules on how doctors must behave when they choose to object.

However, that problem is unlikely to be resolved by forcing gynaecologists or obstetricians to participate in practices they genuinely believe are wrong. Women deserve better care than that provided by people who have been forced to attend to them; those who have a "conscientious commitment" to the service they deliver should provide clinical care.[15]

The reliance of women on professional clinicians is, in any case, being gradually undermined by access to safe, effective, affordable abortion medications available through the Internet. The drugs mifepristone and misoprostol provide an effective, safe method of ending pregnancy—that could, if laws and regulated permitted, place the induction of abortion in the early pregnancy directly into the hands of women.

The drugs, in effect, trigger an early miscarriage by blocking the hormones that sustain the pregnancy and causing the uterus to cramp and shed its lining into which the embryo has implanted. Typically, once a woman has taken the medication, there is no need for further medical intervention. It is simply a matter of allowing the body to act as it does when it rejects a pregnancy naturally.

In most modern Western countries, until recent years, these drugs have been tightly regulated to ensure that abortions by this method are subject to the same controls as those requiring surgery. The COVID pandemic in 2020 encouraged many governments to relax controls to allow abortifacient drugs to be provided by post as a part of telemedical services which minimise the doctor's involvement. The simplification of early abortions is unlikely to be reversible and it is likely that the future will see a decline in the number of medical professionals required. If this is the case, we may find that conscientious objection because less of a problem.

A woman's right to an abortion that is due to her as part of her control of her own body does not extend to the right to force another to act against their morals to provide that care. We surely don't want medical professionals who see their work as simply "following orders." This does not fit with the values of medical practice in modern societies. Clinicians are expected to hold values and make value judgements, including those

---

15 See Bernard M. Dickens (2014). The right to conscience. In Rebecca J. Cook, Joanna N. Erdman and Bernard M. Dickens (Eds.), *Abortion Law in Transnational Perspective: Cases and Controversies*. Philadelphia: University of Pennsylvania Press.

that will, *in good faith*, act in the interests of their patients demonstrating beneficence and an absence of maleficence. If a doctor genuinely believes that abortion is wrong or believes it would cause harm, surely we must, in the same spirit of tolerance that we demand be shown to women, respect that doctor's judgement about his or her own actions?

It is to this matter of conflicting values that we will now turn.

7

Claims of Conscience

When decision-making about the future of pregnancy is put in a doctor's hands, it may place it out of a woman's reach. The balance of power between a doctor and his or her patient is seldom, if ever, equal.

Usually, we have trust and confidence in our medical professionals because we assume both have the same goal. We want to get well; they want to make us better. As patients we rely on the clinical expertise of professionals because they know more about the "condition" we present with, and how best to treat it. Typically, our reliance on the professional increases along with the complexity and seriousness of our condition—and this is reflected in how we access medical care. Complicated diagnoses and complex treatments may require the insight and expertise of specialist consultants; common complaints requiring simple, low-risk medication tend to be self-managed. Typically, we see doctors when we don't know quite what to do, or when what needs to be done requires a specialist's skill and knowledge.

Abortion is a striking exception to this. Usually, the woman is clear what the problem is (being pregnant) and how to resolve it (becoming un-pregnant). With the exception of later abortions, or complex situations when surgery is necessary, the doctor's direct role is often to be

© The Author(s), under exclusive license to Springer Nature
Switzerland AG 2021
A. Furedi, *The Moral Case for Abortion*,
https://doi.org/10.1007/978-3-030-90189-9_7

the gatekeeper of services by means of a consultation to confirm what the woman has said, rather than practice medicine directly. The abortion consultation in most countries is what medical sociologists describe as a "performative" act or encounter. In this case the doctor gives permission to proceed to terminate the pregnancy.

But to "give permission" in this way implies that one approves of, or at least condones, the treatment. And so, in an abortion consultation, the judgement by the doctor about what is best for a patient is one that is based on values more than on fact. Only rarely is there any need to end a pregnancy for a reason that is strictly necessary to preserve the woman's physical health in the way an appendectomy is required to remove an inflamed appendix.

Regardless of how much abortion is accepted and integrated into healthcare systems and despite attempts to "normalise" it as a clinical procedure, it is impossible to release abortion from the ties of moral judgement. When, at a meeting in 2017, the first woman president of the UK Royal College of Obstetricians and Gynaecologists, Professor Lesley Regan, claimed that the requirement for two doctors to certify the grounds for abortion was ludicrous and that the procedure should be seen "no differently to other medical procedures—including something as simple as removing a bunion," this made sense from a clinical point of view. A bunionectomy is considerably more complex than earlier abortion and is riskier since it involves general anesthesia. However, the comment provoked considerable controversy and moral challenge. Writing for conservativewomen.com, a leading anti-choice spokesman claimed it as an example of how contemporary doctors have abandoned their commitment to not just the Hippocratic oath but the Declaration of Geneva (1948) adopted by the World Medical Association in response to the Nazi war atrocities.

Peter Saunders, at that time the leader of the Christian Medical Fellowship pointed out that the oath originally read: "I will maintain the utmost respect for human life from the time of conception, even against threat I will not use my medical knowledge contrary to the laws of humanity," and went on to point out that the British Medical Association affirmed in 1947: "although there have been many changes in medicine, the spirit of the Hippocratic Oath cannot change," and added that "cooperation in the destruction of life by murder, suicide and abortion" was "the greatest crime."[1] Observing how the zeitgeist has changed the role of the medical profession, Saunders claimed: "From being the greatest protectors of innocent human life just 70 years ago, it seems that doctors have now become abortion's greatest proponents and facilitators."

No one disputes the morality of removing an appendix or tonsils but the deliberate removal of an embryo is an act that some people find morally abhorrent. The rightness or wrongness of ending human life—albeit human life in an early and unconscious state—is ever present. Even if, personally, we do not feel compelled to protect the life of an embryo, we know that others do, and many doctors feel that abortion decisions a balance between two competing interests. Many say that what tips them to approve the woman's request is "her story," that is her reasons, because this transforms abortion from something abstract (one life with a beating heart versus another), to an event that impacts on a live being lived. After all, no woman has an abortion without a reason.

But, then again, not *all* doctors can accept the reasons or explanations that women give. Britain is an increasingly secular society but in 2021 the Christian Medical Fellowship claimed more than 6000 clinical members who "accept the Bible as the supreme authority in matters of faith and conduct."[2] Among these, and indeed among other faith groups and those who are humanists or identify with no faith, are doctors who genuinely have a heartfelt belief that abortion is utterly wrong and the equivalent of murder or a death penalty—perhaps worse. Pro-life Humanists claim on their website that embryos must be protected as *the* most marginalised humans.

Since our morals and values are deeply felt as part of our essential identity, we cannot put them on and take them off when we enter and leave our work and they cannot be countered by the presentation of any kind of rational evidence. Whether or not an abortion is safe or unsafe, whether it is associated with long-term depression or trauma, whether it

[1] https://www.conservativewoman.co.uk/dr-peter-saunders-abortion-must-serious-matter-taking-tonsils-bunions accessed 6 April 2021.

[2] https://www.cmf.org.uk/about accessed 6 April 2021.

causes cancer ... these things are matters that can be resolved by medical science and demonstrated by studies. Whether it is right or wrong is a matter of "values" and "beliefs" that many people believe sit outside the scope of medical evidence.

Modern democratic society is built on the tolerance of pluralist values. If we feel strongly that a woman should have the right to decide about her pregnancy, whatever her reasons, and that this is an expression of her autonomy, her right to which is self-evident, surely we must accept that for some people the opposite view may be held just as deeply. A woman's right to end her own pregnancy rests on her bodily integrity and self-determination. Surely a doctor too can make this claim about his or her own actions? Even when healthcare legislation, regulations and guidelines present abortion as a legitimate, legal and safe clinical option, there will be some individual doctors who find termination of pregnancy morally unacceptable and *contra* their own individual values. Some feel morally compelled to be involved in abortion (even when it is outside the law),[3] while some feel obliged to resist it.

This poses a challenge. If a woman has a right to abortion but a doctor has a right to not perform it, whose right triumphs? Should we insist that the only people who can work in reproductive healthcare are those who reject faiths that prohibit abortion? Should we insist that good doctors who cannot approve of abortion wear their values like a casual dress that they leave at home when they come to work? In deciding what is best for a patient, do we expect them to refer only to what is efficacious and cost-effective in their treatment?

Or, perhaps, since medical professionals hold in their hands the power to kill and the responsibility to cure, we may prefer to be treated by clinicians who felt the pull of a strong moral compass?

---

[3] See the excellent account of US sociologist Carole Joffe (1995). *Doctors of Conscience: The Struggle to Provide Abortion Before and After Roe v Wade*. Boston, MA: Beacon Press.

Church and State

In the UK, the relationship between church and state made the issue of conscience particularly pertinent when abortion was legalised. There was, and is today, no formal separation of church and state: rather church and state are bound together in a way that seems paradoxical in a country that has a largely secular population.

As Head of State, the Queen is Head of the Church of England and an allocation of Anglican bishops sit in the House of Lords which provides the established church with a voice in parliament, and a role in law-making. This meant from earliest parliamentary discussion of abortion legislation the concerns of those with deep religious conviction who might oppose abortion[4] were considered in public policy.

The inclusion of a "conscience clause" in the Abortion Act was a recognition of the tension involved in taking abortion into a public healthcare system. Section 4(i) set out a provision that, except in life-threatening emergencies:

> no person shall be under any duty, whether by contract or statutory or other legal requirement to participate in ant treatment authorized by this Act to which he has a conscientious objection:
> Provided that in any legal proceedings the burden of proof of conscientious objection shall rest on the person claiming it.[5]

This approach has subsequently been adopted in many other countries to balance the right to abortion as healthcare with the claims of conscience. Usually, such clauses are supported by professional bodies representing doctors, nurses and midwives and, in their own in their own professional guidelines, they require objecting providers to be forthright about their objection and to provide timely referral to a provider who does not object.

At the level of policy, conscientious objection seems to be a reasonable accommodation as a means to avoid collisions of values. But,

---

[4] Although not all the bishops were opposed to legal abortion, and historically representatives of the Church of England have tended towards support for the Abortion Act.
[5] Abortion Act 1967 S4 (1).

like most compromise solutions, it is constantly challenged and has become increasingly controversial as abortion has become more and more accepted. Many pro-choice advocates make valid claims that the existence of such a clause "exceptionalises" abortion, making it different from other medical procedures. This creates stigma and legitimises, even privileges, the notion that abortion is wrong. The duty of an objecting doctor to "refer on" is a problem for some objectors who see it as enabling abortion, claiming it to be akin to the role of prison-camp guards who, while not actually killing Jews in concentration camps, allowed it to happen.

What conscientious objection means in practice is subject to different interpretations. While in the UK it applies only to individuals, in the USA entire institutions use claims of conscience to opt out of legal abortion provision, despite the insistence by some theologians that only individuals, and not institutions (such as hospitals), can claim a conscience. This is a distinction with practical significance where the public rely on hospitals run by the Catholic Church and where the proscriptive attitudes of the administration are not shared by hospital doctors who, if allowed to exercise their own personal conscience, may be willing to provide abortion care.

Clearly, conscientious objection provision can obstruct care where a significant number of doctors choose to exercise an objection and where institutions fail to provide arrangements to "provide cover." Provision for conscientious objection can be abused and manipulated by doctors who wish to excuse themselves from abortion from all manner of reasons that seem barely related to conscience. In the UK, it is widely acknowledged that trainee doctors use the clause to opt out of abortion simply to give themselves a few more hours to study other topics in a crammed schedule. This, and those who use the clause to opt out because they find the procedure "distasteful" or who, wrongly, believe it is unnecessary in a country where contraception is freely available and free of cost, is a source of much resentment by doctors who struggle to cope with an unfairly distributed workload.

Acknowledging both the reasons for and objections to conscientious objection, academic lawyer Kate Greasley suggests that limits on the rights to conscientious objection must be necessary within the context of permissive abortion regulations. She summarises some key factors that we need to consider:

> One is the imperative that conscientious refusals do not undermine the purpose of abortion regulation and the values and ideals furthered by it. Another is the degree to which the contested activity implicates the objector in giving abortion treatment. A third and final pair of considerations are the cost to individual objectors of shouldering the burden of the objections themselves, and, symmetrically, the cost to others of shouldering the burdens of (presumed) morally erroneous conscientious objections.[6]

In short, it is complicated. Our lives, our work and our beliefs impact on others as well as ourselves. When many doctors "opt out" doctors who provide abortions may also find themselves ostracised for doing what is seen as "the dirty work." A woman facing a doctor who feels her decision is wrong may feel additionally burdened by his or her judgement.

Italy is often used as an example that the conscience clause undermines necessary care. Although the Italian law, despite the institutionalised role of Catholicism, is relatively liberal in early pregnancy,[7] at the time of writing it is estimated that between 82 and 91% of gynaecologists invoke the conscience clause in Article 9 to opt out. As a consequence, 40% of hospitals are unable to provide abortion services.

But the difficulty in providing abortion in Italy is not *necessarily* a result of the existence of the legal clause per se.

How a legal conscience clause impacts on care depends on the broader social context and not on the existence of clause itself. The USA is a manifest example of this. Despite a formal separation of church and state, Catholic hospitals are responsible of so much of the nation's healthcare—particularly that of the poor and disadvantaged. So when a Catholic

---

[6] Kate Greasley (2017). *Arguments About Abortion: Personhood, Motherhood and Law*. Oxford: Oxford University Press, p. 251.

[7] Law No. 194 of 22 May 1978 on the social protection of motherhood and the voluntary termination of pregnancy legalises abortion during the first ninety days of pregnancy for economic, family, health or personal reasons, and allows abortion before twenty-four weeks' gestation when the pregnancy entails a serious threat to the woman's life or when foetal abnormalities constitute a serious threat to the woman's physical or mental health.

hospital refuses to provide abortion (or contraception) it denies access to a community. At first sight it seems obvious that this is a problem caused by the Catholic hospital's "refusal to provide"—but it actually begs this question: is the root of the problem the "opt out" or the absence of an alternative?

Do we really believe that women seeking abortion would wish to be treated in an institution which has, as a core value, a believe that they are sinful in seeking care? It seems paradoxical that a nation with an institutional separation of church and state, which forbids the display of religious symbols in public offices, fails to undermine the religious dominance of a key public function—healthcare by ensuring adequate reproduction healthcare services that sit outside the Catholic faith.

The crucial issue seems to be not the existence of a conscience clause in law, but rather, how many healthcare professionals are prepared to provide abortion care. A clause allowing conscientious exceptions in a social context where only a few want to be excepted has a different impact to one where hostility to abortion dominates public and professional thinking. This creates a catch-22 situation that clouds discussions of the impact of conscientious objection clauses. In countries with a strong liberal and secular tradition, like Sweden, no religious exception clauses exist (why would they?) and typically abortion is well provided and uncontested. In countries with a strong religious and conservative tradition, like Italy, conscientious objection is frequently invoked, and abortion services are often poorly provided and stigmatised. But this does not mean the legal clause is *the problem* or even *the cause of the problem.* The truth of the matter is that, should a conscientious objection provision be introduced into Sweden or Canada, it is likely that it would have negligible impact because hardly anyone would use it, while in countries where many clinicians are morally opposed to abortion, a conscientious objection clause may facilitate a framework where abortion may be provided by those who do feel able.

The experience of European countries such as England and Norway illustrate that it is possible legally to accommodate individuals who object to providing abortion, while still ensuring that women have access to legal healthcare services.[8] In Norway, hardly anyone objects. In Britain, health systems have employed work-arounds. When the Abortion Act was first implemented and many doctors in public hospitals refused to set up services, specialist independent abortion clinics were established, many of which continue to operate offering services on a not-for-profit basis.

Whose Responsibility?

Perhaps many advocates for reproductive choice find it hard to tolerate conscientious objection because they are secular and have little empathy with religious faith. People who would never contemplate compelling a vegan to eat meat at a dinner party feel quite able to argue that doctors who object to abortion have no place in women's healthcare.

However, there are two reasons why toleration of conscience is important. First, to be effective, laws and models for service development need to reflect the views and values of those who live with them. That is an instrumental reason.

However, more important than that is this: in a world where we uphold the moral autonomy of women seeking abortion, we cannot *but* accept that a doctor's objection from a place of conscience is far more than a mere preference. For a true conscientious objector, their objection is a matter of core conviction, which cannot be shed at will.

Some would like to see doctors provide "evidence" of their conscience—although it is difficult to imagine how this could possibly be done. Evidence of church membership is not evidence of belief and besides conscience is not limited to, or even linked to faith. Faith cannot be evidenced; no one can prove that their objection is due to conscience, not just convenience.

---

[8] W. Chavkin, L. Swerdlow, and J. Fifield (2017). Regulation of Conscientious Objection to Abortion: An International Comparative Multiple-Case Study. *Health and Human Rights Journal*, vol. 19, no. 1, pp. 55–68. W. Chavkin, L. Leitman, and K. Polin, (2013) 'Conscientious Objection and Refusal to Provide Reproductive Healthcare: A White Paper Examining Prevalence, Health Consequences, and Policy Responses,' *International Journal of Gynecology and Obstetrics*, 123(3), S41–S56.

Two pro-choice advocates who are vigorous critics of conscientious objection, Austrian doctor Christian Fiala and Canadian activist Joyce Arthur, observe that the absence of evidence for conscience de facto places it outside the realm of legitimate consideration:

> Since it is impossible to determine whether an objector's motivations are genuine, or even to question them, there is no rational evidence-based argument for allowing CO. Laws and policies trying to control and limit CO cannot be effectively applied because consciences are private, subjective things that differ for each individual. It is simply not possible to have any criteria for CO, let alone enforce them. Anyone can cite CO and lie or exaggerate. Or be sincere. Who knows?
>
> … Whether that belief is sincere or pretended, extreme or moderate, is irrelevant because CO is harmful in any case.[9]

In reality however, there is growing evidence that tolerance of those who wish to opt out of abortion provision may help facilitate the provision of services by those who do. Paradoxically, the Republic of Ireland, a country where traditional Catholic values have been situated at the core of national identity, has shown how conscientious objection provision within the law may coexist with, and even facilitate, the development of abortion services.

Ireland's constitution prohibited abortion by according to foetal life equal standing with the life of "the mother" until it was repealed in 2018 by a public referendum. The national vote followed a debate that for several months dominated national political and social discussion in a way that thoroughly engaged the nation. Extensive campaigning by both pro- and anti- choice campaigners was shadowed by discussions about what a good abortion law might look like in a specifically Irish context. A "Citizens' Assembly" of one hundred members was appointed by the government from a random selection of the country's voters to take evidence from international experts on all aspects of the discussion. The assembly made recommendations to the Irish parliament on what a law should be, which then formed the basis of legislation.

---

[9] Christian Fiala and Joyce Arthur (2017). There Is No Defence for "Conscientious Objection" in Reproductive Health Care. *European Journal of Obstetrics and Gynecology*, 216, 254–258.

One contested area was the inclusion of a conscience clause, which was strongly supported by medical bodies but divided pro-choice advocates; some argued that support for conscience was crucial if a liberal law to allow abortion for unwanted early pregnancy were to succeed; others countered that the number of objectors would make an Irish abortion service unimplementable.

The conscience clause was passed and, within months of it becoming law in 2019 a national network of doctors had declared not only that they would provide abortion, but that they would allow their practice details to be publicised as part of a care pathway. In effect, these doctors were announcing their commitment to the service, placing themselves at risk of harassment. After six months of legality, more doctors were registered to provide abortion in Catholic Ireland, where family doctors can prescribe early abortion medication, than in the UK, fifty years after legality where abortion provision is constrained to doctors working from licensed properties.

The situation in Ireland is far from perfect, but it stands as evidence to refute claims that the existence of conscientious objection clauses *necessarily* undermines services. The public and professional engagement in the debates before the referendum resulted in far greater awareness of both why women need abortion and an understanding that Irish society could no longer accept women openly travelling to England to access legal services, or illegally using medication bought online. This greater awareness and understanding seemed to create circumstances where doctors felt conscientiously *committed* to provide abortion services in the spirit discussed by sociologist Carole Joffe's compelling account of the role in doctors' struggles to provide abortions in the USA, risking imprisonment and harassment to do what they believe to be right.[10]

This is unlikely to persuade those who feel that conscience has no place in medicine and who insist that "even if the harm seems minimal refusals are still inherently wrong and harmful … [as] …The provider is deliberately refusing to do part of their job for personal reasons."[11] And Fiala

---

[10] Carole Joffe (1995). *Doctors of Conscience: The Struggle to Provide Abortion Before and After Roe v Wade*. Boston: Beacon Press.

[11] C. Fiala and J. Arthur (2017). There is No Defence for "Conscientious Objection" in Reproductive Health Care. *European Journal of Obstetrics and Gynaecology*, 216, 254–258.

and Arthur are correct to claim that a woman refused care by a conscientiously objecting doctor receives a negative message that stigmatises her and the healthcare she needs. However, if society is truly trying to find accommodation that respects the inherent conflict between women who wish to exercise the moral autonomy to choose abortion as a moral solution, and doctors who wish to abide by their moral conviction that abortion is wrong, then we need mutual tolerance at an *individual* level. This requires that doctors accept their responsibility to assist women to access services from those who are willing provide abortion. We also need *institutional* commitment to provide comprehensive legal services. It is the responsibility for those who commission and manage services to accept responsibility for access to legal abortion, just as it is for any other clinical service.

It hardly matters to a woman *why* a doctor fails to provide a service she needs. Regardless of whether abortion is denied by conscience or by competence the result for her is the same; unless someone else steps in, her pregnancy continues. It is the responsibility of care systems to meet the individual needs of patients and to employ clinicians to do that. Rather than compel doctors to provide abortions unwillingly, or leave their chosen speciality, might it not be better to encourage, enable and mobilise people who *are* willing to provide care?

Where the law allows medication abortion, pregnancies can be ended just as proficiently by midwives, nurses, general practitioners and healthcare assistants. Even in medical systems that have no shortage of doctors to deliver care, abortion services are increasingly "owned" by non-physicians since it is well within their professional competence. Surely it makes more sense to mobilise those who are motivated to provide abortion care than to force doctors who believe it to be wrong to carry out procedures or renounce their profession?

If we understand the right to abortion to be rooted in our understanding of what is "good," and a significant part of that is individual moral autonomy, it seems consistent to apply that principle, as far as possible, to doctors. A society where conscienceless doctors comply with laws and guidelines to do what they think is wrong is simply dystopian.

It seems far better to struggle to win hearts and minds, strengthen conscientious commitment to reproductive choice and widen the pool of providers that to ban conscience clauses and make unwilling doctors provide.

Personal Boundaries and Political Lines

Discussions about conscience and its role in healthcare has become politicised by both sides of the abortion debate, turning it into a regrettable and unnecessary battleground over principles on which minds cannot meet. A pluralist society can only function where there is tolerance and a spirit of reasonable accommodation. Those values require compromise, not in respect of one's own beliefs but as to how others operate on their equally strongly held views. So it is regrettable that conscience clauses are "weaponised."

Abortion's opponents have, on occasion, treated conscience clauses as instruments to drive a disruptive wedge into the provision of services. In the UK the boundaries of what constitutes the abortion procedure to which an objector may excuse him or herself have been tested by court challenges.[12] Is the managing of correspondence relating to abortion, for example the typing of a letter referring or discharging a patient an activity to which someone may conscientiously object? What about the preparation of a work schedule for nurses on an abortion ward? In both of these cases the court said, "No." Medical guidelines advise consciously objecting doctors to refer patients requesting abortions to a colleague who will assist, but is this complicity in the act itself?[13]

Testing these issues in the courts has been a way to achieve publicity and to suggest discrimination against people who hold "pro-life" values. It's notable that a major international anti-choice organisations funded

---

[12] See the cases of *Janaway v Salford Area Health Authority* [1989] AC 537 and *Doogan and Wood v Greater Glasgow Health Board* [2013] CSIH 36 as discussed in Kate Greasley (2017). *Arguments About Abortion: Personhood, Morality, and Law.* Oxford: Oxford University Press, pp. 247–251.

[13] J. W. Gerrard (2009). Is It Ethical for a General Practitioner to Claim a Conscientious Objection When Asked to Refer for Abortion? *Journal of Medical Ethics*, 35(10), 599–602.

the widely publicised case in Sweden, in which a midwife appealed to the European Court of Human Rights after a national court ruling in 2017 found against her claim that she was discriminated against when she was denied employment because of her refusal to provide abortion care. It is hard to see these cases as anything other than instrumental grandstanding that casts anti-abortion stalwarts as victims of a conscienceless society. It is the same political strategy that has been used by individuals who claim denial of freedom of speech or assembly, when prevented from disrupting women's access to abortion clinics by what they claim to be "pavement counselling" but the clinics see it as attempts to intimidate.

Court rulings tell us what is legal now, and by establishing precedent, set legal boundaries for the future; the "conscience cases" that come before them are attempts to claim an absolute right, but are something that in practice needs to be negotiated. In the world of day-to-day hospital management, as in any other area of normal life, clashes of values and different "ways of seeing things" are usually negotiated and subject to accommodation. Medical practice is riddled with areas where doctors disagree—sometimes on principle and sometimes because of different interpretations of the evidence.

For example, whether hormone replacement therapy is an appropriate treatment for menopause is an area that remains contested and is unlikely to be resolved by the clinical guidelines, because different views on treatment rely so heavily on different interpretations of what the menopause represents. Usually in a healthcare setting, a clinic manager will try to balance out the prejudices of her workforce in whatever way works best to balance patients' needs for HRT with doctors' idiosyncratic beliefs. It seems a better solution than insisting that doctors obey rules they don't believe in.

Conscience matters to women, who are just as concerned with the rightness and wrongness of their actions, as they make decisions about pregnancy that affect lives other than their own. The complications of moral reasoning present themselves in very tangible but complex real-life forms that they can never step out of. A pregnant woman requesting abortion knows this perhaps better than anyone, since she lives with the knowledge that, having weighed up everything, decided it was best to end this pregnancy, or to have this child.

We think of conscience as a way of feeling that draws on more than reason and argument. It is often associated with Christian faith with its origins in God's law and, indeed, the catechism of the Catholic Church expresses with special elegance what it sees as the origins of conscience and its application in life as imposed upon us from without.

> Deep within his conscience man discovers a law which he has not laid upon himself but which he must obey. Its voice, ever calling him to love and to do what is good and to avoid evil, sounds in his heart at the right moment. ... For man has in his heart a law inscribed by God. ... His conscience is man's most secret core and his sanctuary. There he is alone with God whose voice echoes in his depths. (CCC 1776)

Conscience as a religious phenomenon is associated with Catholicism, but it is beyond being "a catholic thing." The seventeenth-century theologian William Perkins, who famously described conscience as "a little God sitting in the middle of men's hearts"[14] was one of the founders of the Puritan movement. For some committed Christians the notion that conscience calls to a law which is "not laid upon himself" may be true that decisions are more simple since it leaves no "choice" for the individual but to obey.

The religious association of "conscience clauses" is an obvious and easy target for secularists who object to the accommodation of doctors who practice religion[15] and who prefer to understand it simply as "dishonourable disobedience" or "conscientious obstruction" as in this strident denunciation:

> Those who want to preserve "conscientious objection" (CO) as a right in reproductive healthcare seem to treat it like a sacred cow, a religious belief that cannot be questioned. But mixing religion with evidence-based

---

[14] William Perkins, *A Discourse on Conscience*, cited in Mika Ojankangas (2013). *The Voice of Conscience: A Political Genealogy of Western Ethical Experience*. London: Bloomsbury.

[15] C. Fiala, K. G. Danielsson, O. Keikinheimo, et al. (2016). Yes We Can! Successful Examples of Disallowing "Conscientious Objection" in Reproductive Health Care. *European Journal of Contraception and Reproductive Healthcare*, 21(3), 201. C. Fiala and J. H. Arthur (2014). "Dishonourable Disobedience"—Why Refusal to Treat in Reproductive Health Care Is Not Conscientious Objection. *Woman—Psychosom Gynaecol Obstetr*, 1, 12–23.

medicine does not work and has negative consequences. ... Societies should still work to implement recommendations to mitigate CO and its harms, and robustly enforce existing CO regulations. Such measures are essential and will hopefully have positive effects over time. But the primary, transparent objective of these efforts should be to steadily reduce the number of objectors and eventually *abolish CO, not save it*. That should include the repeal of discriminatory policies and laws[4] that mistakenly treat CO as a "right" of health care professionals. Instead, CO should be recognized as fundamentally unethical. It is "dishonourable disobedience" and has no place in reproductive health care.[16]

Paradoxically, this denial of choice and absence of personal judgement in decision-making is a flip side of that imposed by opponents of conscientious objection, who replace the law of God by a secular law of clinical risk management or formulation of harm reduction. A world without personal moral judgement can be a world according to God, or a world according to clinical guidelines. Both seem detached from the lived lives in which contextual, contingent choices are made.

Where Does Conscience Come From?

In many ways it seems difficult to see conscience as related to obedience (or disobedience) or detached from reasoned thinking. One way of understanding conscience is as an internal discussion. The philosopher Hannah Arendt describes conflicts of conscience as "deliberations between me and myself."[17]

To banish conscience from our lives is to remove a kernel of our humanity. The notion of the importance and power of individual internal dialogue is one of the singular aspects of Western thought that differentiates it from other traditions and has remained constant despite historical changes and ideological disputes. A fundamental tenet of Western thinking is that truth and justice come "from within" and

---

[16] C. Fiala and J. Arthur (2017). There Is No Defence for "Conscientious Objection" in Reproductive Health Care. *European Journal of Obstetrics and Gynaecology*, 216, 254–258.

[17] Hannah Arendt (2003). *Responsibility and Judgement*. New York: Random House, p. 108.

that it is insufficient, and somehow wrong, to always rely on traditions, public norms and opinions. There is a rebelliousness and individualistic element in Western ethical and political traditions, even when they are conservative at heart, and the founding of laws to govern society has carefully regarded the importance of the individual.

Finnish professor of political thought, Mika Ojakangas, explains that a key principle of the construction of Western political and legal principles has been that it, "has not only tirelessly strived for the *displacement* of external laws by the disorientating experience of conscience but also wanted to *found* these laws and regulations on this very experience."[18] He argues that through conscience we hold ourselves to account for our values and actions and that society is built upon the assumption that each of us does this: "without the voice of conscience, the Western tradition has assumed, there is no sin, no guilt, no virtue, no obligation, no duty, no force of law, no freedom, no responsibility, no humanity, not even consciousness." This is because it is through conscience that we hold ourselves to account for our values and actions.

Dismissing conscience as a superstitious and irrational hangover from a religious past betrays a profound ignorance and shallow understanding of what it is. To understand the voice of a "God within" may be the way that people of faith understand it in the context of their system of beliefs. But paradoxically, it is when conscience loses its connection with God that its importance can really be understood.

Writers concerned with the secular Enlightenment traditions of individual freedom, such as Kant, Hegel and Sartre, demonstrate through their writings how the authority and strength of the voice of conscience increases when it no longer requires supernatural external assistance.

The loneliness of a decision based on conscience is what faces women when they make decisions about pregnancy. Women, when asked *why?* do not respond with a template of clinical evidence weighing up the relative risks of abortion, but with moral reasoning.

For those of us who do not have a relationship with any God, individual conscience puts us in a lonely place where we are forced to set our

---

[18] Mika Ojankangas (2013). *The Voice of Conscience: A Political Genealogy of Western Ethical Experience.* London: Bloomsbury, pp. 2–3.

own moral compass, thinking things through for ourselves by weighing up what is right or wrong.

Why Conscience Matters

In 1820, in the *Philosophy of Right*, Hegel considered that: "Conscience is the deepest internal solitude from which both limit and the external have disappeared."[19] The inner voice of conscience that we hear is not the voice of God, but the voice of our own self, and in what Arendt describes as the conversation between "I" and "me" are the different and conflicting views we hold. In practice, this means: "I can think abortion is wrong in the abstract because … but yet it is right for me because …".

The notion of conscience as a phenomenon that is at the core of our self is central to why it is crucial to defend the claims of those who morally object to abortion to opt out of services. Common sense tells us that any abortion service will be woefully inadequate if it is provided by people who resent being forced to do what they think is wrong. It is far better to allow people to act on their conscience and, in leaving the room, make space for those who regard the work as a privilege.

More fundamental however, is the possibility of what happens when conscience is denied. When discussions of what is right and wrong are stripped out of clinical care and are reduced to a simple rational weighing of evidence, our humanity is stripped away.

Doctors who are required to be "obedient" to moral codes, to be functionaries of prevailing mores, are surely not what we want. A clinician who considers his or her conscience, who engages in a dialogue about what is right or wrong in a specific situation, who draws back from the obvious options and decides specifically what is the right thing for "this" and for "now" is surely preferable to one who robotically follows an algorithm in a clinic guideline. We want doctors, nurses, midwives, counsellors and administrators who think and feel and empathise and

---

[19] G. W. F. Hegel (2001). *Philosophy of Right*, trans. S. W. Dyde. Kitchener: Batoche Books, p. 115.

act on this—even if it means they sometimes withdraw from services and present challenges for those who disagree.

Today modern societies accept, indeed expect, medical services to be provided within an evidence-based framework by providers where little is left to subjective judgement. Contemporary clinical practice is based on guidelines which in turn are based on evidence reviews. Frameworks for good practice aim to ensure that there is consistency and that doctors can draw on opinion that has been informed by objective reviews of all the available research. Evidence-based medicine (EBM) is now regarded as the standard to which medical systems should strive. From the international experts at the World Health Organisation to family doctors the rule is: when in doubt, look to the evidence.

A key reason why some pro-choice advocates claim that conscientious objection is simply an abandonment of the professional obligation to patients, a violation of medical ethics, and the denial of the right to lawful healthcare[20] is because it steps away from this medical model. When someone conscientiously objects to abortion they deliberately step back from evidence and reject the principle of non-judgementalism.[21] Furthermore, in doing so they insist—explicitly or implicitly—that abortion is different to other forms of healthcare. Abortion is once again exceptionalised and stigmatised, regardless of whether this is what the objector intends.

Pro-choice advocates have long argued that abortion should be seen as a normal medical procedure—and so it should be. It is "normal" in that it is necessary and sought by about one-third of all women for the reasons explored in Chapter 1, and as such legal and healthcare systems should make it safely available. But that claim for abortion does not imply that we should deny its particular differences.

---

[20] C. Fiala, K. G. Danielsson, O. Keikinheimo, et al. (2016). Yes We Can! Successful Examples of Disallowing "Conscientious Objection" in Reproductive Health Care. *European Journal of Contraception and Reproductive Health Care*, 21(3), 201. C. Fiala and J. H. Arthur (2014). "Dishonourable Disobedience"—Why Refusal to Treat in Reproductive Health Care Is Not Conscientious Objection. *Woman—Psychosom Gynaecol Obstetr* [Internet] [cited 2015 October 13], 1, 12–23.

[21] We will return to non-judgementalism later, since judgement and any kind of moral reckoning are wedded and simply cannot be divorced.

Abortion is healthcare, but it is not just healthcare. It has a voluntaristic element; a woman seeks abortion because she wants to end her pregnancy for any number of reasons that may or may not be connected to her health. The evidence that abortion is statistically safer than childbirth, which is cited in many evidence-based guidelines on abortion,[22] is helpful to doctors who wish to help women in circumstances where legal abortion is conditional on a health benefit, and to help women understand how small the risks are. But it is not evidence that we would expect to see applied to the "treatment" of pregnancy in the way that we might expect evidence to be applied to the treatment of uterine cancer, because pregnancy is not a disease like cancer.

Based on an assessment of risks and evidence no sane pregnant woman would choose childbirth. She chooses childbirth not because she wants to minimise or maximise the health benefit to her own life, but because she wants a child. Subject to that primary and fundamental decision, she will consider what the safest way is to achieve that objective. This is one reason why the exaggerated claims about the relationship between abortion and breast cancer fall on deaf ears. The abortion decision is not made according to the medical evidence in relation to a percentage increase in the risk of a possible disease, it hangs on an altogether different set of thoughts based on non-clinical matters—mainly in relation to motherhood. If the principle of evidence-based medicine was mindlessly applied to the management of pregnancy—every pregnant woman would be advised that the risks she faces could be most comprehensively reduced by an early abortion. But it is not—nor would we want it to be. We expect clinicians to step back from evidence. We expect them to make a value-judgement: to value a woman's judgement about the future of her pregnancy requires judgement on the part of clinical staff.

The notion that the medical profession should limit the "judgement" part of the clinical judgement is much more complex than it seems. When those of us who support abortion services say that women seeking abortion should receive a non-judgemental service, we do not mean that that nurses, doctors, counsellors, administrators and everyone else in the service put aside their personal notions of what is right and wrong.

---

[22] See, for example, the RCOG evidence-based guideline on induced abortion.

We do not want healthcare staff to exist in an a-human state of non-thinkingness. We understand and expect that abortion carers will have their own views about whether a woman's decision is right or wrong, but we expect them to hold their opinion, keeping it to themselves, and acknowledging that it is impressionistic and partial. Only the woman is fully able to know what her decision will mean for herself and those in her world. And, of course, she will literally live with her decision while for everyone else, their responsibility ends with the workday.

When Hannah Arendt watched the trial in Jerusalem in 1961 of the Nazi Albert Eichmann, the coordinator of Hitler's attempt to exterminate the Jewish people, she noted that his lawyer twice remarked that what happened in Auschwitz and other extermination camps had been a "medical matter" and she commented:

> It was as though morality at the very moment of its total collapse within an old and highly civilized nation, stood revealed in the original meaning of the word as a set of *mores*, which could be exchanged for another set with no more trouble than it would take to change the table manners of a whole people.[23]

What was needed, she insisted, was for people at this time to make moral judgements for themselves, and to draw on their own sense of right and wrong. For Arendt, this was not a retreat into any reliance on religious belief—or a hiding behind general principles. She explained: "The precondition for this kind of judging is not a highly developed intelligence or sophistication in moral matters, but rather the disposition to live with oneself, to have intercourse with oneself, that is, to be engaged in that silent dialogue between me and myself which, since Socrates and Plato, we usually call thinking." Later she called this: "The status of being human."[24]

Arendt's point is that humanity relies on us determine for ourselves as individuals *as a matter of conscience* what is right and wrong and how much wrongness we will be complicit with or tolerate. An institution can

---

[23] Hannah Arendt (2003). *Responsibility and Judgement*. New York: Random House, p. 43.
[24] Ibid., p. 45.

have values and principles, but it has no conscience. The responsibility for that sits singularly with every one of us.

And this is why—despite the inconvenience to health systems and institutions, and possibly even the problems it may cause women seeking care, there is something appalling in trying to cut conscience out of healthcare and requiring "obedience" from clinicians. It is far better to have a situation that understands and negotiates accommodation in a spirit of tolerance, than that conscience be condemned.

8

New Challenges to Choice

My central claim throughout this book has been that a woman's *choice* about the future of her pregnancy is personal and private and should be disentangled from the arguments for birth control based on claims about what is best for society.

Ruling elites have, throughout history, had strong opinions about which people should and should not have children, and in which circumstances.

Arguments based on demography, whether to increase or reduce the population, have no place in our arguments. Nor do claims about what is best for the ecology or the environment. Women do not become pregnant with, or give birth to, populations; they have babies. Nor, in modern democracies do women typically shape their family with an expressivist intent—that is to serve as an example of what others should do. Large families are not conceived to cast shame on the childless.

Traditionally, modern democracies have accepted that our personal, private choices are based on personal private needs, and it is accepted that social problems require social solutions based on political and economic policies. While it is not uncommon for governments to seek to influence family decisions by, for example, offering childcare to make it easier to combine motherhood with paid employment, and even offering incentives to maintain what they consider to be optimal family size, it is becoming increasing rare for coercive measures to be taken. Countries as diverse as Hungary, France, Singapore and Russia offer benefits to multiparous parents while England, on the other hand, restricts child benefit payments in families with more than three children, but all these governments would say that, ultimately, the choice of family size is not for them to set. The example of Ceausescu's regime (1967–1989) under which Romanian women were prevented from using contraception or abortion, is widely discussed because it is a rare example. Even China, famous for its one-child policy, has needed to step back from its totalitarian attitude as the price to be paid for acceptance and integration with global institutions.

My arguments about pregnancy quite deliberately subjugate state policy to three inviolable principles: (i) that modern society grants us the autonomy to make moral decisions for ourselves; (ii) that within capitalist democracy we are free to enjoy a private family life; and that (ii) that our bodies are "our own" and that inventions that comprise our physical integrity require consent.

Those of us who argue for a woman's right to abortion, place our emphasis on the defence of her own right to make "the choice"; her ability to make the decision and act on what she has chosen, whatever that may be. We use the word "choice" because it speaks to the woman's autonomy or self-determination. It acknowledges that the woman is deciding for herself how to proceed in a situation where she is confronted with a decision between different options. No one else is deciding for her—nor is she being driven by circumstance, although her circumstances may profoundly influence what she does, her decision is not predetermined.

This is not to deny that the decision is sometimes difficult beyond imagining, involving a course of action a woman would prefer not to take. Sometimes what we *want* and what we *choose* are not the same thing.

Our focus on the word "choice" is specific and deliberate because it has special relevance as we go into the third decade of the twenty-first century. This is a time when the zeitgeist in modern democratic countries treats claims of the individual freedom with scepticism. It is not within the scope of this book to discuss why and how the post-modern consensus has shifted from notions of personal choice and responsibility to explain behaviour in terms of various determinisms (genetic determinism, neuro determinism, psychological determinism, economic and social determinism to name a few). But now, perhaps more than at any time in the last fifty years, it is important to reassert the principle of reproductive choice and to be clear that in situating abortion in the context of a *choice*, it marks a way of affirming moral responsibility and accountability for it.

An abortion forced upon you is not your choice and you cannot be held accountable or responsible for the procedure. By choosing it, by determining it, it becomes *your* action for which you are morally responsible and accountable.

A focus on choice in reproductive rights advocacy has not always had this emphasis. Especially in the USA, the term "choice" has sometimes been used as a polite or coded reference to abortion. The slogans "a woman's right to choose" and "my body, my choice" became popular among campaigners because they seemed less provocative than a direct reference to abortion. But it has never been possible to evade the question of the nature of the choice. To say that you are "pro-choice" begs the question about the nature of the choice that you are "pro."

Paradoxically, to say that a woman "chooses" abortion is now seen as provocative and less sympathetic than a formulation that suggests it is essential healthcare. Whereas previous generations of activists looked to "choice" as a more acceptable euphemism for "abortion," today campaigners consider "reproductive health" to be a more acceptable frame than "choice." Furthermore, sometimes the very reason for selecting the language of health is to imply that abortion is *not a choice* and a woman's abortion is beyond criticism because it is necessary for her well-being.

The linkage of abortion to individual decision making—the right to freely act according to our own morals that is expressed through the language of choice has not always been as central to the abortion debate as it is now.

In the 1970s, the early days of women's liberation movements, abortion was situated in the context of women's social and political empowerment rather than that of personal agency. Few countries had legal abortion and activists demonstrated under banners bearing legends such as, "Abortion on Demand," because they saw its availability as essential to women's equality in all areas of life. If women were to enjoy equality with men, we not only needed equal education, job opportunities and pay, but we needed the ability to learn, work and engage in politics as men did. Also, to take advantage of this, we needed the means to plan and manage family life. This led to the demands for free contraception and abortion (which would allow to control if and when we had children), and free childcare to allow women to combine parenting with work and other social responsibilities and activity outside the home.

The individual choices that women might make if these "demands" were granted were beside the point. Politics for this generation of social activists were not so concerned with how or why individuals made choices; it was more about "the sphere of politics and social change."[1]

In the UK, the language shift to a "woman's right to choose" was deliberate and tactical, and the pros and cons were debated in the feminist magazines of the time. One prominent writer, the well-known radical feminist Eileen Fairweather, observed in *Spare Rib* that "there is a tendency to pose abortion as though it is an end in itself. 'Free abortion on demand' the second demand of the women's liberation movement, has something of that ring." While acknowledging that the slogan, like all slogans, stood for something more complex, Fairweather observed that her badge "Abortion: a Woman's Right to Choose," "always produced more sympathetic chats on the bus." She suggested that it was "pretty lazy" to use the phrase "pro-abortion" and not "pro-choice" and that it "restricted support for the aims of the campaigns."[2]

Clearly, this argument had merit since it was (and is still) possible to support another woman's right to make a choice even if you personally believe abortion is wrong. A paper in *Feminist Review* by a member of the

---

[1] Ann Furedi writing as Ann Burton (1988). The Dangers of Being Defensive. *Confrontation*, no. 3.
[2] Eileen Fairweather (1979). The Feelings Behind the Slogans. *Spare Rib*, October.

grassroots National Abortion Campaign noted, "Even anti-abortionists have signed [petitions] on the grounds that while they themselves would never have an abortion, they do not see why they should prevent others coming to their own decisions."[3]

Activists in the USA also shifted to the language of choice as it became clear, after Medicaid funding was restricted for abortion services in 1977, that the main problem faced by economically disadvantaged women was not the constitutional right to abortion (at least in early pregnancy) but the money to pay for it. While in the UK, a publicly funded national health service provided free services (at least for some women) but not the right to access it without a medical need, in the USA the constitution allowed abortion to be a private decision although one a woman must pay for. Slogans concerning the "choice" in the USA, were concerned more with funding than political rights.

In time, the distinct nature of the term "pro-choice," either as an expression of an "agnostic" support for a woman's right to decide about her pregnancy (regardless of what that decision might be) or for the means to exercise that decision, became less distinct. The pro-choice label began to be attached to different campaign garments. In Europe, there has been a tendency to expand pro-choiceness to include all areas of reproductive choice gathering the need for decisions about fertility and infertility to rest with the individual concerned. Indeed, in the 1980s, the pro-choice movement divided between those who wished to focus on abortion rights and those who wanted to develop feminist resistance to forced sterilisation and racially motivated promotion of contraception injections and sterilisation in addition to the traditional women's liberation demands for contraception and abortion. Both wings of the movement identified themselves as "pro-choice."

In the USA however, to describe oneself as pro-choice became synonymous with support for abortion. By the early 2000, this became so much the case, that those who felt uneasy being associated with abortion began to drop that term, lest they be seen to have a bias towards pregnancy termination. In her excellent account of the politics of abortion

---

[3] Sue Himmelweit (1980). Abortion: Individual Choice or Social Control. *Feminist Review*, no. 5.

in the USA, journalist Katha Pollitt describes how in 2013 the Planned Parenthood Federation of America, a major national provider of women's reproductive health services, announced that it was moving away from the term "pro-choice." In mass media messaging, the term "defending Roe" (i.e., the current legal framework for abortion) was more likely to be used instead.[4]

There are seldom, if ever, linguistic solutions to political problems and substituting the term "pro-choice" to avoid the "A-word" has done little, if anything, to defuse opposition to abortion. Battles over whether a woman can decide on the future of her own pregnancy will not be settled by negotiations about whether a procedure is called an "abortion" or a "pregnancy termination," or whether a movement's badge claims to be "Pro-Child, Pro-Choice" or "Abortion on Demand." Similarly, it seems to make little difference whether we refer to those who oppose abortion as "pro-life" (their preference) or "anti-choice" (our preference).

Although it has become common in recent decades to obsess over nuanced language—causing millions of dollars and euros to be invested in "messaging,"[5] and strategies to "nudge" (as opposed to convincing) people to adopt a viewpoint—it seems unlikely that people are really pushed over fundamental lines of moral principles by the use of one word instead of another. Were the two-thirds majority who voted for changes to allow legal abortion in the Republic of Ireland swayed by whether canvassers talked about the "right to choose" or the "right to decide"? It is much more probable that they understood both meant the right for a woman to have an abortion and that they agreed with the principle.

That said, there are ways in which language matters significantly. To support a woman's right to choose abortion is not to say that you think she is right to choose one. If we believe the choice is hers then it follows that she is free to make a decision with which we disagree.

As regards abortion there is nothing more important than the matter of *who decides*. If it is a woman's own choice to have an abortion, the procedure is an expression of her agency; it represents the triumph of

---

[4] Katha Pollitt (2014). *Pro: Reclaiming Abortion Rights*. New York: Picador.

[5] One of the better examples is *Getting the Edge: Pro-active abortion messaging to seize the debate*, a campaign guide published by NARAL-Pro Choice America in 2021.

her will and reasoning over nature. If someone else makes the decision, and the abortion is the unwanted termination of a wanted pregnancy, the procedure is a crime against her own humanity and an abhorrence. To compel a woman to have an abortion is as profoundly awful as to compel her to have a child. Here, without doubt or ambiguity, *her choice matters*—and in this sense there is a fundamental difference in what it means to be pro-choice and pro-abortion.

The birth control movements in Europe and North America have been profoundly influenced—and were in most places established—by policy-makers and intellectual thinkers who believed that governments or medical specialists should be the ones to choose who should, and who should not, procreate. Early twentieth-century birth control advocates Margaret Sanger in the USA and Marie Stopes in the UK, may sometimes have spoken of the need to free women from the burden of pregnancy, but their underlying agenda was a eugenic intent to free society from the burden of unhealthy babies and unfit mothers.

To the radical intellectuals of the day, eugenics was an exciting application of Darwin's evolutionary theories. "Positive eugenics" was seen as a way to improve the human species by selectively mating people with specific desirable hereditary traits. "Negative eugenics" aimed to reduce human suffering by "breeding out" disease, disabilities and so-called undesirable characteristics from the human population. Both were seen as the application of rationalism and science to improve humanity. The eugenic project, was of course, massively discredited by the rise of Naziism and Hitler's final genocidal solution. We tend to associate population engineering with fascism, but the eugenic zeitgeist of the 1920s and 1930s swept up liberal and social democrats quite as much as it did fascists. The targeting of social groups for birth control interventions for the good of society is an enduring tradition.

In 1990s, a decade of government interventions and targets to reduce teenage pregnancies in the UK resulted in many benefits for young people. Access to contraceptive services was expanded, nurses skilled to advise on sexual health and education were funded for schools, and abortion services were expanded and linked their treatment with contraception. Sometimes, the language of "choice" was used—but the emphasis of the public health departments was always on a particular kind of choice: the "healthy" choice. And the best healthy choice and so the promoted choice was to remain unpregnant, preferably by not having sex, but otherwise using the recommended long-acting method of contraception. Should a teenage girl become pregnant, then the best choice, in the eyes of most people was now abortion. A teenage abortion might be a mark of some reckless failure—but teenage motherhood carried far greater stigma.

As regards teenagers in the UK at the end of the twentieth century, abortion had come to be seen as careless, but becoming a mother was seen as reckless. There is a credible claim that while reproductive behaviour is not coerced for some sections of the population, reproductive choice is compromised.

A small but growing number of younger people seem to be drawn to a pro-abortion, as against a pro-choice stance. Perhaps there are some environmentalists who believe that the planet cannot sustain more babies, or some who believe that it is morally wrong to bring into the world children who carry "defective genes," or when their parents cannot support them financially. Social policies may be engineered to push women into limiting their family size by all manner of measures, including abortion.

This gives us a particular reason to insist that *choice* is absolutely centred in how we think about abortion. And it makes it deeply troubling that there is an increasingly popular view, emanating from social and reproductive justice movements in the USA, that the language of choice should be changed.

Feminists Against Choice

There are several contemporary objections to the "C-word". For some, the word "choice" is seen as trivialising and there is a claim that it encourages decisions about fertility to be compared with something superficial, say, a choice of shoes or lipstick colour.[6] Others claim it is individualist and consumerist and fails to take account of "all the social, economic

---

[6] See Renata Salecl (2010). *The Tyranny of Choice*. London: Profile Books.

and political conditions that frame the so-called choices that women are forced to make."[7]

This latter complaint has become a much-voiced claim within what is now referred to as the Reproductive Justice movement in the USA, and among legal feminist academics in Europe who identify with various branches of critical theory, all which are deliberate attempts to move away from post-Enlightenment rational discourse, embracing subjective, identitarian schools of thought.[8]

In her introduction to a collection of academic essays, *Reproductive Justice: A Global Concern,* American psychology professor Joan C. Chrisler claims the Reproductive Justice movement emerged from discussions by women of colour who had attended a global conference in 1994, the International Conference on Population and Development (ICPD). The event, sponsored by the United Nations, and often referred to as the Cairo conference (since it was held in Cairo) gathered together an audience that might accurately bes described as "the great and the good" to set shared global priorities and in particular development goals. By the 1990, governments and elite donor agencies were extremely sensitive about previous associations between development programmes and coercive population control.[9] This conference was intended to cast off suspicions about its intentions by putting women at the front and centre of initiatives. And it succeeded with the future of women in the Global South and the future prospects of girl-children becoming the visible focus of international efforts.

Increasingly Reproductive Justice concerns have come to dominate international and domestic movements that formally identified as pro-choice. The discourse has shifted from the problems of individual agency

---

[7] Andrea Smith (2017). Beyond Pro-Choice and Pro-Life: Women of Color and Reproductive Justice. In Loretta J. Ross, Lynn Roberts, Erika Derkas, Whitney Peoples, and Pamela Bridgewater Toure (Eds.), *Radical Reproductive Justice: Foundations, Theory, Practice, Critique.* New York City: Feminist Press, p. 160.

[8] A critical and helpful guide to critical theory is: Helen Pluckrose and James Lindsay (2020). *How Universities Made Everything About Race, Gender, and Identity—And Why This Harms Everybody.* London: Swift. See also Kathleen Stock (2021). *Material Girls: Why Reality Matters for Feminism.* London: Fleet.

[9] See Frank Furedi (1997). *Population and Development: A Critical Introduction.* London: Polity Press, for a discussion of the shift in the policy narrative of Governments, aid donors and recipients.

to those of social organisation and consequences of "white supremacy" and its attendant capitalist social relations. The discourse has focussed the on claim that globally, women's "ability to control what happens to our bodies is constantly challenged by poverty, racism, environmental degradation, sexism, homophobia and injustice ...".[10]

These longstanding social justice concerns were seen by activists to need "community" grassroots-based initiatives. They were beyond the power of governments; fundamental social change could only be achieved through anti-capitalism. Activists believed that what was needed was a redirection of resources away from those with privilege, to "level up" those without it. This, they considered, would not be possible from within the existing systems. It required the disruption of the social and economic relations of patriarchal capitalism.

The campaigns for justice, which were to achieve both notoriety and influence when the Black Lives Matter movement achieved a global profile in 2021, were not campaigns for rights under the law, or even for the inalienable natural rights (life, liberty and property) that were informed by Enlightenment thinking and foundational to the American Constitution. Indeed, the concept of "the inalienable rights of man" were not where movements based on equity rather than traditional notions of equality were trying to head. From their perspective, equal treatment would perpetuate existing privileges which they wished to disrupt. Consequently, the Reproductive Justice movement aligned with the movements for racial and economic justice seeking to reconstitute and re-educate society around communitarian values.

Among this constituency, talk of rights, even reproductive rights, became problematised. Rights were seen as a threat to communitarianism, since they were (correctly) perceived to be more individual and concerned with freedom and liberty, and crucially with independence from the state. In the USA, it seemed to many that as the twenty-first century advanced, so individual freedom was associated with the political right. The notion that state intervention should be limited, and personal decisions in particular should be outwith state interest, seemed to have

---

[10] Loretta Ross cited in J. Silliman, M. G. Fried, L. Ross, and E. R. Gutierrez (2004). *Undivided Rights: Women of Color Organize for Reproductive Justice*. Boston: South End Press.

been owned by Conservatives. The successful resistance of the gun-lobby, which wrapped itself in the language of freedom and individual rights seemed to taint the concepts for everyone else. Instead of challenging the ownership of rights and freedom by conservatives and insisting that concepts such as choice were as essential to disadvantaged people as they were to anyone else, the "left" demonised and encouraged its association with the libertarian right.

"Individual rights," and even the notion of equality, became seen as a problem. In the eyes of "social-justice warriors," demands for rights addressed what each individual perceived was necessary for them personally, rather than trying to level everyone to a place where everyone has the same. It was, from their perspective, more "just" for "those with" to have less and "those without" to have more.

In the USA, abortion tumbled across this contested ground. The constitutional protection of abortion under the *Roe v Wade* ruling, which had been championed by the pro-choice movement throughout the last century, allows the right to choose abortion in early pregnancy under the rubric of the protection of private decision-making in an area that should properly be outside the intervention of the state. Consequently, the constitutional protection of abortion had never addressed the issue of funding, so access to poor people remained an issue, while women with private means could exercise their choices. This made it indefensible to some in the Reproductive Justice movement. Furthermore, women of colour were conscious that eugenic imperatives and public-health assumptions about which kind of babies would be "at risk," meant that they were the target of birth control initiatives.

Joan Chrisler summed up the problem of choice as the Reproductive Justice movement had come to see it. The "rhetoric of 'choice'," she says, "suggests a 'marketplace of options,' much like the array of goods presented to consumers in a shopping mall, where many options are appealing." However, she argues, reproductive decisions are different and so cannot be seen truly as choices:

> In reality, reproductive decisions are often painful and difficult. For example, if a woman uses contraception or seeks abortion because she cannot afford to raise a child, because of her own ill health (or a

serious medical condition of the fetus) or because of insecurity, due to war or natural disaster, does she experience her decision as a choice? What if women choose to become parents but cannot get pregnant (e.g., no partner, partner resistance, infertility, forced sterilization) and are prevented from using adoption services (e.g., by economic status, by discrimination), or lose their children to early death or revocation of custody as a result of divorce or government action (e.g., substance abuse, physical or mental illness, disability)?[11]

Of course, it is absolutely true that we do not get to live the lives we want. We might even say, in a rhetorical sense, "we don't always get to live the lives we might choose." But even if we do not *always* get to make a choice, *sometimes* we do and, when we do, it gives a different texture to how we feel.

Consider Chrisler's example of women "who choose to become parents but cannot get pregnant." Here it is evident how different the reasons for the problem are, and the consequently how different are the degrees of control that a person can have over them. While some are totally outside the scope of personal choice some are not. Infertility is a good example of this.

Infertility may be the consequence of an untreatable medical condition that is perhaps an abnormality of an individual's reproductive biology caused by no person. There may be no solution or redress; it is no one's fault and there is no one to blame and possibly nothing to be done. Infertility caused by forced sterilisation is entirely different. This is the result of a deliberate action. Some individual or agency has acted on *their* (not her) decision to prevent what should have been have been her choice to become pregnant. Her own agency has been deliberately obliterated. Unlike untreatable "natural" infertility this woman's infertility is the consequence of political and social problems that call on us to act in support of her.

If we compare this to "not having a partner," or "partner resistance," we can see that these are problems of a different order. These issues are outside the realm of social and political action. The absence of a

---

[11] Joan C. Chrisler (Ed.) (2012). *Reproductive Justice: A Global Concern*. California: Praeger, p. 3.

male partner willing to be collaborate in a woman's desire for pregnancy can be resolved only by the individuals involved because the problem is located in their personal, private lives. Even the most effective justice warriors cannot deliver up a partner to impregnate someone who aspires to motherhood. Nor can any movement cause a "resistant partner" to stop resisting. There may be many socio-economic reasons why women remain in relationships that do not allow them to make the choices they wish to make—but ultimately the only person with the ability to make that change to her life is the woman herself. Society is to blame for many of the burdens that we bear, but not all. Bracketing together all the causes of a distressing outcome erases the differences between what is "natural," what is "social" and what is "personal."

It is easy rhetoric to blame the material relations of capitalist socio-economic society for our absence of freedom to live as we wish. Indeed, the structures of capitalism can legitimately be seen as responsible for the framework of women's oppression,[12] but even within those structures, we are not slaves without personal agency. Ironically, just as capitalism creates a web of social and economic control that denies rights, so it also generates a personal sphere and the possibility of personal freedoms.[13] Ultimately there are potential solutions that a woman may choose to consider and decide to take. Not being able to have a child with the man with whom you live is not the same as not being able to have a child because you have no ovaries.

The basic point is this: not everything that seems unfair can be resolved by laws, because there are aspects of our lives that sit outside the spheres in which justice can be delivered. The claim that: "partner selection is essential to reproductive justice"[14] suggests that the law, or other arbiters of justice can, even should, interfere in areas of life that are deeply personal and intimate. I may feel it is "unjust" that a man does not want to be the biological father of a child with me but a man would surely find it "unjust" to be forced into fatherhood. But there are some

---

[12] See Fredrich Engels (1884). *The Origin of the Family, Private Property and the State* and many subsequent materialist explanations for how capitalism relies on and shapes family life.

[13] Those wishing to explore this will find the work of Hannah Arendt particularly enriching.

[14] Makiko Kasai and S. Craig Rooney, The Choice Before the Choice: Partner Selection Is Essential to Reproductive Justice. In Crisler (2012), pp. 11–21.

areas of inequality in life that are outwith any external intervention and should stay that way.

"Justice," as Chrisler states, "implies that people are treated fairly, equitably, and respectfully. Thus, the term *reproductive justice* situates the work in the context in the context of the greater social justice movement." This makes sense when we think about many aspects of what are required from society to enable access to resources. But it is not the whole story, and elevating justice while ignoring the capacity for personal choice offers a very partial narrative.

A New Anti-choice Opposition

By 2020, the Reproductive Justice movement had started to frame commitment to "choice" as problem. For some justice advocates, the Choice became symbolic of a focus on middle-class white women's priorities and failure to meet the needs of women of colour. For them, the pro-choice framework and reference to rights failed to take into account the many ways that women of colour and other marginalised women had difficulty accessing abortion even in places where it is legally allowed. Women of colour, it was argued, experienced systematic oppression and not self-determination as their problem.[15] Organisations, particularly in the USA, that had been synonymous with abortion care, began to adapt to claims that only the privileged could make choices and therefore a focus on choice did not only *fail to include* those who were not privileged; it was *deliberately exclusionary*.

An open letter to the pro-choice movement[16] from the Sistersong Women of Color Reproductive Justice Collective spelt out why it saw choice as a problem. In their opinion the concepts of self-determination and individual freedom were insufficiently inclusive of all matters of concern, and all peoples who were concerned. From their perspective,

---

[15] See Loretta Ross and Rickie Solinger (2019). *Reproductive Justice*. Berkeley: University of California Press.

[16] Monica Simpson et al. (2014). Reproductive Justice and "Choice": An Open Letter to Planned Parenthood. Accessible at https://rewirenewsgroup.com/article/2014/08/05/reproductive-justice-choice-open-letter-planned-parenthood.

issues pertaining to reproduction could only be addressed if the other aspects of individual life were addressed with which they intersected were tackled too. Reproductive justice was understood to be inseparable from the struggle against racism, poverty, homelessness, educational disadvantage and be obtained as a freestanding aim. Furthermore, from this perspective the priority for action should be set by the disadvantaged, not the long-standing campaigns for choice which were increasing dismissed as being influenced by white supremacy. Pro-choice advocates continued to direct attention to abortion, when people of colour thought effort should be turned elsewhere.

The letter, with many co-signatories from groups known for previous pro-choice abortion activism, made the choice between choice and justice stark. From their perspective, it was not simply that an orientation to choice ignored the needs of non-privileged by an act of omission communities, rather it ignored an opportunity for solidarity with the oppressed, disadvantaged and excluded. It stated:

> Although the coining of RJ did not explicitly name every injustice experienced by every oppressed group, we believe it was a catalyst that opened up the discussion of the intersection of justice and health that is experienced by a myriad of communities—the trans community, undocumented youth, persons with disabilities, those who are incarcerated, sex workers, and those who are living with HIV, to name a few. We are seeing a sense of unity grow from the relationships built based on the shared experience of these communities. This growth simply would not have been possible under the pro-choice framing.

In response, organisations that had previously focussed on "pro-choice" advocacy began to pivot to intersectionality, diversity and inclusivity. In the USA, Planned Parenthood (ironically the nation's main provider of contraceptive and abortion services to the economically disadvantaged) issued a self-flagellatory statement for publication in the *New York Times*. An op-ed by a president and chief executive, newly appointed following investigations into institutional racism, apologised for its past focus on maintaining contraception and abortion, and in rallying under the banner of women's rights:

> By privileging whiteness, we've contributed to America harming Black women and other women of color. And when we focus too narrowly on "women's health," we have excluded trans and nonbinary people. …
>
> As we face relentless attacks on our ability to keep providing sexual and reproductive health care, including abortion, we've claimed the mantle of women's rights, to the exclusion of other causes that women of color and trans people cannot afford to ignore.[17]

How the privileging of concerns relating to diversity and inclusion came about and its impact on abortion advocacy is a complicated story that outside the scope of this book. Where this turn will take advocacy for abortion is currently unresolved. There is no clear consensus within the movement itself. In one essay in a foundational collection of essays on reproductive justice, an activist-academic observes: "Currently, there is general agreement within the movement about the need to reframe abortion rights and reproductive choice, but no agreement on the frame itself" (Marlene Gerber Freed, p. 142). While the author of the final essay of the same book, also by an activist-academic, Aaronette White, claims that her own "personal anthem" (p. 412) remains a 1989 black feminist statement that centres on "choice."

> Choice is the essence of freedom. It's what we African Americans have struggled for all these years. The right to choose where we would sit on the bus. The right to vote. The right for each of us to select our own paths, to dream and reach for our dreams. The right to choose how we would and would not live our lives.
>
> This freedom—to choose and exercise our choices—is what we've fought and died for …

This point that "choice is the essence of freedom" is foundational to the moral case for abortion. To be pro-choice, and in such a way that privileges a personal individual private decision over against public

---

social policy, is our fundamental defence against assaults on reproductive freedom and is particularly important to the marginalised and disadvantaged communities, as we will come to discuss.

Why Personal Choice Matters

A woman's demand for control over her body and the future of her pregnancy has its own integrity whether or not it intersects with other concerns. It stands regardless of her standing as to class, race or any way in which society defines her, or she defines herself. It is as true for a woman who is a white, wealthy republican gun-enthusiast as it is for a trans eco-warrior or socially-deprived woman of colour from an inner-city project. The ownership of our own bodies (bodily autonomy) is a universal principle that has existed throughout civilisation throughout all modern times. It is common to us all, part of our respect for human life, and it cannot be jettisoned without renouncing that respect. Pregnancy does not make a woman less human, and it should never reduce her bodily integrity, since to do that would mean she was less entitled to respect as a human being than the rest of us.

It is woeful that some advocates in the Reproductive Justice movement set the concept of a pregnant woman's right to choose abortion against the principles of equity and justice. And it is wrong to claim that the defence of an individual's autonomy, agency and privacy contradicts the values of social inclusion.

A legal right does not always guarantee a chosen result. But legal prohibition is a different kind of prohibition to being unable afford something we might otherwise have. This became starkly clear when countries closed their borders in the 2020 pandemic and international travel was banned whether a person could afford it or not. Previously, I simply could not afford my bucket-list ambition to visit the Galapagos Islands; during the pandemic it was no longer a matter of what resources I could muster because I was not "allowed" to travel. Prohibition by law *is* different to denial by circumstances, and it *feels* different even though, for whatever reason, the not-being-able-to-go amounts to the same denial.

This difference in how legal and resource restrictions on reproductive choice is impeded is particularly familiar to women who cannot conceive naturally. There is one important way in which abortion is different from assisted conception. While ending a pregnancy is always possible, even the most expert infertility doctors may fail to help a woman become pregnant since we don't have the knowledge or means to overcome every obstacle. This might be described as a natural limitation on choice. Limitations on choice due to the law, or lack of funds, are both socially set. Natural limits and social limits are substantially different and feel substantially different to us, as every account of prisoners awaiting execution reveals. Knowing you will die because of an illness that no one can cure is profoundly different to knowing you will die because of a judges decision, which could, if she wished, be reversed.

Just because the state grants a legal right, this does not guarantee that everyone can exercise that right. The *Roe v. Wade* 1974 judgment that accorded women in the USA the right to abortion in early pregnancy (defining it as a private decision that was outside government concern) simply removed legal barriers to a woman wishing to exercise her abortion decision. The state did not guarantee that she would be able to afford the procedure, nor that a clinic would be accessible. Indeed, it has been argued that the decision did women a disadvantage in that, by defining abortion as a private affair, it allowed the government to shrug off responsibility for all manner of birth control.[18]

This has led to some arguments in the USA that constitutional defence of a woman's right to make a private decision means nothing at all for poor women. They conclude that the *Roe v. Wade* judgment is irrelevant except to the privileged and defence of this legal right only matters to those committed to the maintenance of white supremacy, a term that has come to mean what was previously known as "western civilisation"— not the specific belief that caucasians are superior.

In truth, women need rights *and* the resources to exercise them. So in Cambridge Massachusetts, women have a right to early abortion that

---

[18] See William Saletan (2004). *Bearing Right: How Conservatives Won the Abortion War*. Los Angeles: University of California Press, p. 43.

is protected under their right to privacy, but the service may be unaffordable. In Cambridge England, a woman has no capacity to choose abortion because she thinks it is best for her, but she may access a service that is conditional on the approval of those in authority. Both Cambridge women face obstacles in exercising their choice, but these are problems of a different kind. Which form of denial is worse? For those who look to the principles of justice and equity, the UK situation will probably appear preferable since all women, in theory at least, face the same tests and the same obstacles regardless of their social standing. The law applies equally to the disadvantaged and the privileged. All are equally denied self-determination. All are denied "the choice" of abortion because society has decided that they *may not* make that reproductive decision, regardless of whether they are able to act on it. The seeming "trade off"—access to abortion with medical permission—is fragile and can be removed at any time.

Of course, in many societies, the granting of rights and freedoms has failed to impact on the lives of particular groups of women, and a pro-choice movement needs to pay more attention to this reality. As we have discussed, economically deprived women may be encouraged to have abortions. Many women of colour have a different experience of social pressures around abortion, often being encouraged to terminate pregnancies for racist and eugenic reasons. But this is an argument to fight harder for reproductive choice, not a reason to give up on it. This is no new discovery by millennial reproductive warriors. One of the most influential women in the late twentieth-century abortion advocacy movement, Kate Michelman, as former president of the National Abortion Rights Action League[19] spelled out a vision of "a truly pro-choice America" that captures much of today's reproductive justice orientation before its Generation-Z warriors were born. In a keynote speech in 1987[20] she argued that the fight pro-choice fight was:

---

[19] Later to be known as NARAL-Pro Choice America.

[20] Cited in Saletan p. 43. Saletan claims that the emphasis on privacy was a significant error that cost the pro-choice movement state funding for abortion.

Not just for an America where women had the legal right to choose abortion, but an America where women have the social and economic freedom to choose from a full range of reproductive options ... We know the difference between a real choice and the least disastrous option. We know that a welfare mother of six living on $400 a month, the "right" to have a $240 abortion is no right at all. She doesn't have the choice to have an abortion, just as she doesn't have the right to go back to school or the choice to feed her children three square meals a day ... We must talk about the social and economic conditions under which choices are made.

To address these preconditions of choice, Michelman pledged to fight not just for privacy but for government activity in the public domain:

We must insist that contraceptives be safe, reliable and accessible. We must help women get the counseling they need ... We must lend our voices to the demands for adequate pre-natal and post-natal care. We must join the call for improved health care for women and their children, for nutrition programs and for affordable childcare ... When groups get together to talk about economic equity, we should be there. When groups get together to talk about childcare and nutrition issues, we should be there.

But the rationale for freedom of choice, constitutionally captured in the right to privacy was, to Michelman, essential. She understood that the constitutional right to abortion was not just important to those who could afford to exercise it, but to all people regardless of colour or status or privilege. She explained it like this:

[The Constitution] guarantees our rights ... in a sort of roundabout way—by carving out those spheres of American life which are off-bounds to state regulation. It defines what we *can* do by telling the government what it *cannot* do ... **We simply contend that it should be a woman and her family, not the state who should provide the answers.** (my emphasis)

In other words, at the heart of the matter is this question: who decides? And in this context "personal choice" matters precisely *because* its locus is in the individual self. It is a decision made by a woman in her own self-interest—regardless of what is best for others, or society or the claims of justice. And as we have seen earlier, in this fundamental of a woman's person, her physical self, her self-interest must stand prior to everything else. She must have the right to decide what her body will endure in relation to pregnancy.

Our understanding that choice is paramount but limited to the extent that women can exercise that choice is not a relic of the 1980s. In 2012, a meeting of influential global advocates, providers and interested academics organised in London by Jon O'Brien, then president of Catholics for Choice based in the USA and the British Pregnancy Advisory Service, the main provider of abortions in the UK, issued this declaration of what was required of a movement for abortion rights:

> We believe in a woman's autonomy and her right to choose whether to continue or end a pregnancy. Every woman should have the right to decide the future of her pregnancy according to her conscience, whatever her reasons or circumstances. A just society does not compel women to continue undesired pregnancies.
>
> We recognize that support for choice itself is not enough. Access to abortion is an integral part of women's reproductive health care, and we uphold the right to receive this. Women need access to resources and services, including the counsel of professionals, friends and family that they choose to involve. Legal, political, social and economic changes are necessary to allow the exercise of reproductive choice, and a commitment to such changes is part of a commitment to choice.
>
> We express solidarity with those who provide abortion care, and we recognize the moral value of their work. We recognized and respect that some health personnel may choose not to provide abortions but we believe it is ethically imperative for them to ensure that a woman receives a referral to a willing provider.
>
> We believe there is profound moral case for freedom of reproductive choice, and that women are competent to make decisions for themselves, and to act on them responsibly.
>
> To be pro-choice is to be committed to the right of women to make their own reproductive decisions and to:

- strive to create the conditions in which reproductive choice can be exercised;
- support reproductive autonomy;
- advocate for legal frameworks that allow autonomous decision-making;
- educate the public and policy makers globally about the value of reproductive choice.[21]

These commitments are as necessary and relevant today as they have been in preceding decades.

Who Decides?

Ironically, in rejecting the concept of "choice" to replace it with those of "justice" and "equity," and in dismissing the principle of individual freedom as neo-liberal and of benefit only to the "privileged," the Reproductive Justice movement is jettisoning the single most important protection the marginaliszed and disadvantaged can claim: the personal moral status that each of us has as a human individual to self-determination.

It is a bizarre paradox that those who are at the front of arguing most loudly that personal freedom is meaningless are organisations that claim to be representing people of colour, and that draw on the history of colonialism and oppression in their demands for justice. The rejection of slavery was propelled by the notion that all of us—as human beings—are entitled to the same dignity and freedoms. The notion that no man may "own" another as property sits with the principle that our bodies, our existent physical selves, are our own. Each of us has a "body and soul" that is a fundamental entitlement; it is our *self*.

There is a huge philosophical and psychological literature that discusses the constitution of self, and there is insufficient space here to

---

[21] The London Declaration of Pro-Choice Principles as reproduced in *Select Proceedings from the International Summit on Reproductive Choice*, Lisbon 2014 published by Catholics for Choice, Washington, DC.

attempt even the most basic critique.[22] However, the notion that *integrity* of both our bodies and our conscience is essential to our human dignity is a basic tenet of many faiths beyond that of the Judaeo-Christian beliefs of Western modernity.

The view that our individual capabilities—our agency—is overwritten by our economic and social resources is a form of determinism that belittles the internal struggles that people face. Our circumstances may set out the play that we act in, the scenery on the stage, the role in which we are cast and even the audience we play before. But the lines we deliver are our own. Faced with insufficient income, we decide what to privilege and what to sacrifice. Even in the most degraded circumstances, faced with the confinement of colonial slavery or the Nazi concentration camps, individuals fought to maintain their dignity through control of themselves. Tiny choices, when to eat a crust or with whom to associate, mattered because the deliberateness of chosen action is an expression of self.

Surely, those who consider women *should* be able to choose freely should strive to stretch those areas where we are able to exercise that control, rather than degrading the aspiration as neoliberal. Surely the answer to the question of whether abortion is "right" or "wrong" in both moral theory and moral practice comes down to the matter of "who decides."

---

[22] Personally, I am drawn to Christine Korsgaard's neo-Kantian arguments about self-constitution expressed in Onora O'Neill (Ed.) (1996). *The Sources of Normativity*. Cambridge: Cambridge University Press. And Christine M. Korsgaard (2009). *Self Constitution: Agency, Identity and Integrity*. Oxford: Oxford University Press.

9

Self-Determination

Every previous chapter leads us to this place: abortion should be a woman's choice. This means no more and no less than that a woman should be able to make a personal and private decision about the future of her pregnancy. She should have the freedom to make that decision according to her own beliefs, and she should be able to act on her decision, following her own values and her own conscience. The philosophical and moral foundation for reproductive choice is the principle of autonomy— sometimes referred to as "self-determination."

Respect for autonomy, that respect for our ability to make our own life choices, sits behind the principle of respect for bodily integrity, the belief that our bodies are our own for us to control and that, providing we cause no harm to others, no one may interfere with us without our consent.

Our autonomy is expressed in the choices we make. These choices are themselves a reflection of who we are, since they are an expression of what we think is best for us. The way we make a choice does not matter. It may be the outcome of serious thoughtful deliberation, or a snap spur-of-the-moment decision, but that is not the crucial factor. The point is

A. Furedi, *The Moral Case for Abortion*, https://doi.org/10.1007/978-3-030-90189-9_9

simply that we have willed it; we have faced different options and decided which one is best.

Our capacity for autonomy is as important as our DNA in defining what it is to be a human person. Choice is not simply about making a decision that is right for us. It also serves as a vehicle through which we cultivate our capacity for self-conscious, self-aware and self-determining behaviour. The development of these capacities is integral to the emergence of the unique qualities that distinguish humans from all other beings.

Emily Jackson's description of the expression of autonomy as "writing our own biography" is especially apt.[1] People are shaped by their life circumstances; class, ethnicity, sex, gender-expression and the values and beliefs of the community into which they are born intersect with and influence everything about human life. But they do not dictate the story of a person's life. Different people, from the same background, faced with the same circumstances, respond in different ways. A person's life course is not drafted in advance; we write it as we live it, and the decisions we reach do not just produce the chosen "outcome"—they shape us and those around us.

There is no clearer illustration of the way choice matters than the consequences of a woman's decision about her pregnancy.

When a woman knows that she is pregnant, she stands at a fork in the road of her life's path. If she follows one route and allows her pregnancy to continue, she will become a mother (perhaps, for the first time, perhaps again). She will extend her family, with all of the consequences that follow from that. If she follows the other route and ends her pregnancy, consequences will also follow from that. The impact of her decision is not just about the birth (or not) of a baby. The option she chooses will almost certainly have a profound effect on the lives of those around her, and those relationships.

If she chooses to continue her pregnancy, the man with whom she has conceived becomes a father, with all the consequential decisions that this brings to his life, and her parents gain a grandchild. All of the woman's familial relatives are cast in new roles, whether or not they choose to

---

[1] Emily Jackson (2001). *Regulating Reproduction: Law, Technology and Autonomy.* Oxford: Hart.

assume involvement or responsibility in raising the new life. As a baby's mother, a woman may need to redefine her role in relation to paid work (she may now need employment, or to scale down her employment), she may find that her friendships change; she may develop new links within her community and perhaps relinquish others.

Making these decisions and being responsible for them affects not only the woman's circumstances but also the woman herself. Her choice will, in some essential way, cast her as a different person.

For a woman to know that she has decided to bear a man's child is a very different thing than to know that she has decided against it. And importantly, for her to know that *she* has made this choice is significantly different to knowing that she was forced to accept her lot. It matters to all of us when decisions are of our own making.

This is not to say that when a woman looks at a positive pregnancy test, and considers which of the paths to follow, she is fully aware of the complex and nuanced consequences that follow from her decision. How could she be? How much rationality and reasoning a woman applies to her decision, how well informed she is, and how realistic her intentions may be are in many ways irrelevant. For some women the choice is clearly deliberative, intentional and expressly conscious. Others are indecisive, ambivalent, unable to conclude what they want and seek to "hand over" the decision to someone else, or place themselves in a situation where personal choice is effectively short-circuited by delaying disclosure until it is too late for abortion.[2] But, when the woman "knows," even denial is a decision of sorts.

The claim that human thinking is rational and based on reason does not imply that we always apply a high-level of abstract, learned knowledge, or that our decision is based on a detailed consideration. It means simply this: when we are faced with two or more alternatives, we are able to consider our circumstances and all things considered arrive at the best course of action.

This "knowing" is what marks the pregnant woman out from the pregnant female of any other species. For a dog, a horse or a chimpanzee

---

[2] See Ann Furedi (1995). *Unplanned Pregnancy: Your Choices.* Oxford: Oxford University Press.

pregnancy is *followed* by birth or miscarriage. It is simply a matter of nature taking its course. One thing inexorably follows the other.

At no time does an animal weigh up which is the best option and what consequences are likely to follow. Natural instinct leads the cat to give birth in the warm comfy laundry basket and not on the hard cold back-doorstep. There is no feline birth plan or cat-consideration of the pros and cons of birthing places. That we, alone of all animals, can and do reflect and apply our knowledge makes our lives different from all other kinds of lives.[3]

The Essence of Ourselves

The right to choose our own life course, to work out what we believe is right and wrong, to frame our values privately for ourselves, and live according to the dictates of our own consciences, is a unique and wonderful human project. It took shape in the Enlightenment of the eighteenth century, that period in Europe and America when notions of rationality, rights and responsibility began to dominate the cultural climate. This was the period of the American Declaration of Independence, the French Revolution and the radical intellectual climate influenced by the European *philosophes* who explored the nature of humanity with confidence in a rational, scientific, secular society based on reason.

Conceptually, the principle of autonomy resonated with the spirit of the time as both a *condition* of individual freedom, and an *expression* of individual freedom.[4] This was a time of questioning notions that people's lives were (and should be) shaped by forces outside of their control, whether those forces were those of God and the Church, or the natural order of birthright. Humanity was seen as possessing a degree of free will and able to act voluntarily. The spirit of liberty and freedom was

[3] See Daniel C. Dennett (1996). *Kinds of Minds: Towards an Understanding of Consciousness*. New York: HarperCollins, for an excellent exploration of the difference between the intentionality in humans and animals.

[4] See Frank Furedi (2013). *Authority: A Sociological History*. Cambridge: Cambridge University Press.

in the air, and with it, the sense that people controlled their destiny. Two centuries later, in the twentieth century, that spirit was revived and infused into existentialist thinking that people were (and should be) free to determine what to value and how to live.[5]

Although today it is common for human rights lawyers to assert that there is no hierarchy of rights and so no one "right" can be seen as more important than any other, most moral philosophy retains the notion that there are fundamental and inalienable principles, sometimes called "first order principles,"[6] and sometimes thought of as deontological principles or truths.

The right to personal autonomy has been considered important as far back in Western thought as the ancient Greeks. The word "autonomy" is itself derived from the ancient Greek, *auto* meaning self and *nomos* meaning law—self-law—the government of ourselves by ourselves. Originally, for the Greeks autonomy referred to the self-rule or self-governance of independent city-states, but now we think of it in terms of individuals. The autonomous individual "acts freely in accordance with a self-chosen plan, analogous to the way an independent government manages its territories and sets its policies."[7] Hence "autonomy" is sometimes called "self determination," and this is a particularly useful way to understand its importance in our lives.

Two great philosophers with very different approaches are responsible for placing autonomy at the heart of the tradition of modern Western liberal thought. Both Immanuel Kant and John Stuart Mill saw autonomy as more than just a freedom, as essential to the development of individuals.[8] Warnock describes Kant as "pivotal"[9] in understanding the application of free will, in that even when people know they are subject to a moral law, sometimes they need to decide whether or not to follow

---

[5] See Mary Warnock (1970). *Existentialism*. Oxford: Oxford University Press.

[6] See the explanation of first- and second-order principles in Robin Barrow (2007). *An Introduction to Moral Philosophy and Moral Education*. London: Routledge, pp. 71–82.

[7] Tom E. Beauchamp and James F. Childress (2013). *Principles of Biomedical Ethics*, 7th edn. Oxford: Oxford University Press, p. 101.

[8] Raanan Gillon (1986). *Philosophical Medical Ethics*. Chichester: Wiley.

[9] Mary Warnock (1970). *Existentialism*. Oxford: Oxford University Press, p. 4.

it. His notion of a *human agent*, faced with *decisions*, bringing his or her *will* to bear on them, is what creates a sense of moral value.

In his exploration *Groundwork of the Metaphysic of Morals*, Kant deploys the concept of autonomy as the foundation for human dignity, which he then uses to define the concept of personhood. Published in 1785, this was Kant's consideration of "foundational ethics," the core concepts of moral theory, which attempted to isolate the fundamental principle of morality. His argument that the rightness of an action is determined by the character of the principle that a person chooses to act on, has influenced thinking ever since.

For Kant, autonomy and rationality were the two criteria for a meaningful, truly human life. Without autonomy, Kant argues, there can be no moral accountability. If the course of action you take involves no personal decision, then it has no value. Actions are merely functional, and our lives are just an accumulation of actions with no meaning that are neither blameworthy nor praiseworthy. If that is the case, then our lives are not enriched with meaning and are equivalent to the lives of plants or insects. Kant leads us, in valuing autonomy, to acknowledge the sovereignty of the individual conscience—especially when society is divided by moral doubts in relation to a particular issue. And it follows from Kant that we recognise that those who must personally bear the responsibility for their moral choices should have the right to make those choices, and that our lives are enriched by being able to make choices in accordance with our own values. Kant held the view that it was preferable to make the wrong choice through the exercise of moral independence, than to take the right actions without thinking for oneself:

> It is so easy to be immature. If I have a book to serve as my understanding, a pastor to serve as my conscience, a physician to determine my diet for me, and so on, I need not exert myself at all. I need not think ...[10]

Thinking and working through one's own independent conclusions was, for Kant, what mattered most.

---

[10] Immanuel Kant (1784). *An Answer to the Question: What Is Enlightenment?* 2009 edn. Harmondsworth: Penguin.

Mill stressed a different element: the importance of decision-making itself. He held that through the exercise of moral autonomy, individuals develop personality and the experience necessary for maturity, and that the cultivation of moral independence requires that people are free to deliberate and draw their own conclusions about how best to live. For Mill, it was the very process of deciding what we want that shapes our character: "The human faculties of perception, judgment, discriminative feeling, mental activity and even moral preference, are exercised *only* in making a choice"[11] (my emphasis). Mill went on to say:

> He who lets the world, or his own portion of it, choose his life plan for him has no need of any other faculty than the ape-like one of imitation. He who chooses his plan for himself employs all his faculties. He must use observation to see, reasoning and judgment to foresee, activity to gather materials for decision, discrimination to decide, and when he has decided, firmness and self-control to hold to his deliberate decision. And these qualities he requires and exercises exactly in proportion as the part of his conduct which he determines according to his own judgment and feelings is a large one.

That it is necessary for a person to exercise the faculties that Mill describes "according to his own judgment and feeling" is important. It means that not only is our humanity exercised in making choices, but it is also exercised in our decisions about how we make that choice.

The vital importance of choice, and the role choices play in constructing ourselves, possibly found its most significant expression in the writings of Jean-Paul Sartre, for whom the decision-making capacity of humans mattered more than anything. It was the capacity for choice and acting on it, having self-interest and being able to follow it, which gave people worth. For Sartre, there is no "essence" of what it is to be human—nothing matters—except our consciousness that we can make

---

[11] John Stuart Mill (1863a). *On Liberty*. In Mary Warnock (Ed.), *Utilitarianism, On Liberty, Essay on Bentham*. Glasgow: William Collins & Sons, pp. 187–188.

ourselves in whichever way that we choose. The most important thing about human consciousness is our awareness that we are self-aware.[12]

Of course, Sartre understood that we live in "society" and that the social context of our lives shapes the challenges and opportunities that confront us. He identified strongly with Marxism with its focus on class and the material basis of ideology. He understood however, that as individuals we are still capable of shaping our lives through the decisions we make; only when every freedom we have is taken away—including the power to end our own lives—are we completely victims of our circumstances.

For Sartre and his existentialist colleagues, the moral questions could only be answered by people individually in their approach to the choices in front of them and by the decisions they took. To him, if people did not recognise that they themselves were the source of their values, they could not recognise themselves as the moral agents that they were.[13]

From this perspective, it becomes clear how important "choice" is to our lives—not just in arriving at a decision but also in becoming ourselves. If we deny people the ability to make choices for themselves we stunt and constrain them; we deny them the potential to construct themselves and to take responsibility for the people they are. Many psychologists argue that allowing the woman to make the choice that is right for her is essential for her mental well-being. But perhaps it is also true for her existential well-being.

No one can be in doubt that abortion begins with an intentional decision by *someone*, and it follows that the key question is: who should that be? Should a woman's abortion be a matter for religious leaders? Politicians? Lawyers? Doctors? Or should the woman decide because she most understands the circumstances in which the biological accident of pregnancy has occurred? Because she will be affected most by the outcome of the decision and must bear the risks and consequences; because only if she makes that that decision for herself can she hold herself morally accountable.

---

[12] Jean-Paul Sartre (1943). *Being and Nothingness: An Essay on Phenomenological Ontology*, 2003 edn. London: Routledge.

[13] Jean-Paul Sartre (1946). *Existentialism and Humanism*, 2007 edn. New Haven: Yale University Press.

Challenges to Autonomy

From the outset, autonomy was contested by religious leaders, traditional conservatives and others who were distrustful of people making decisions for themselves. Traditionally, abortion's opponents have objected to autonomy-based demands for a woman's right to choose abortion on the grounds that abortion is not an exercise of self-determination *that causes no harm to another*.[14] Clearly, if one holds that the unborn entity is fully human and deserving of legal protection, there will be two lives to consider, although the considerations we have outlined in respect of personhood, and those about whether we can be compelled to use our bodies to support others, provides a moral defence of abortion choice that seems overriding.

More challenging arguments against autonomy are those that have been explored within feminism. These tend to come from two perspectives, which are related. Some critics disparage autonomy as a "masculinist" obsession linked to freedom, individualism and self-reliance at the expense of "social solidarity." This is seen to belittle the importance of co-dependence, which is understood to be of more concern to women, and to encourage "separation, and isolation in the war against all."[15]

An alternative but related critique of autonomy draws on a structuralist feminism approach. This holds that that the subordinate position of women which results from their oppression in patriarchal, capitalist society, leaves them with little—or even no—scope for autonomy. Thus it follows that any type of reasoning that links discussions of rights, freedom and autonomy to abortion is fallacious and treats pregnant women as self-interested and isolated, detached from the network of relationships and social circumstances by which their personal preferences are constructed.

Currently, especially in North America, as we considered in the previous chapter, a number of these arguments have enjoyed a revival.

---

[14] Francis J. Beckwith (2007). *Defending Life: A Moral and Legal Case Against Abortion*. Cambridge: Cambridge University Press, p. 124.

[15] M. A. Glendon (1987). *Abortion and Divorce in Western Law: American Failures, European Challenges*. Cambridge, MA: Harvard University Press, p. 58.

The protagonists have taken communitarian arguments previously asso-ciated with socialist feminism in the 1970s and 1980s and rebadged them as claims for reproductive justice that pay special attention to the connectedness of others, especially to the way different aspects of our lives intersect.

Self or Community?

Some feminist thinkers believe that the different reproductive roles of men and women lead women to view "individuality" in a different way. This means that women's experience of "being human" is significantly different to that of men because it "includes the counter-autonomous experience of a shared physical identity between woman and fetus, as well as the counter-autonomous experience of the emotional and psychological bond between mother and infant."[16]

Catherine MacKinnon, a professor at the University of Michigan law school, a foundational voice among the more radical feminist critics, frames notions of autonomy and private decision-making as a major problem for women because, she argues, "women have no privacy," in the sense that privacy can be understood in a positive way, because in the private world, especially the privacy of sex and intimate relation-ships, men are most able to dominate women. She sees abortion not as a means for women to exercise a choice, but for men to dominate them more. "Abortion," she says, "facilitates women's heterosexual availability" because under conditions of gender inequality, "sexual liberation in this sense does not free women; it frees male sexual aggression."[17] This is an expression of the view that women are, by their nature, and the nature of society, victims of men, and reluctantly *submit* to heterosexual sex. This is the same view that led the poet and essayist Adrienne Rich to write: "Abortion is violence ... It is the offspring, and will continue to

---

16 Robin West (1992). The Difference in Women's Hedonic Lives: A Phenomenological Critique of Feminist Legal Theory. In Mary Joe Frug (Ed.), *Women and the Law*. Westbury: Foundation Press, p. 823.

17 Catherine A. MacKinnon (1987). Roe v. Wade: A Study in Male Ideology. In *Feminism Unmodified, Discourses on Life and Law*. Cambridge, MA: Harvard University Press.

be the accuser of a more persuasive and prevalent violence, the violence of rapism."[18]

Women, then, are seen as having an impaired autonomy—either as a generalised consequence of socialisation, or specifically because of the inferior position they occupy within the social hierarchy. MacKinnon goes as far as to conclude: "women are in fact not full people in the sense that men are allowed to become." The experience of "growing up female in a male-dominated society," she observes, has an effect that "can be understood as a distortion of self." And so it follows that "understanding women's conditions leads to the conclusion that women are damaged."[19] This sits uncomfortably with demands for women's equality because women *are* competent to take responsibility for their lives and make decisions for themselves. It has also laid the basis for an opposition to abortion based on the need to protect women from themselves, which is a role that some groups with a more traditional anti-abortion perspective have been happy to assume.

Taking possession of the rhetoric around the need for a feminist "ethic of care,"[20] some opponents of abortion have turned to offering practical support for women in the form of "pro-life" pregnancy counselling. For some, it has been a cynical manoeuvre to exploit the complexity of women's decision-making and direct them to "choose life,"[21] but others genuinely see themselves as applying feminist values to an area in which women are damaged by their ability to make an unbiased choice for themselves.[22]

As Joan Chrisler reminds us, reproductive decisions are often painful and difficult:

---

[18] Adrienne Rich (1976). *Of Woman Born* cited in Louis P. Pojman and Francis J. Beckwith (1998). *The Abortion Controversy: 25 Years After Roe v. Wade, A Reader*, 2nd edn. London: Wadsworth, p. 96.

[19] Catherine MacKinnon (1991). *Towards a Feminist Theory of the State*. Cambridge, MA: Harvard University Press, p. 103.

[20] Carol Gilligan (1982). *In a Different Voice: Psychological Theory and Women's Development*. Cambridge, MA: Harvard University Press.

[21] Melanie Symonds (1996). *And Still They Weep: Personal Stories of Abortion*. London: SPUC Educational Research Trust.

[22] Angela Kennedy (Ed.) (1997). *Swimming Against the Tide: Feminist Dissent on the Issue of Abortion*. Dublin: Open Air Press.

For example, if a woman uses contraceptives or seeks abortion because she cannot afford to raise a child, because of her own ill health (or a serious medical condition of the fetus) or because of insecurity due to war or natural disaster, does she experience her decision as a choice?[23]

Yet surely the answer to this rhetorical question must be: "Yes." Daily life routinely requires people to decide which is the least bad option. That we cannot always make a choice that we want does not invalidate our ability to decide.

Freedom of choice does not guarantee that a woman will benefit from choosing between those options available to her. Even if we have some degree of control over our reproductive lives, it may be the case that we have few realistic alternatives. A 15-year-old girl may want to have her child, but have no means to care for it. And the decision to have an abortion at twenty-three weeks may appear to mean nothing when no doctor will perform it.

Emily Jackson argues: "The space within which reproductive autonomy can be exercised will always be comparatively small but [...] possessing some control over the direction of one's life is a necessary constituent part of a 'good' or agreeable existence."[24] In other words, we want the control we can and do have because those choices we can make matter to us. Furthermore, the limitations on the ability of individuals to lead self-authored lives should be a reason to extend the scope of autonomy, not to give up on it altogether.

The demand that women have the right to exercise their reproductive choice, to make an autonomous decision for themselves, is a demand that has as much relevance to a woman in the ghetto as it does for the woman in the mansion.

The liberal, humanist tradition associating personhood with rationality and consciousness, and emphasising the importance of liberty and self-determination, invokes a universalistic standard to which all, regardless of poverty and privilege, race or religion can lay claim. This was the philosophical basis for the anti-slavery and feminist movements in the

---

[23] Joan Chrisler (Ed.) (2012). *Reproductive Justice: A Global Concern*. Santa Barbara: Praeger, pp. 2–3.

[24] Emily Jackson (2001). *Regulating Reproduction: Law, Technology and Autonomy*. Oxford: Hart.

nineteenth century, which argued that neither rationality nor reason was the exclusive preserve of white male property owners, and that autonomy should be accorded to all with the capacity to exercise it.

Petchesky remarks that liberation movements of that time "did *not* argue that *because* women and slaves breathe, have human bodies, or are able to copulate and produce human offspring they should be accorded full rights as citizens. Such an argument would have been perceived as intrinsically degrading in a rationalistic-humanistic culture and yielding to the very stereotypes used to oppress women and blacks." Nor did they argue simply for better housing, payment for work, education or health-care. Rather it was the claim to "dignity" and "humanity" that comes from possessing reason, consciousness and free will that underpinned the claim that feminist and black leaders invoked in asserting their claims to full personhood—with the self-determination and freedom that follows from that.[25]

Of course, no woman chooses to have an abortion as an expression of her autonomy or freedom. She does so to resolve a specific practical problem and usually these are the kinds of problems that others are sympathetic to. Abortion opponents conjure up fanciful examples of what unqualified support for abortion might mean: support for an abortion so that a girl can "fit into her prom dress," "go on a skiing holiday," "avoid looking fat at a party." Abortion supporters counter that women do not, in practice, request abortion for trivial reasons and there is always a "good reason," even if the woman does not disclose it.

This may, or may not, be true. But qualified support for abortion—supporting a woman's decision only if it fits with someone else's view of what is right—is simply not supporting a woman's choice at all.

As we considered earlier, today it has become fashionable to demonise autonomy as "neoliberal" or "conservative." The concept of "reproductive justice" is presented as an alternative that is more representative of what people need in a diverse society, since it takes note of a range of social concerns.

---

[25] Rosalind Pollack Petchesky (1986). *Abortion and Woman's Choice: The State, Sexuality and Reproductive Freedom*. London: Verso, p. 330.

It is unfortunate that justice and autonomy have been counter-posed in this way. Justice is a vague term, which is defined in many ways. Not only do different nations have different ideas of justice, but even in our own individual minds, our sense of what is just and unjust may be driven by different standards at different times. We may resolve our view of what is "just punishment" (should a sentence be set to punish an individual or to send a message to society?) in a different way according to the crime that has been committed. We might arrive at a view of "just punishment" through different routes of thinking than the way that we arrive at ideas about "just distribution of resources."

J. S. Mill saw the idea of justice as being connected to Kant's fundamental principle of morals, which he understood to be "we ought to shape our conduct by a rule which all rational beings might adopt *with benefit to their collective interest*" (original emphasis).[26] Mill's definition is broad and general, and more helpful that any we can lift from modern charters and declarations, because it is based on a clear foundational principle. Mill described justice as "a name for certain classes of moral rules, which concern the essentials of human well-being more nearly … than any other rules for the guidance of life."

Mill insisted that central to the moral rules that comprise justice were "[t]he moral rules which forbid mankind to hurt one another (in which *we must never forget to include wrongful interference with each other's freedom*)" (my emphasis).

These he saw as "more vital to human well-being than any other maxims." So, in valuing autonomy, Mill did not deride justice—rather he described it as "the chief part, and incomparably the most binding part, of all morality."[27]

The principles of "individual freedom," "autonomy" or "self- determination," which emphasise the importance of choice, should not be seen as hostile to notions of what is just. Instead we see them as foundational to what is just, and understand that there can be no justice without them.

---

[26] John Stuart Mill (1863b). *Utilitarianism*. In Mary Warnock (Ed.), *Utilitarianism, On Liberty, Essay on Bentham*. Glasgow: William Collins & Sons, p. 308.

[27] John Stuart Mill (1863b). *Utilitarianism*. In Mary Warnock (Ed.), *Utilitarianism, On Liberty, Essay on Bentham*. Glasgow: William Collins & Sons, pp. 315–316.

Reproductive justice is a particularly thin and imprecise concept that means a range of things to different thinkers and activists. One of its champions suggests that broadly it "implies that people are treated fairly, equitably and respectfully," and "situates the work in the concept of the greater social justice movement."[28]

The principal beliefs of Kant and Mill, which emphasise the importance of the integrity of the individual and their own agency, are thought to diminish the "interconnectedness" of people as social beings; "it disregards that the necessary premise for such persons to exist is the prior human world of interrelationships, interdependence—in short, of social life."[29]

Such a caricatured version of autonomy as a brutal expression of individualism which fails to acknowledge community is an invention of conservative thinking that has been repeated so often that it has acquired an assumed truth, particularly within some schools of feminist thought.

It is beyond doubt that we are shaped by cultural expectations and relationships, and that our decisions are influenced by economic, social and emotional contexts. However, the fact that we are not always able to get what we want should not lead us to conclude that it is meaningless to want it.

Our preferences may well be socially constructed and shaped by our life circumstances, but that does not make them invalid. Our values and beliefs are not all of our own creative invention. Class, nationality, religion and parents heavily influence them. Society plays a huge role in shaping us into the people we are. We are not people of our own making, however much we wish this were so. But the fact that we cannot choose who we *are* does not mean that we should not be allowed to choose what we do. Our reproductive choices are shaped by multiple external influences, but they are the only choices we have, and they are, therefore, of critical importance to our sense of self.

The decision to have an abortion for example, is made because for a variety of reasons this particular woman does not want to carry her

---

[28] Joan Chrisler (Ed.) (2012). *Reproductive Justice: A Global Concern.* Santa Barbara: Praeger, p. 3.

[29] Rosalind Pollack Petchesky (1986). *Abortion and Woman's Choice: The State, Sexuality and Reproductive Freedom.* London: Verso, p. 343.

pregnancy to term. Many of the reasons behind her decision will almost certainly be beyond her control, but that does not mean that she does not have strong preferences about what happens to her now. And the fact that her social and economic circumstances are reasons should not lead us to ignore what are *her* deeply preferences. As Jackson explains:

> Even if we recognize that social forces may shape and constrain our choices, our sense of being the author of our own actions, especially when they pertain to something as personal as reproduction, is profoundly valuable to us. We cannot believe that all our preferences are irredeemably "not ours" without our sense of self effectively collapsing.[30]

The principle of autonomy does not, and has never meant, "going it alone," or "doing it for yourself," without reference to or concern for others. Far from it; our understanding of autonomy cannot be separated from a sense of community and the role that we, as individuals play in it, and how we are affected by it, but also where public interests stop and where private interests triumph. Helen Reece, Associate Professor of Law at the London School of Economics, has studied the impact of rejecting the concept of women's autonomy on divorce, since this is also an area of life in which women's ability to make choices is questioned.

Reece sees liberalism and communitarianism as having different conceptions of shared relations: "While liberalism envisages *contingently shared* relations, communitarianism endorses *essentially shared* relations."[31] The difference is essentially in how we believe our identity (our innerself) is constructed. Are we as individuals primarily a product of the shared relationships we have in our communities? Or do we bring to our communities an identity that is more than the sum of its influences? This is important to the way that we see ourselves, because without a private, separate identity that is our own, we are truly nothing other than what others want us to be.

---

[30] Emily Jackson (2001). *Regulating Reproduction: Law, Technology and Autonomy.* Oxford: Hart, p. 7.

[31] Helen Reece (2003). *Divorcing Responsibly.* Oxford: Hart, p. 21.

For a woman to be herself, she needs to "make and follow her own life plan according to her convictions"[32] but that is not to say she is pursuing her own interests, selfishly, with disregard for those around her. And it is certainly not the case, as the communitarian case seems to imply, that strong individuals make for a fragmented society. It is rather the opposite: the stronger our sense of self-identity and purpose, the more effectively we can take on our social roles. As the philosopher Alasdair MacIntyre puts it:

> I am someone's son or daughter, someone else's cousin or uncle; I am a citizen of this or that city, a member of this or that guild or profession; I belong to this clan, that tribe, this nation. Hence what is good for me has to be good for one who inhabits these roles.[33]

The feminist thinker, Robin West, sees this too:

> Women need the freedom to make reproductive decisions not merely to vindicate a right to be left alone, but often to strengthen their ties with others; to plan responsibly and have a family for which they can provide, to pursue professional or work commitments made to the outside world, or to continue supporting their families and communities.[34]

West acknowledges that for some women, decisions are driven by the "harsh reality of a financially irresponsible partner, a society indifferent to the care of children, and a workplace incapable of accommodating or supporting the needs of working parents." She concludes:

> Whatever the reason, the decision to abort is almost invariably made within a web of interlocking, competing and often irreconcilable responsibilities and commitments.

The twentieth and early twenty-first centuries seem to have been dominated by battles between natural determinism (through the expression

---

[32] See for example Will Kymlicka (1989). *Liberalism, Community and Culture.* Oxford: Oxford University Press, pp. 9–19.

[33] Alasdair MacIntyre (1985). *After Virtue: A Study in Moral Theory.* London: Duckworth, p. 220.

[34] Robin West (1990). Taking Freedom Seriously. *Harvard Law Review,* 43(104), 84–85.

of our genes) and social determinism (through the dominance of social norms). The one determination that has been utterly neglected is that of the self. Contemporary society diminishes and denies an individual's sense of self-determination to the point where we are seen as being driven (or nudged) along our life course with little control over where we end up.

If people are simply products of their environments, it seems fatuous to maintain that our agency has any importance or significance. If our decisions are entirely socially constructed, then choices become just a function determined by their context. Individuals' conception of what is the right action, even of what is in their own self-interest, is merely a function of their particular social position, and not a matter of personal moral judgement at all. But as Warnock wisely observes:

> Freedom cannot emerge except against a background of unchosen elements. But these elements do not *restrict* freedom; we are totally free in the manner in which we experience these elements. Our freedom to choose ourselves is limitless.[35]

While we cannot choose the circumstances we confront, we can choose how we react to them. Along with Warnock: "I can choose my reaction to my facticity."

Individual reproductive choice and personal autonomy are two notions that are indivisibly bound together and specifically relate to the previous discussion to personhood. The exercise of personal choice with regard to abortion as with anything else, requires two things: the *liberty* from controlling influences to be able to make a decision for oneself, and *agency*, which means the capacity for intentional action.

The importance of bodily integrity—the belief that our bodies are our own—is one important aspect of our claim to our self-determination. Equally important is our freedom to make decisions for ourselves. Our *right* to follow the course we think is right, along with our *responsibility* and moral accountability for what we do, is vital to our standing as "persons." When a woman, upon discovering that she is pregnant, weighs

[35] Mary Warnock (1970). *Existentialism*. Oxford: Oxford University Press, p. 112.

her options to work out what is best for herself (and others), considers how she feels about what is "right" and decides on a course of action for which she will be responsible, she is demonstrating what it is to be an autonomous moral agent. When society denies her that right and that responsibility it undermines the very essence of her personhood. In making a choice about the future of her pregnancy, a woman engages in an act of moral self-governance. She decides for herself, according to her own conscience, what is right for her. The fact that it is *she* who decides what is right for her—and not anyone else—is important in itself.

This ability to work out a plan for our lives, to be authors of our own biographies, is fundamental to our sense of self, because it is an expression of our self-consciousness. The Canadian philosopher Charles Taylor goes as far as to claim that "To be a person, the individual's life plan, choices and sense of self must be attributed to the individual as their point of origin."[36] If we turn that around, we can see that to strip away an individual's life plan, choices and sense of self is to strip away part of their personhood.

Making a choice is in itself a demonstration of a freedom of sorts—the freedom to influence and take responsibility for what happens next. Our lives are made richer if we can direct them according to our personal values and convictions—even if our lives are not made richer by the options available to us. The point is this: life is full of decisions, and it is who makes them that matters.

Socially constructed value systems do not predetermine all the decisions we make, although they can shape them. People in similar situations make different choices based on their values. The abject poverty that drives one woman to have an abortion may drive another to decide to have a child that she places for adoption. A diagnosis of Down Syndrome may compel one woman to end her pregnancy, while another decides to embrace the child as "special." The fact that a woman is black, or poor, or alone or stigmatised clearly will influence her decision—but that does not take away her capacity to decide, to make a choice.

---

[36] Charles Taylor (1985). The Concept of a Person. In C. Taylor (Ed.), *Human Agency and Language: Philosophical Papers 1*. Cambridge: Cambridge University Press, p. 97.

This is not a "masculinist" argument. Dworkin argues[37] "that women are often dominated by men makes it more rather than less important to insist that women should have a constitutionally protected right to control the use of their own bodies."

Our ability to make moral judgements, decisions and choices is a precondition of human development in a free society. To deny that women have the capacity to make reproductive choices denies their moral agency; it denies their humanity. It is unfortunate that in denying the importance of individual autonomy, certain strands of feminism have taken positioned themselves in opposition to the just fight for choice.

---

[37] Ronald Dworkin (1996). *Life's Dominion: An Argument About Abortion, Euthanasia, and Individual Freedom.* London: HarperCollins, p. 53.

10

The Most Important Freedom

This journey started with a discussion about where abortion sits in modern life; it closes with thoughts on where our thinking about abortion needs to be.

There is a strong and compelling case for a woman to make her own choices about the future of her pregnancy—and for abortion—if that is her choice. That choice should be legitimate and legal without regard to her reasons or her circumstances.

Abortion is a fact of modern life. It is necessary in a society where women expect to be more than mothers and where they expect to plan their futures. It may be essential to a society that aims for "planned parenthood" and families made up of responsible, willing parents and wanted children. And in those societies that do not yet benefit from the infrastructure that comes with development, safe, legal abortion services may be necessary to reduce the damage and death that follows repeated unwanted deliveries and desperate, unsafe abortions.

However, all these reasons for abortion are beside the point. What matters most of all is that women should have the right to make their own decisions about pregnancy, privately and accountable to no person except those whom they invite to share in their decision. Just as women

© The Author(s), under exclusive license to Springer Nature Switzerland AG 2021
A. Furedi, *The Moral Case for Abortion*,
https://doi.org/10.1007/978-3-030-90189-9_10

are responsible for the children they bring into the world, so they are responsible for the pregnancies that they terminate.

No society that truly respects women's equality and individual conscience can tolerate interference with how a woman comes to decide on the future of her pregnancy. The contents of her womb are hers and hers alone, by virtue of their location in her womb. How she values the embryo or foetus that she carries inside her body is for her to decide.

The responsibility for bringing a potential child into the world, allowing it to develop into a person with human interests of its own, is hers because it requires her body. This is a commitment no one else can give, and, in a society that values freedom, the commitment to childbirth should be freely given, and a woman can only *freely* commit when she has an alternative choice.

While the foetus is still in her body, its life is hers and the decisions as to its future must be hers, because its future is her future.

The decision to choose abortion—to end a foetal life before it knows it is alive—will always be contested. Different people have their own views on when life begins and ends. But if we believe in personal freedom and liberty, and uphold the right to freedom of conscience, then on the fundamentally moral matter of abortion the choice must be the woman's. A compassionate and humane society will provide the means for her to exercise that choice as early as possible and as late as necessary.

Medicine has had its own scheme of ethics for more than 2500 years.[1] The notion of *Primum non nocere*—above all do no harm—is key to the Hippocratic tradition. Those who see the termination of pregnancy as killing, causing offence and "depriving others of the goods of life," cite it often as an ethical prohibition on abortion since these are regarded as rules of nonmaleficence.[2]

Ultimately, unless we follow a code of religious belief, our only way of verifying whether something is right or wrong is by assessing its impact on human life—that is, by considering its effect on the welfare and consciousness of those persons who make up our human community.

---

[1] See Raanan Gillon (1986). *Philosophical Medical Ethics*. Chichester: Wiley, pp. 9–14.

[2] Tom L. Beauchamp and James F. Childress (2013). *Principles of Biomedical Ethics*, 7th edn. Oxford: Oxford University Press, pp. 150–154.

Whether a woman can be compelled to carry a foetus and give birth to a baby is just as much a moral question as those raised about the value of the foetus. If the benefit of abortion is that it enables women to exercise their freedom, clearly the maleficence (the harm) is in its denial.

Abortion concerns the value of life, more than death. A woman chooses abortion because she values *her* life and her future more than she values the life in her womb. And why should she not make that decision for herself? If we assume she is self-conscious, self-aware and capable of moral determination (and why should we not?) why should her choice to live her life according to her conscience be subject to veto?

To deprive a woman of the right to choose abortion deprives her of "the goods of life" since it deprives her of the future she wants for herself. It deprives her of returning to a "non-pregnant" present, and the future that she planned, even though this is an option that modern medicine can deliver to her safely.

Yes, abortion involves a "killing," in the sense that it stops a beating heart, but not in the sense that it stops a person from living. The end of a life in the womb does not compare with infanticide, euthanasia or any other taking of human life. Abortion does not assault an individual that is living a biologically independent existence of its own. Whatever the foetus experiences, it is not human life as we know it with its joys or sorrows, fears, hopes and expectations. It knows nothing of itself, nor of others. And others know nothing of it.

Claims that the foetus is part of human society, that the embryo is "one of us," are irrational. The only person with whom the foetus has a relationship is the woman in whose body it resides—and even that relationship is one of unconscious physical dependence. The reason why expectant mothers often talk about "meeting their baby" at birth is because this is the first time it is separate and distinct from her.

Comparisons between abortion and the killing of people betray an appalling and degraded sense of what it means to be human. Can opponents of abortion be serious when they compare society's tolerance of abortion to the Nazi genocide against Jews?[3] Who can truly compare the grievous suffering of those rounded up, impounded and executed

---

[3] F. Lagard Smith (1990). *When Choice Becomes God.* Oregon: Harvest House, pp. 171–172.

or worked to death, to the death of an entity with no human understanding? The qualities that the embryo lacks are precisely those that make the terror of extermination so dreadful for individual people: the capacity for self-consciousness, the capacity for rational thought, the capacity to imagine a future for oneself, the capacity to remember a past involving oneself and the capacity for being a subject of non-momentary interests.[4] The qualities that make us individuals who want to live are the same qualities as those that make us want to choose the path of our lives, which may sometimes include the choice of abortion.

If we respect an individual's autonomy and their bodily integrity, and if we believe that people should be allowed to make private personal decisions according to their own conscience, there can be no moral offence in making or assisting the choice of abortion. We can value all that the embryo or foetus is, and we can respect its potential, but still accept that however significant it is as a human life's biological beginning, a woman's complete life (which is so much more than a beating heart and DNA) matters more.

It is a travesty of our freedom for abortion to be restricted by criminal law. The criminalisation of abortion, which has undermined reproductive rights and freedoms in almost every country for centuries, has no place in a modern liberal society. Currently, few national laws recognise abortion as a private moral decision to be made by the woman herself, throughout pregnancy. Even countries with relatively liberal laws assume that abortion is an exceptional procedure requiring explanations and justifications. Why should termination of pregnancy not be subject only to the laws and regulations and consents and permissions that apply to treatments of equivalent complexity and risk? Criminal statutes do not control when other medical procedures should be allowed, and it is bizarre for doctors to be criminalised when they accede to a woman's request to a safe and consented procedure.

Even when abortion laws are interpreted liberally by progressive doctors, they exceptionalise abortion by requiring a woman to account for her decision. They ignore the principles of autonomy and self-determination and fail to accept that our bodies are our own—always.

---

[4] Michael Tooley (1983). *Abortion and Infanticide*. Oxford: Clarendon Press, p. 170.

A woman's right to her body does not lessen when she is pregnant; she is just as much a person as she was before.

Abortion needs to be acknowledged for what it is—a safe, effective means of birth control that can be subject to the same clinical governance and regulatory requirements as other treatments. The clinical risks of an early abortion are not significantly higher than those of contraception, so why should it matter morally or legally if a woman chooses to practise birth control through this method instead of another? After all, "bringing a period on" was common practice in the 1920s and 1930s—and now medicine provides safe, effective, reliable medication that is conveniently packaged, complete with instructions. In most countries, only the law and judgemental attitudes get in the way.

Whether an ethical divide exists between abortion and contraception is a matter of moral judgement based on the rightness of one and the wrongness of the other. Technically and legally, there is a bright line of difference between abortion and contraception: abortion *ends* a pregnancy; contraception *prevents* one. But the moral significance of this distinction is less clear. It can only be determined by conscience and never be determined by courts.

Reproductive choice matters for women. Naturally, reproductive health is important, but choice matters just as much, and the choices that women make about abortion should not be exceptionalised and seen as so very different from the many reproductive choices that they make during their lives and manage without difficulty. They choose their method of contraception; they choose whether they want to have children (and how many and when); they choose how to give birth, and how to feed their newborn. Of course, women may not receive what they want, but usually they have a preference.

Women make moral choices all the time. An abortion may be a difficult choice that a woman would rather not make. She may have little control over her circumstances and wish her decision could be different. But this is no different than many decisions we make and women are no less competent to make pregnancy choices than they are to make other life-changing decisions—such as whether or not to marry, or whether or not to divorce. And, certainly, no one else is better situated to make a choice in this regard than the person whose life will be most affected by the outcome.

This is not to say women are always right. Abortion may not always be the right choice for the woman who makes it. She may come to feel she was mistaken, just as a woman may feel her choice to bear a child was wrong. While it is in our nature to have hopes for the future, we can never see into the future, or predict what will happen. But this is not exclusive to pregnancy choices; it is the nature of choice itself that we gamble that the decision we make will be the right one for as at that time. That we *personally* have actively selected an outcome gives us responsibility for that decision.

The responsibility of personal, individual choice is a burden that we might often prefer to avoid, but responsibility is the price we pay for the right to shape our own destinies.

The language of "autonomy," "bodily integrity," "rights" and "self-determination" is as relevant today as it was during the struggles of the Enlightenment, and it is as relevant to the world female world as is to that of men.

Always when we think of abortion we should consider this: a woman who is unwillingly pregnant faces a terrifying loss of control over her life and her future. Although she cannot control all of the facts of her life, she can choose how she responds to them. Every woman should be allowed to decide for herself the nature and scope of the obligations she chooses to assume towards her developing foetus. A civilised society would allow that choice to be as free it could possibly and practicably be.

The importance of abortion choice is not only the solution it delivers, but also what the act of choosing does to us. Considering abortion, Dworkin wisely commented:

> Decisions about life and death are the most important, the most crucial for forming or expressing personality that anyone makes; we think it crucial to get these decisions right, but also to make them in character, and for ourselves.[5]

---

[5] Ronald Dworkin (1996). *Life's Dominion: An Argument about Abortion, Euthanasia, and Individual Freedom.* London: HarperCollins, p. 239.

The freedom to make moral choices is the most important freedom we have; the freedom to act on our moral choices is the most important privilege we can claim.

Select Bibliography

Learned journal references, statistical sources and citations are included in the notes. These are the books I have considered most useful.

Aristotle. (2004 ed.). *Nicomachean Ethics*. Harmondsworth: Penguin Classics.

Arendt, Hannah. (2003). *Responsibility and Judgement*. New York: Random House.

Barrow, R. (2007). *An Introduction to Moral Philosophy and Moral Education*. London: Routledge.

Beauchamp, T. E., & Childress, J. F. (2013). *Principles of Biomedical Ethics*, 7th edn. Oxford: Oxford University Press.

Beckwith, F. J. (2007). *Defending Life: A Moral and Legal Case Against Abortion Choice*. Cambridge: Cambridge University Press.

Beckwith, J. (1998). *The Abortion Controversy: 25 Years After* Roe v. Wade, *a Reader*, 2nd edn. London: Wadsworth.

Bristow, J. (2009). *Standing Up to Supernanny*. Exeter: Societas Imprint Academic.

British Social Attitudes Survey. (2015). London: NatCen Social Research.

Cecil, R. (Ed.). (1996). *The Anthropology of Pregnancy Loss: Comparative Studies in Miscarriage, Stillbirth and Neonatal Death*. Oxford: Berg.

Chrisler, J. (Ed.). (2012). *Reproductive Justice: A Global Concern.* Santa Barbara: Praeger.

Clinton, H. R. (1996). *It Takes a Village: And Other Lessons Children Teach Us.* New York: Simon & Schuster.

Coote, A., & Campbell, B. (1987). *Sweet Freedom: The Struggle for Women's Liberation.* London: Virago.

Dennett, D. C. (1996). *Kinds of Minds: Towards an Understanding of Consciousness.* New York: HarperCollins.

Derr, M. K., MacNair, R., & Naranjo-Huebl, L. (2005). *Prolife Feminism: Yesterday and Today.* Kansas City: Feminism and Non-Violent Studies Association.

Devereux, G. (1955). *A Study of Abortion in Primitive Societies; A Typological, Distributional, and Dynamic Analysis of the Prevention of Birth in 400 Pre-industrial Societies.* New York: Julian Press.

Dickens, B. M. (2014). The Right to Conscience. In R. J. Cook, J. N. Erdman, & B. M. Dickens (Eds.), *Abortion Law in Transnational Perspectives: Cases and Controversies.* Philadelphia: University of Pennsylvania Press.

Dombrowski, D. A., & Deltete, R. (2000). *A Brief, Liberal, Catholic Defense of Abortion.* Urbana: University of Illinois Press.

Dubow, S. (2011). *Ourselves Unborn: A History of the Fetus in Modern America.* Oxford: Oxford University Press.

Duncan, S., Edwards, R., & Alexander, C. (2010). *Teenage Parenthood: What's the Problem?* London: Tufnell Press.

Dworkin, R. (1993). *Life's Dominion: An Argument about Abortion, Euthanasia, and Individual Freedom.* London: HarperCollins.

Dworkin, R. (2013). *Religion Without God.* Cambridge, MA: Harvard University Press.

Edwards, R. (1989). *Life Before Birth.* London: Hutchinson.

Engels, Fredrich. (1884). *The Origin of the Family, Private Property and the State.* Harmondsworth: Penguin.

Fryer, P. (1965). *The Birth Controllers.* London: Secker & Warburg.

Furedi, A. (1988). Wrong But the Right Thing to Do: Public Opinion and Abortion. In E. Lee (Ed.), *Abortion Law and Politics Today.* London: Macmillan.

Furedi, A. (1995). *Unplanned Pregnancy: Your Choices.* Oxford: Oxford University Press.

Furedi, F. (1997). *Population and Development: A Critical Introduction.* Cambridge: Polity Press.

Furedi, F. (2004). *Therapy Culture: Cultivating Vulnerability in an Uncertain Age.* London: Routledge.

Furedi, F. (2008). *Paranoid Parenting: Why Ignoring the Experts May Be Best for Your Child*. London: Bloomsbury.

Furedi, F. (2013). *Authority: A Sociological History*. Cambridge: Cambridge University Press.

Furedi, F. (2020). *Why Borders Matter: Why Humanity Must Relearn the Art of Drawing Boundaries*. London: Routledge.

George, R., & Tollesfen, C. (2011). *Embryo: A Defense of Human Life*. Princeton: The Witherspoon Institute.

Gilligan, C. (1982). *In a Different Voice: Psychological Theory and Women's Development*. Cambridge, MA: Harvard University Press.

Gillon, R. (1986). *Philosophical Medical Ethics*. Chichester: Wiley.

Glendon, M. A. (1987). *Abortion and Divorce in Western Law: American Failures, European Challenges*. Cambridge, MA: Harvard University Press.

Greasley, Kate. (2017). *Arguments About Abortion: Personhood, Motherhood and Law*. Oxford: Oxford University Press.

Hadley, J. (1996). *Abortion: Between Freedom and Necessity*. London: Virago.

Hallesby, O. (1933). *Conscience*, 1950 edn. London: Intervarsity Fellowship.

Harris, J. (1985). *The Value of Life: An Introduction to Medical Ethics*. London: Routledge.

Harris, John and Soren Holm ed. (1998). *The Future of Human Reproduction*, Oxford University Press: Oxford

Hegel, G. W. F. (2001). *Philosophy of Right*, trans. S. W. Dyde. Kitchener: Batoche Books.

Hindell, K., & Simms, M. (1971). *Abortion Law Reformed*. London: Peter Owen.

Irving J. (1985). *The Cider House Rules*. Jonathon Cape: London

Jackson, E. (2001). *Regulating Reproduction: Law, Technology and Autonomy*. Oxford: Hart.

Joffe, Carole. (1995). *Doctors of Conscience: The Struggle to Provide Abortion Before and After*. Boston, MA: Roe v Wade Beacon Press.

Jones, R. K., & Dreweke, J. (2011). *Countering Conventional Wisdom: New Evidence on Religion and Contraceptive Use*. Washington, DC: Guttmacher Institute.

Kant, I. (1784). *An Answer to the Question: What Is Enlightenment?* 2009 edn. Harmondsworth: Penguin.

Kennedy, A. (Ed.). (1997). *Swimming Against the Tide: Feminist Dissent on the Issue of Abortion*. Dublin: Open Air Press.

Kenyon, E. (1986). *The Dilemma of Abortion*. London: Faber & Faber.

Keown, J. (1988). *Abortion Doctors and the Law: Some Aspects of the Legal Regulation of Abortion in England for 1803 to 1982*. Cambridge: Cambridge University Press.

Kevles, D. J. (1985). *In the Name of Eugenics: Genetics and the Uses of Human Heredity*. Harmondsworth: Penguin.

Korsgaard, Christine M. (2009). *Self Constitution: Agency, Identity and Integrity*. Oxford: Oxford University Press.

Kuhse, H., & Singer, P. (1985). *Should the Baby Live? The Problem of Handicapped Infants*. Oxford: Oxford University Press.

Kymlicka, W. (1989). *Liberalism, Community and Culture*. Oxford: Oxford University Press.

Lee, E. (2003). *Abortion, Motherhood and Mental Health: Medicalizing Reproduction in the United States and Great Britain*. New York: Aldine de Gruyter.

Lee, E. (Ed.), *Abortion Law and Politics Today*. Basingstoke: Palgrave Macmillan.

Lee, E., Bristow, J., Faircloth, C., & Macvarish, J. (2014). *Parenting Culture Studies*. London: Palgrave Macmillan.

Litchfield, M., & Kentish, S. (1974). *Babies for Burning*. London: Serpentine Press.

Locke, J. (1689). *An Essay Concerning Human Understanding*. Oxford: Oxford University Press

Luker, K. (1984). *Abortion and the Politics of Motherhood*. Berkeley: University of California Press.

MacIntyre, A. (1985). *After Virtue: A Study in Moral Theory*. London: Duckworth.

MacKinnon, C. A. (1987). *Roe v. Wade*: A Study in Male Ideology. In *Feminism Unmodified: Discourses on Life and Law*. Cambridge, MA: Harvard University Press.

MacKinnon, C. (1991). *Towards a Feminist Theory of the State*. Cambridge, MA: Harvard University Press.

Marshall, K. (1985). *Moral Panics and Victorian Values: Women and the Family in Thatcher's Britain*. London: Junius.

Mill, J. S. (1863a). *On Liberty*. In M. Warnock (Ed.), *Utilitarianism, On Liberty, Essay on Bentham*. Glasgow: William Collins & Sons.

Mill, J. S. (1863b). *Utilitarianism*. In M. Warnock (Ed.), *Utilitarianism, on Liberty, Essay on Bentham*. Glasgow: William Collins & Sons.

Mohr, C. J. (1978). *Abortion in America: The Origins and Evolution of National Policy*. Oxford: Oxford University Press.

Newman, K. (1996). *Fetal Positions: Individualism, Science and Visuality*. Stanford: Stanford University Press.

Nilsson, L. (1990). *A Child Is Born*. London: Doubleday.

Oderberg, D. S. (2000a). *Applied Ethics: A Non-Consequentialist Approach*. Oxford: Blackwell.

Oderberg, D. S. (2000b). *Moral Theory: A Non-Consequentialist Approach*. Oxford: Blackwell.

Ojankangas, Mika. (2013). *The Voice of Conscience: A political genealogy of Western ethical experience*, Bloomsbury: London

O'Neill, O ed. (1996). *The Sources of Normativity*. Cambridge: Cambridge University Press.

Overy, R. (2009). *The Morbid Age: Britain between the Wars*. London: Allen Lane.

Parker W. (2017). *Lifes's Work: A Moral Argument for Choice* New York: Atria

Petchesky, R. P. (1986). *Abortion and Women's Choice: The State, Sexuality, and Reproductive Freedom*. London: Verso.

Pluckrose, Helen and James Lindsay (2020) *How Universities Made Everything about Race, Gender, and Identity – and Why this Harms Everybody*, London: Swift

Pojman, L., & Beckwith, F. J. (1998). *The Abortion Controversy: 25 Years After Roe v. Wade, a Reader*, 2nd edn. Belmont: Wadsworth.

Pollitt, K. (2014). *Pro: Reclaiming Abortion Rights*. New York: Picador.

Prija, J. V. (1992). *Birth Traditions and Modern Pregnancy Care*. Shaftesbury, Dorset: Element.

Ramsey, P. (1968). The Morality of Abortion. In E. Shils et al. (Eds.), *Life or Death: Ethics and Options*. Portland: Reed College.

Reece, H. (2003). *Divorcing Responsibly*. Oxford: Hart.

Ross, L. J., Roberts, L., Derkas, E., Peoples, W., and Bridgewater, P. Toure ed. (2017). *Radical Reproductive Justice: Foundations, Theory, Practice, Critique*. New York City: Feminist Press.

Rue, V. M. (1995). Post-abortion Syndrome: A Variant of Post-traumatic Stress Disorder. In P. Doherty (Ed.), *Post-abortion Syndrome: Its Wide Ramifications*. Dublin: Four Courts Press.

Russell, B. (1946). *The History of Western Philosophy and Its Connection with Political and Social Circumstances from the Earliest Times to the Present Day*. London: George Allen and Unwin.

Salecl, Renata. (2010). *The Tyranny of Choice*. Profile Books: London

Saletan, W. (2004). *Bearing Right: How Conservatives Won the Abortion Wars.* Berkeley: University of California Press.

Sartre, J.-P. (1943). *Being and Nothingness: An Essay on Phenomenological Ontology,* 2003 edn. London: Routledge.

Sartre, J.-P. (1945). *The Age of Reason,* 1986 edn. Penguin: London.

Sartre, J.-P. (1946). *Existentialism and Humanism,* 2007 edn. New Haven: Yale University Press.

Schneider, W. H. (1990). *Quality and Quantity: The Quest for Biological Regeneration in Twentieth-Century France.* Cambridge: Cambridge University Press.

Schwarz, S. D. (1990). *The Moral Question of Abortion.* Chicago: Loyola University Press.

Sheldon, S. (1997). *Beyond Control: Medical Power and Abortion Law.* London: Pluto Press.

Silliman, J., Fried, M. G., Ross, L., & Gutiérrez, E. R. (2004). *Undivided Rights: Women of Color Organise for Reproductive Justice,* 1st edn. Boston: South End Press.

Singer, P. (1995). *Animal Liberation,* 2nd edn. London: Thorsons.

Smith, F. L. (1990). *When Choice Becomes God.* Oregon: Harvest House

Stock, K. (2021). *Material Girls: Why Reality Matters for Feminism.* London: Fleet

Stopes, M. C. (1929). *Mother England: A Contemporary History.* London: John Bale, Sons and Danielsson, p. 137.

Symonds, M. (1996). *And Still They Weep: Personal Stories of Abortion.* London: SPUC Educational Research Trust.

Thaler, R. H., & Sunstein, C. R. (2009). *Nudge: Improving Decisions about Health, Wealth and Happiness.* London: Penguin Books.

Tooley, M. (1983). *Abortion and Infanticide.* Oxford: Clarendon Press

Trussell, J. (2011). Contraceptive Failure. In R. A. Hatcher, J. Trussell, A. L. Nelson, W. Cates, D. Kowal & M Policar (Eds.), *Contraceptive Technology: Twentieth Revised Edition.* New York: Ardent Media.

Warnock, M. (1970). *Existentialism.* Oxford: Oxford University Press.

Weitz, T. A. (2015). Rethinking the Mantra That Abortion Should Be "Safe, Legal, and Rare". In C. Joffe & J. Reich (Eds.), *Reproduction and Society: Interdisciplinary Readings.* New York: Routledge.

WHO Department of Reproductive Health and Research. (2012). *Safe Abortion: Technical and Policy Guidance for Health Systems.* Geneva: WHO 2012.

Wicclair, M. (2011). *Conscientious Objection in Health Care: An Ethical Analysis*. Cambridge: Cambridge University Press.

Williams, G. L. (1983). *Textbook of Criminal Law*, 2nd edn. London: Stevens.

Index